'GRACE AND INTEGRITY'

A Portrait of The Lady Eleanor Holles School

'GRACE AND INTEGRITY'

A Portrait of The Lady Eleanor Holles School

ELIZABETH HOSSAIN

THIRD MILLENNIUM
PUBLISHING, LONDON

'Grace and Integrity'
A Portrait of The Lady Eleanor Holles School

© The Lady Eleanor Holles School and Third Millennium Publishing Limited.
Elizabeth Hossain has asserted her right to be identified as the author of
this work in accordance with the Copyright, Designs and Patents Act 1988.

First published in 2011 by Third Millennium Publishing Limited,
a subsidiary of Third Millennium Information Limited.
2–5 Benjamin Street
London
United Kingdom
EC1M 5QL
www.tmiltd.com

ISBN 978 1 906507 32 9

British Library Cataloguing in Publication Data
A CIP catalogue record for this book is available from the British Library.

Project Manager: Susan Millership
Designer: Susan Pugsley
Production: Bonnie Murray
Reprographics: Studio Fasoli, Italy
Printer: Gorenjski Tisk, Slovenia

PICTURE ACKNOWLEDGEMENTS
Most of the images have been sourced from the LEH archives by the author
with the help of Trish White. LEH and TMI Publishers would like to thank the
following people and organisations for granting permission for material to be
reproduced on the following pages: p7 Boo Beaumont; p8 Courtesy of Trustees
of Dr Johnson's House Trust; pp45 (below), 52 (top) National Portrait Gallery;
pp40,41, Private Collection; pp42 (top left), 47, 48/49 © Motco Enterprises
Ltd; p43 V & A Images; pp44 (left), 51, 56 (below) Heritage Images/Diomedia,
p44 (right) Roger Stenson; p45 (top) Courtesy James Saunders Watson,
Rockingham Castle; p46 Huntington Library, San Marino, California; p47
(top) National Archives, Crown copyright; pp50, 60 London Metropolitan
Archives, pp52 (below), 69 Alamy; p59 Getty Images; p61 Bridgeman; pp67,
90 (below), 124 (below), 126 (left), 127 (below) Mary Evans Photo Library; p69
(inset) Whitelands Archive, University of Roehampton; p71 (top) TopFoto;
p76 (below) Courtesy of Lincoln Joyce Fine Art of Great Bookham Surrey,
miniature on ivory by Harriet Frances S Mackreth (1803–1850s); pp81, 86
North London Collegiate School; p83 Susan Pugsley; p98 provided by Martin
Connor, grandson of Edith Thornton, a former pupil at Hackney; pp116, 124
(top), 125 Corbis; pp120/21 English Heritage. NMR Aerofilms Collections;
p127 (top) Charterhouse School; p128 (left) © Museum of London/By Kind
Permission of The Commissioner of the City of London Police; p144 supplied
by Julia Gaffyne; p149 (top) supplied by Gillian Cumberland; p150 supplied
by Christine Bates; p151 (below) supplied by Pamela Ireland-Brown; p159
(top) taken by Jane Allden; pp157, 163, 164 supplied by Elizabeth Candy; p166
supplied by Christine Brown; p171 supplied by Stephen Harris.

Every effort has been made to contact copyright holders but if you have been
inadvertently overlooked, please contact TMI Publishers.

Acknowledgements

This history could not have been written without the support of Mrs Trish
White (née Bush 1947–55), staff member from 1958 who retired as a Deputy
Headmistress in 1996 and is now the School Archivist. Trish's encyclopaedic
knowledge of LEH, its staff and pupils has been of enormous help.

I am indebted to many former pupils, staff, past and present, and current
pupils who have contributed, either by sending in reminiscences or through
interviews. I have tried to use as many extracts as possible and all the material
makes a valuable contribution to the school archives. I should like to thank,
in particular, Joan Blythe (1932–8) and Peggy Morris (née Clark 1924–39), two
of the pupils who moved from Hackney to Hampton in 1936, and Barbara
Megson (1936–48). I was particularly pleased to meet Barbara, who, as a
15-year-old student in 1945, took on the challenge of writing a history of the
school. From my experience, I know what an achievement that was. Thanks,
too, to Ceridwen Roberts (1957–66) and Rosemary Cole (née Heath 1958–66)
for their work on the beginnings of a database for the Mare Street registers.

I should like to thank the staff of the London Metropolitan Archives for
their assistance as I read my way through the 20 or so volumes of records of
the school from 1710 to the mid-twentieth century.

I am also grateful to a number of academics, researchers and others who
suggested lines of research or answered specific questions. Thanks go to Sue
Bennett, Martyn Bennett, Robert Bucholz, Hannah Greig, Anne Laurence, Lois
Louden and PR Seddon.

Finally, I would like to thank Richard Nicholson, Assistant Head, for his
encouragement, and all the support staff at LEH for their help, in particular
Andy Clarkson of the ITC support team for his technical expertise and
unfailing good humour, and Shelley Newton for her help in sourcing pictures
for the twenty-first-century school.

Elizabeth Hossain

Contents

Foreword

We always knew that Elizabeth Hossain's research into the history of our great school would unearth a fascinating story; little did we expect that we would learn so much about the school's original foundation and its remarkable transformation into the school we know and love today.

A school is a living community and the stories contained in these pages tell of pupils, teachers and governors whose link across the centuries is a shared sense of commitment to the educational ideals of their age. These philosophies have changed radically since the early years of the eighteenth century, yet what is striking is that a desire for excellence permeates so much of our history. That the school survived at all from its humble beginnings speaks of the tenacity and vision of its leaders; that it thrives today is testament to the examples set by those educational pioneers, which have cascaded down the generations.

Equally fascinating is the indefatigable spirit of the LEH girls, which shines through this book and provides a striking commonality between pupils past and present. Whilst I am sure that neither the Hon. Anne Watson nor Lady Eleanor Holles could have had any idea of the great educational institution they were to create, I feel certain they would be proud of the opportunities their foresight and generosity have given to countless thousands of girls over the past 300 years. I hope, too, that they would approve of the sense of empowerment amongst the LEH girls of today, who are encouraged to follow their dreams, whatever they may be.

Those of us fortunate enough to be associated with the school are custodians of its distinguished history and share in the responsibility for both its success today and its future prosperity. We enter our fourth century with confidence, but without complacency, attributes which have defined the school and stood it in good stead since 1710. It is at once a great privilege and deeply humbling to be Head Mistress, as we, the LEH community of today, chart a course through the educational vicissitudes of the present, with the same determination and sense of purpose as our forebears.

Gillian Low
Head Mistress

Introduction

On 26 December 1707 a noblewoman of 71, Lady Eleanor Holles, a parishioner of St Giles-in-the-Fields, was writing her will. She dealt first with bequests of money, her house, jewellery and paintings, to her relatives and servants. She then instructed that her executrix, a kinswoman, the Honourable Anne Watson, should dispose of the 'overplus' to whatever charitable purposes Anne thought fit. It was common practice at the time to leave bequests to charity. This legacy, and how it was used, began the process which, 300 years later, has given us a leading independent school for girls, The Lady Eleanor Holles School (LEH) in Hampton, Middlesex.

At the time of writing in 2010, the profile of the school has never been higher. *The Good Schools Guide 2010* called it, 'Absolutely superb – one of the top academic schools in the country'. The Head Mistress, Mrs Gillian Low, was President of the Girls' Schools Association and was named in the *London Evening Standard*'s list of 1,000 most influential Londoners. The Lady Eleanor Holles School is proud to be one of the oldest foundations for girls, not only in London, but in the country. The story of the rise to pre-eminence of the school is a remarkable one. How was it that a school with humble beginnings not only survived, but was able to adapt to the changing expectations of society and emerge to become the distinguished school it is today?

As someone who had taught history at the school for 16 years, I thought I had some idea of the school's development, but, as research progressed, I discovered that there were more twists and turns in the story than I had imagined. The minute and account books, dating back to 1710, detail the decisions, first of the Trustees and then of the Governors, and have provided a rich vein of information, albeit they offer hints rather than details of how the schools were managed. These were practical records and were not written with the idea that, three centuries later, they would be pored over for glimpses of what life was like for the first girls who attended the Lady Holles' Charity School (Lady Holles' School).

What has emerged is a wonderful story of how a charity school for 50 poor girls, founded in 1710 in the parish of St Giles', Cripplegate, has developed into one of the leading independent schools for girls in Britain. This is all the more remarkable as so many of the charity schools, started during an explosion of such foundations in London and Westminster in the first quarter of the eighteenth century, did not survive. That the Lady Holles' School (LHS) not only survived the vicissitudes of time, but thrived, and developed into the lively and creative establishment we see in the early twenty-first century, is a tribute to the integrity of many associated with the school. Perhaps above all, first, the Trustees and then, from 1875, the Governors played a key role in the development of the school. From the late nineteenth century the Governors had to adapt, sometimes uncomfortably, to a succession of Acts of Parliament, each of which was to have a major impact on the development of the school. The role of the Charity Commission, set up in the nineteenth century, to make sure that all trusts did their best to respect the original intent of the benefactors, was to be of critical importance and to set the school on the path to the establishment we see today.

I am grateful to Mrs Low for giving me the opportunity to dust off my historical skills and to uncover the key stages in the development of The Lady Eleanor Holles School. I hope you will enjoy reading the story as much as I have enjoyed researching and writing it.

Elizabeth Hossain

John Wesley preaching in Old Cripplegate church. A group of charity school girls, dressed in their distinctive uniform, can clearly be seen in the congregation.

The Lady Eleanor Holles School in the twenty-first century

Snapshot of 2010

October 2010, a warm autumn afternoon. The sound of 'Summertime' by Gershwin drifts from the oak-panelled Nora Nickalls Assembly Hall. A Music Scholar is singing for a group of prospective parents and pupils at an Open Afternoon for the Senior Department. They are waiting for the Head Mistress, Mrs Gillian Low, to begin her talk. Later they will tour the school, which occupies a spacious and attractive 24-acre site in Hampton, Middlesex. The extensive playing fields and green space which surround the Senior Department are linked to the Junior Department, housed in Burlington House, by a tiny bridge over a stream leading to the Longford River. In these leafy, country-like surroundings it seems hard to believe that the school is only 16 miles or so from the parish of

St Giles', Cripplegate, in the City of London, where the first Lady Holles' School was founded. The distinction and reputation of the school attracts around 180 girls aged 7 to 11 to the Junior Department, and about 700 aged between 11 and 18 to the Senior Department, which includes a thriving Sixth Form of around 180 girls. Girls come from a wide area, as far north as Ealing, as far south as Woking and Byfleet, as far east as Chelsea and as far west as Windsor and Ascot. Many arrive by the coach service which is shared with Hampton School.

Left to right: Senior School; Senior Department pupils; Junior Department pupils.

Opposite: Aerial view of Senior School.

Above: Senior Department pupils.

Right: Burlington House.

Why do parents send their girls to LEH?

Many of those who come to visit on an Open Afternoon have initially been attracted by the school's impressive academic record. Entry to both Junior and Senior Departments is by examination, and the combination of able girls, who work hard, and expert teachers results in outstanding academic achievement. The GCSE results in the summer of 2010 were the best yet, with 74 per cent of candidates gaining the highest grade of A* and over 98 per cent of candidates gaining A* or A grades. Upper Sixth Form (UVI) results were also excellent. In 2010 the A* grade was awarded for the first time at A level for performance above 90 per cent. Over one-third of the grades earned were at A* level.

Results such as these are encouraged by superb teaching and learning facilities. Girls at LEH are extremely fortunate that, with the exception of the Boat House which is a short distance from the school, everything they could want is available on-site. The Juniors in Burlington House are taught in attractive classrooms with specialist rooms for ICT, art, design technology, science and music. Senior work is supported by specialist facilities, such as state-of-the-art science laboratories, design and technology rooms, music and art suites, language laboratories, comprehensive information technology support and the

Learning Resources Centre. The Sixth Form has its own suite of classrooms, a dedicated Sixth Form Library known as the Margaret Lacey Library, and Sixth Form common rooms. Sporting facilities are superb, with a magnificent Sports Hall, swimming pool and vast playing fields, with tennis and netball courts, and space for several pitches for lacrosse and athletics. The governing body, which meets regularly at the school, has always looked ahead to make sure that the curriculum and facilities meet the needs of each generation. These needs have changed dramatically in the course of the school's history and 2010 was no

Below: Portable staging in use for a concert.

exception. The Governors' plans for a new Arts Centre, which will include new accommodation for the Music, Drama and Art Departments and a 300-plus seat theatre, were unveiled in the spring of 2010.

Parents, through membership of The Friends of The Lady Eleanor Holles School, support the educational experience and build on the sense of community at the school. In 2010, for example, they provided an A-frame play den for the Juniors' play area and over £29,000 for portable staging for the Senior Department.

Being a member of The Friends has great advantages for parents at LEH. I enjoyed making new friends at the New Parents' social evening when my daughter joined the Junior Department, in 2003. Since that point, the Form Reps helped to ensure that we got to know other parents, which included social evenings, forming a team for Quiz Night and helping out at the Christmas Bazaar and Second Hand Uniform sales.

Since I was appointed Chair in 2009 it has been a pleasure working with others to organise and host New Parents' evenings, Wine Tasting evenings, the Christmas Bazaar, the ever popular Quiz Night, a Summer Spectacular Music evening with the most amazing firework display and the recent Barn Dance.

Mrs Lisa Prior, Chair of The Friends

'As this book celebrates 300 years of The Lady Eleanor Holles School, I reflect on my own long association with the school, from being a pupil in the fifties and sixties to now as Chairman of Governors.

I was lucky to be in the school at the time of the 250th anniversary and remember well the special train with the school badge on the front that took us to Stratford-upon-Avon to see a performance of *Much Ado About Nothing*.

When I look at the school today I see many similarities; the building is very recognisable although much extended in line with the development and growth of the school, and those wonderful grass tennis courts at the front are still there. LEH has moved with the times though, and more. The range of activities and the facilities now available are things we could not have imagined in the sixties. How wonderful not to have to traipse down to Hampton Baths in a crocodile to learn to swim in that freezing cold water. The style of teaching has moved from the "chalk and talk" era, with an element of fear, to the modern interactive approach with the great developments in technology. Today's girls are provided with a broader education and a huge range of extracurricular activities which offer so many opportunities for young women to take an active role in all aspects of society.

Through my regular visits to "old girl" events and as Holly Club Treasurer I have been able to observe many of these changes taking place. Now in my role as Chairman of Governors I am privileged to see and experience at first hand the level of excellence in the school. As Governors we try to spend a day in the school every year, sitting in on a variety of lessons across the age range. We all find it a fascinating and hugely enjoyable day and (almost) wish we were back at school.

I have always been proud to be associated with LEH and I am so pleased to be the Chairman at this particularly special time.'

Mrs Jane Ross (née Lester 1957–64)
Chairman of Governors from 2002

A rich curriculum

“

A well-rounded and challenging education in a very happy, purposeful environment, preparing them well for higher education and their future lives. ”

LEH website, 2010

Below: Junior Department girls explore the globe.

Right: On the catwalk at the Ethical Fashion Show.

In theory, every opportunity in British society in the twenty-first century is available to a woman. Although debate is still strong about whether there is a 'glass ceiling' for women and whether they can 'have it all', by combining a successful working life with that of a wife and mother, many girls from LEH now occupy top positions in the professions. The school aims to prepare its pupils not just to take their place in the working life of the country, but also to help their development as individuals and citizens in a global community.

In school

Terms at LEH are action-packed and fun. There are plenty of opportunities, both inside and outside the classroom, for girls to be busy in a productive and purposeful way. Even a brief glance at the newsletters produced each term for the Senior and Junior Departments shows the rich variety of stimulating and enjoyable ways in which the curriculum is enhanced. The Junior Department's Africa Week in February 2010, for example, benefited from visitors from UK Fairtrade, talks from former parents about the work of the Baraka Community, which has partnerships in Morocco and Zambia, and a visit from the African Children's Choir. A highlight of the week for many was enjoying an African drumming workshop under the expert guidance of Martin Hanson, who also accompanied the choir as they sang 'Siyahamba' – an African song meaning 'walking in the light of God'.

❝ Wow! The African drumming workshop was amazing. Martin, the professional drummer, taught us a lot of amazing things about how to hold the drums, how they made different noises if they were bigger. There were different drums to play: some were big and some were small; they had different patterns and designs. I learned how you could make a simple tune into something really good. There were other instruments as well, like maracas and triangles. ❞

Annabel Suter (LII)

Both Junior and Senior Departments take every opportunity to encourage pupils to engage with their subject and to develop as citizens, so on 24 June 2010, pupils took part in Schools Low Carbon Day. This was part of a national initiative to educate a million pupils across Britain about climate change. Girls from the Junior Department worked alongside Thirds (III) from the Senior Department, in a day which included practical investigations to find out more about renewable energy, insulation and the carbon cycle and to inspire them to reduce carbon emissions. As one Third reflected, 'It really made me think about how much the world could change in fifty years if we carry on releasing carbon emissions'.

In a similar attempt to make pupils think about their values, the Geography Department ran an Ethical Fashion Show, in which Upper Fourth (UIV) classes showcased an amazing array of outfits to show how much useful material is discarded each year.

World Days are firm favourites in the school. World Book Day is popularly celebrated by the Thirds each year, when each girl is encouraged to dress up as a character from her favourite novel, play or poem. In March 2010, first place in the group category went to a troupe of seven characters from *Alice's Adventures in Wonderland*.

On World Maths Day in March 2010, the Junior girls had a wonderful time playing mental arithmetic games online against children worldwide. As Jasmine Quah (UII) said, 'I really enjoyed World Maths Day and the game was so addictive! It was also interesting to see how many

Top left: Paying close attention at the African drumming workshop.

Top right: Practical investigations on Low Carbon Day.

Bottom right: Alice's Adventures in Wonderland *winners.*

Left: Junior Department pupils enjoying the sponsored aerobics which raised £4,000 for Baraka Community Partnerships.

countries were taking part in it, and it was really fun to play against people from all over the world.'

Jennifer Adams, Head of the Junior Department, explained that there were other benefits too. 'We were thrilled that, at various times during the practice period and the event itself, some of our classes and individual pupils made it onto the worldwide Hall of Fame, with the highest position being Form 1C at eleventh in the world at one stage. There was huge excitement during the competition, and a marked improvement in mental arithmetic skills!'

Guest speakers are frequently welcomed into school to enrich the curriculum and to introduce challenging ideas. In 2010, author Linda Buckley-Archer spoke to the Thirds about *Time Quake*, her trilogy set in eighteenth-century London, and first-time author Jason Wallace visited the Lower Fifth (LV) just weeks before being catapulted to fame with the nomination of his novel, *Out of Shadows*, for the Booktrust Teenage Prize.

Meanwhile, at the Senior Cafe for Upper Fifth (UV) and Sixth Forms, students welcomed speakers on topics as varied as the scientific achievements of the Hubble space telescope, US foreign policy and the work of the Managing Editor of *Tatler*, an old girl.

Out of school

Since its days in Hackney, the school has made good use of its proximity to the museums, theatres and other opportunities in and around London. This tradition is well maintained. In February 2010, both Form Is visited the Science Museum, and Lower IIs (LII) learnt how to create stop motion animation films at the BBC's 21st Century Classroom in White City. As Molly Mercurio (LII) explained, 'The animation workshop at the BBC was probably one of the best school trips I ever went on. We based our animations on myths, and drew and coloured our characters before lunch. In the afternoon we animated them, which was the best part. We added effects and put in voice-overs. Before we left, we watched everyone else's. It was a brilliant day, and I would love to go there again.'

The Upper Is (UI), who had been studying the rainforest in the spring of 2010, had their geography brought to life in the Tropical Forest at Syon Park, and some of them had a close encounter with a python! Ellie

Wastle thought that this was the best part of the trip. 'I loved it when I got to hold the different creatures, like the stick insect and the millipede. The very best part was when the tour guide put a python on our laps!'

LEH girls love to get involved, and the pond-dipping, birdwatching, meadow-sweeping and nature trail on the Bushy Park visit provide just the sort of opportunities the LIIs love.

The Senior Department is not left out, with over 140 day visits each year. They may be to build team spirit, such as the IIIs' visit to Hillingdon Outdoor Activity Centre; to stimulate further subject curiosity such as the UIV visit to Fishbourne to get a feel for life in Roman Britain; or to take part in local or national competitions. Whatever the purpose, you may be sure they are well organised and staff and pupils have a great time.

Top right: Raft building for IIIs at Hillingdon.

Bottom right: Upper Is with a python in the Tropical Forest at Syon Park.

Sixth formers enjoying the warmth of a naturally heated pool in Iceland.

"

At no time were we in any danger and we were really impressed by the calmness of the Icelandic people and the efficiency of the emergency operation. We heard of other schools which had to be evacuated and had their trip cut short, but we were staying in a safe location and the eruption allowed us to enjoy some wonderful sights and experiences.

The highlight of the trip for most was a visit to the 'Blue Lagoon of the North', a geothermally heated pool in the remote lava fields of north Iceland. We enjoyed bathing in the warm water whilst the air temperature of −6°C meant that our hair froze! Our Icelandic guide Oli organised a pizza delivery to the pool.

"

Sarah Coggin, Head of Geography Department on the volcanic eruption in Iceland

Away from school

Extended school trips are popular in both Departments. LIIs enjoyed a residential stay at Barton Hall in Devon. On this multi-activity trip, girls took part in team-building sessions as well as new outdoor challenges, such as abseiling and learning to trapeze. The girls returned brimming with enthusiasm and proud of their new skills. Their experiences there topped the list when they were asked to recall their favourite memory of 2010.

In the Senior Department there are over 40 residential trips a year. In 2010 these included the Geography field trip to Iceland and modern foreign language trips and exchanges to Paris, Munich, Konstanz and Salamanca. In the autumn of 2010, a group of students in the History Department even got as far as China.

On occasion, trips turned out to be even more exciting than anticipated, as we saw from the Geography

Department's Lower Sixth (LVI) trip to Iceland in April, which, as a result of the Eyjafjallajökull eruption, lasted four days longer than planned.

The LV French exchange to Paris and the UV visit to Salamanca in Spain, by contrast, went according to plan. Students on both trips enjoyed their immersion in the culture and the opportunity to practise their language skills.

Stephanie Powell (LV), having overcome her initial anxiety, became a firm advocate of the advantages of the French exchange made with a school in Paris during the

Easter holidays. 'Despite being a bit nervous before we arrived, many of us found we could speak French better than expected. All of us found our families to be really welcoming and hospitable, which made the experience much less daunting than anticipated!'

In Salamanca, Emma Allden (UV) also felt the advantages of being immersed in the language, as well as enjoying other aspects of the lifestyle. 'Every evening we had dinner with our families, and when surrounded by the Spanish language we soon found it much easier to dive into conversation, great practice for our looming GCSE orals.' She also reported the group's approval of their first taste of churros and chocolate. 'On Tuesday, after visiting the stunning cathedral, Miss Pla-Miró tore us away from the intricate architecture to a cafe where we all had our first churros: fried pastry sticks dipped into a bowl of melted chocolate and sugar. Delicious!'

Above: History Department pupils try out their Tai-chi skills in China.

Left: LEH and Hampton School pupils in Konstanz.

These examples are just a taste of a huge range of exchanges and trips organised by staff, for the most part, in the school holidays. A number, such as the German Department's UV exchange with Konstanz, are joint ventures with Hampton School.

Joint LEH and Hampton School production of Oklahoma!, *October 2009.*

Links with Hampton School

A major benefit for the girls is the close cooperation, nurtured by regular meetings between the heads, Gillian Low and Barry Martin, which has developed between LEH and the neighbouring boys' school, Hampton School. Relations have come a very long way since the days when even speaking to a Hampton boy would result in a fearsome dressing down! Tessa Sauven (née Sherriff 1961–72) remembers the fear she had that she and friends would be caught 'chatting to Hampton Grammar boys through the fence behind the Garden Club shed'. Marilyn Garrod (née Virgo 1950–63) remembers that girls had to avoid the field between Hampton (Grammar as was) School and the path to Burlington House, 'as fraternisation was not allowed'. Trish White (née Bush 1947–55) also remembers, 'on our side of the boundary fence there was a "no-man's land", a strip of grass five feet wide which was patrolled by the member of staff on outside duty'. As a young member of staff in 1959 she hated that particular duty!

Girls and boys now enjoy a number of shared activities, ranging from concerts, musicals, drama and charity events to the Combined Cadet Force (CCF) and Sixth Form talks and lectures. Sixth formers are welcome visitors in each other's common rooms. Barry Martin, Headmaster of Hampton School, interviewed in October 2010, describes this as a 'dream scenario'. Proximity and good fortune have, in his view, enabled two powerful schools in their own right to preserve the integrity of single-sex education, whilst adding a range of joint opportunities to provide the benefits of co-educational schools. The positive synergy created gives a better result than could be achieved without these important links. He sees this as having reciprocal benefits for both schools, and it means that each is offering another route through secondary education, what might be called a model of single-sex plus.

Barry Martin singled out the musical *Oklahoma!* in October 2009 and the Hampton School CCF as outstanding examples of cooperation between the two schools.

The Hampton School CCF, with 278 cadets in the autumn of 2010, is one of the largest day school cadet forces and has an Army and an RAF section. The contingent now also includes staff and pupils from Hampton Academy. Around 100 girls from LEH take part, and the experience often leads to wonderful opportunities, such as the one which Warrant Officer Kirsty Dixon experienced in 2010, when she was awarded an International Air Cadets Exchange Scholarship to the US.

Far left: LEH
members of the
Hampton School
CCF learning the
tricks of camouflage
on an Army Field
Day.

Left: Advertising
the Art Club at the
Extra-curricular
Fair.

Below: Working
together on an
experiment at
Science Club.

'The other half'

> " Rewarding activities where you can contribute to the wider life of the school and the local community. "
>
> **Extra-curricular handbook, 2010**

As Mrs Low emphasises in her talks to prospective parents, The Lady Eleanor Holles School is about much more than academic achievement. As important as providing opportunities for a girl to achieve her best academically is encouraging personal development and enabling girls to develop as citizens. In the mid-twentieth century, the Head Mistress, Miss Ruth Garwood Scott (1949–73), in a revision of the school prospectus, introduced her aim for the school that 'our girls should "grow up to be women of grace and integrity" serving their generation'. In 2010, although the phrase may seem a little old-fashioned, this aim still stands. LEH is committed to helping girls to develop integrity, in the sense of helping them to develop a strong set of personal values, and grace, by encouraging them to treat others with respect and kindness. Girls are encouraged to be friendly, outgoing and generous-hearted. These qualities are promoted and encouraged not only within the classroom, but also in the extensive range of opportunities available outside the classroom. A stroll round the school at any lunchtime will reveal the myriad activities on offer. There is a buzz of activity. In the Nora Nickalls Hall, you might see girls rehearsing for the inter-house drama festival; in practice rooms, musicians preparing material for concerts, for music examinations or just for sheer enjoyment; and out on the sports field, lacrosse. In and around classrooms, you might see meetings of the Science and Engineering Club; the Amnesty group writing letters to support prisoners of conscience; the Fairtrade group selling chocolate bars; or representatives to the Model United Nations researching their new roles. There are clubs and societies for all interests; over 100 are offered each week.

23

Performers at the Rock, Pop and Jazz concert.

Music and drama

Music is part of the school's heritage. From the school's foundation in 1710, girls were coached in psalmody for the Sunday service, for the occasional national event and for the annual gathering of all the pupils at charity schools in London and Westminster.

The breadth and range of music making at LEH in 2010 was impressive. There were groups for lovers of classical music, rock, pop, jazz and more, with regular concerts, such as the May 2010 Soloists and Ensembles' Concert in the Junior Department. *Junior Focus* reported:

From the opening bars of Haydn's Minuet … we knew we were in for an evening of stunning music when, at times, we needed to remind ourselves that the performers were no older than 11 and some considerably younger.

The programme featured an impressive variety of instruments and styles and the diversity ensured that we were constantly surprised by the sheer scope of the girls' musical ability. Extra special highlights were Olivia Deru (LII) who showed her considerable talent on the piano, playing a Chopin Waltz in E minor. We heard very moving performances on the violin from Esther Duffy, who has achieved a Music Scholarship to the Senior Department … The Piano Trio, Ailin Cheng (piano), Esther Duffy (violin) and Millie Hughes (cello), brought the evening to a wonderful conclusion by playing three Piano Miniatures by Frank Bridge.

Houses

Although the Junior Department has had a house system with four houses – Burlington, Summerleigh, St Giles and Hackney – for many years, the Senior Department had focused instead on the year system. The house system was introduced again into the Senior Department in the academic year 2008–9, after a gap of over 50 years. Many activities in the Senior Department now centre around the house system. This encourages a sense of loyalty to a group within the school community and fosters friendships between girls from different year groups. The four houses provide, in Mrs Low's words, 'different chances for different girls to shine'.

The vertical structure of the four houses – De Vere, Fitzwilliam, Holles and Tyrconnel – provides many opportunities for individuals not only to showcase talents and interests, but also to develop new skills and work with girls in different years. The House Drama Festival is an excellent example of this. The introduction of houses has also reinvigorated Sports Day. It seems hard to believe that within two years the house system has already become embedded in the life of the school.

The introduction of a house system has brought new life to Sports Day and to the Drama Festival.

Concerts give both soloists and groups the chance to share their impressive level of music making.

In the Senior Department there are some 30 music groups, ranging from choirs and orchestras to chamber groups and bands, directed and coached by the full-time music staff and a large number of visiting teachers. A taste of the rich variety of music making by the Senior Department can be found in the programme for the summer concert, Summer Spectacular, held in July 2010. As Miranda Ashe, Director of Music, reported:

> *This concert certainly lived up to its name – a spectacular evening of dazzling solos, orchestras, ensembles and choirs performed by the immensely talented LEH musicians. The buzz in the air was centred around the leaving Sixth Form musicians, for whom this was the final opportunity to perform before going on study leave. They provided a magical showcase of virtuosity and skill.*
>
> *The school's top ensembles and choirs were also on show, and the evening began with a powerful trumpet fanfare, especially written by Dr Hughes for*

the occasion. Symphony Orchestra maintained its energetic and ebullient reputation with Mars *and a John Williams Tribute, and Percussion Ensemble gave a classy performance of Albeniz's* Asturias. *The rich sound of the Senior Strings in Ireland's* Downland Suite *was a perfect foil to the jazz idiom of the Brass Group. The choirs continue to excel: Junior Choir gave us an enchanting medley from* Oliver!, *Senior Choir performed a haunting setting of* The Lamb *followed by a witty arrangement by Dr Hughes, and Cantata gave a stylish performance of music by Cole Porter and Neil Diamond. The joint LEH–Hampton School SATB[1] choir sang some luscious Lauridsen and tongue-twisting Rutter with great aplomb. The Holles Singers performed the programme with which they won the BBC Radio 3 Choir of the Year auditions. An impressive variety of music at a wonderful standard – congratulations!*

The Holles Singers went on to win the prestigious Youth Choir Category Finals of the BBC Choir of the Year Competition on Saturday 6 November 2010, in the splendid surroundings of Birmingham's Symphony Hall. The choir performed a Latin choral fanfare called *Veni Veni*, especially written for them by their accompanist, Brendan Ashe; then changed its sound completely for a wild Bulgarian piece called 'Erghen Diado', and, finally, the girls gave a spirited account of songs from Queen. The judges, Mary King, Stuart Barr and Eugene Skeef, described how impressed they were by the extraordinary versatility of the choir and its 'wall of sound'.

The Music and Drama Departments cooperate each year in the annual joint LEH and Hampton School musical. In 2010, this was the rock musical *We Will Rock You*.

There are many other opportunities for girls across the school to take part in productions. The then Head of Drama, Pauline Flannery, in recalling the highlights of 2010, spoke of the wide range of productions, from *The Rivals* by Sheridan, another joint LEH and Hampton School Sixth Form production, through *Chatterton*, a devised piece of theatre for GCSE, and *Tejas Verdes*, a very

moving account of the Chilean 'disappeared', to the IIIs' play, *Race Around the World*.

Drama also figures strongly in the Junior Department, which holds a House Drama Competition and leavers' production. With so many opportunities for performance, it is no wonder that the talents of individual pupils are regularly recognised at national level, with pupils earning places in the National Children's Orchestra, the National Youth Orchestra, the National Youth Choir and the National Youth Theatre.

Above: The Holles Singers under the direction of Miranda Ashe, Director of Music.

Left: We Will Rock You, *2010.*

Above: In race position – Sally Gunnell with some of the LEH national sportsgirls.

Right: Floor work at the Annual Gymnastics Display.

Sport

Competitive sports were not considered suitable for girls until the beginning of the twentieth century, but hockey fixtures were a regular feature after 1902. The range of sports now available to LEH girls is vast, and there are many opportunities for girls to take part in sporting activities, either just for fun or at a competitive level. The very high standards reached can be gauged by the fact that in 2010 over 20 LEH pupils represented their country in their chosen sport and over 60 played at county level.

As Director of Sport, Mrs Vicky Sumner, says:

My colleagues and I see sport as vitally important in a successful school such as LEH. We have five, well-qualified full-time staff and a team of visiting coaches, many of them national performers in their own right, who work to help pupils to achieve excellence.

Our pupils are given opportunities to compete in local school fixtures, county tournaments and national tournaments. We are proud of our record in tournaments such as Middlesex County Netball, National Schools Netball and Lacrosse Tournaments, London Schools Trampolining Competition, London Regional Carita House Gymnastics Championships, National Schools' Regatta, English Schools' Swimming Association National Finals, to name but a few of the many events in which we regularly compete and do well.

Girls also take part in inter-house competitions within curriculum time. These experiences mean pupils learn how to compete against each other, as well as challenging them to improve their own performances.

We are proud of the number of pupils who participate in sport and we include a wide range of disciplines in our curricular and extra-curricular programmes, to cater for all tastes. Sports include lacrosse, netball, gymnastics, trampolining, swimming, rowing, rounders, tennis, athletics, hockey, cross country, skiing and fencing.

We are very fortunate to have fantastic facilities, supportive parents, dedicated staff and highly motivated pupils, which all help to maintain our excellent reputation at national competitions.

Mrs Sumner selected the following as particularly memorable moments in 2010:
- The Junior Swimming Team finishing in Bronze Medal position at the National Finals of the English Schools' Swimming Championships.
- LEH hosting the Girls' Schools Association (GSA) Girls Go Gold Sports Conference, at which Gabby Logan and Sally Gunnell were the keynote speakers. The conference was for girls in Years 10–13 (aged 14 to 18) who represent either their county or their country in their chosen sport. More than 400 girls from all over the country attended.

From top left: Junior Department swimming team success at Richmond Borough Gala; J16 Coxed Fours heading for start of race; J16 Coxed Fours with National Schools Trophy; Winning Senior First team at the South Schools Lacrosse Tournament.

In addition, Senior Department teams showed their excellence in a range of fields. Six teams, including the U19s, were county champions in lacrosse, with the First team also winning the South Schools Lacrosse Tournament. Four netball teams, including the U19s, were county champions.

In the Junior Department, PE lessons concentrate on developing a range of skills in games, swimming and gymnastics, whilst gradually introducing more formal games and rules. Netball is the main winter sport, but the girls also have units such as pop lacrosse to give them tasters of other team games. In summer, the school's magnificent fields give junior girls the chance to experience sprinting, long and high jump and other athletic disciplines.

With two PE specialist teachers based in the Junior Department, matches against other schools are frequent, especially in netball and swimming. The Junior Department's membership of the Independent Association of Preparatory Schools (IAPS) since 2004 has enabled its pupils to take part in many local and national IAPS sporting events.

Rowing

LEH is one of the country's best rowing schools, sharing the Millennium Boat House, opened in 2000 on the Lower Sunbury Road in Hampton, with Hampton School. Over 100 girls between 13 and 18 are coached by a team of ten, including past Olympians and Great Britain (GB) rowers, plus current senior GB rowers. Their enthusiasm and dedicated hard work bring impressive results at national and international level. In 2010, LEH won 25 medals at the National Schools Rowing Championships and five girls were unbeaten in the J16 Coxed Fours, winning the National Schools' and Women's Henley Regatta 2010 events.

At international level, Thea Vukasinovic and Louisa Bolton represented Great Britain at the Coupe De La Jeunesse (European Rowing Championships) and each won three bronze medals.

For two girls, their success in rowing led to them gaining full rowing scholarships at Virginia and Yale Universities in the US.

Right: Duke of Edinburgh's Award expedition.

Below: Spending part of the lunch break reading with local infant pupils.

Values for life

Whilst many clubs and societies enrich curriculum subjects, others encourage girls to engage with the wider community, locally, nationally and globally, and to develop a set of ethical values for life. Many girls enjoy the range of challenges of the Duke of Edinburgh's Award and find the experiences very rewarding, as Eleanor van Klaveren (LVI) makes clear in her description of a three-day Silver Award expedition walk in the New Forest.

While walking we encountered some interesting marshy terrain, with many of us sinking up to our knees in the mud! At the campsites we enjoyed our evening meals, along with the local ponies, who tried to steal our food! On Thursday, after three days, having walked a total of 60km, we reached the familiar sight of Brockenhurst Station and we boarded the train home.

We were exhausted and had very sore feet, but we took with us some great memories. Although challenging, this was a very rewarding experience, with many laughs along the way.

From helping with crafts and reading at local infant and primary schools, to mentoring Year 11 pupils at local

secondary schools with GCSE work in maths and science, girls are actively encouraged to contribute to the local community. These opportunities to interact with their peers outside school are popular and well supported by LEH girls. These comments from Dr Sue Demont, Principal of Hampton Academy, make clear the value of such links.

We at Hampton Academy, formerly Hampton Community College, place great value on our successful

*Top left and right:
SHINE activities.*

*Left: Service
Volunteers,
Christmas party for
local elderly people.*

*working partnership with LEH. Over the years this
has included combined activities in music, science,
citizenship and literature, our latest venture being
the successful Literary Quiz Team against a combined
team from Kingston schools. Our GCSE students have
benefited from coaching and mentoring in maths and
science by LEH Sixth Formers since 2007, with pleasing
results for all parties. Our annual sports day at the LEH
athletics track is always a very special occasion for the
whole school.*

*The ISSP[2] has broadened the horizons of all
participating students. We believe that our students
gain greatly from their access to one of the country's
top performing girls' schools; and equally believe
that our young people enrich the experiences of LEH
students through sharing some of their particular skills
and experiences. Such partnerships make a significant
contribution to a healthy, egalitarian and fair society in
which young people are enabled to flourish regardless
of their starting point in life. Hampton Academy is
delighted to be part of this movement.*

LEH also hosts 'Serious Fun on Saturdays' as part of the
SHINE[3] Trust's initiative to provide enrichment activities
across a wide range of subjects for Gifted and Talented

pupils from maintained primary schools. Some 20
members of the teaching staff from both Senior and Junior
Departments, with members of the Sixth Form acting
as mentors, run sessions over a period of 14 weeks. The
culmination each year is a celebration event where parents
are invited to view a selection of the girls' work and plays
which have been devised in the drama sessions.

Service Volunteers (SV) provides another opportunity
for girls from LEH to work with boys from Hampton
School to help members of the local community of all
ages. Regular events include a Splash and Gym afternoon,
hosted annually and described by Swarna Jeyabraba (UVI):

*Children with special needs come to spend leisure time
in our pool and Sports Hall. Eager helpers from LEH
and Hampton School volunteer to be lifeguards, play
games with the children in the pool and help them*

Make Poverty History

Right: Model United Nations.

Far right: Members of Make Poverty History.

Below: Enjoying the fairytales theme at the 2010 Charity Week.

have a wonderful time. The pool was covered with an assortment of toys, from woggles to rings to basketballs. The children never ran out of things to do. After swimming the children played in the Sports Hall, with lively music and enthusiastic helpers, who organised a football game that everyone could play together. The afternoon was hugely enjoyable and the event is a firm favourite in the Service Volunteers' calendar.

Another mainstay of the SV calendar is the annual Christmas party for local elderly residents, an event which is enjoyed immensely by both hosts and guests, as the many letters of thanks received after the event reveal. Over 200 guests attended the 2010 Christmas Party. To support the occasion, a mufti day was held in November, with girls

bringing in a range of Christmas gifts for the visitors. With Service Volunteers from both LEH and Hampton School joining forces, and support from staff, parents and friends, the guests enjoyed a festive Christmas tea, a wonderful mix of entertainment, including songs from the choir, and several games of bingo.

Girls can get to grips with international issues by joining groups such as Amnesty, Model United Nations and Make Poverty History. As well as encouraging awareness of global issues, the Fairtrade group manages the Fairtrade Friday tuck shop, a win-win situation. As well as indulging their passion for chocolate, girls know that the producer has received a fair return and that, in addition, the profits of the tuck shop are being used to sponsor a child in Ethiopia.

Since Lady Holles' Middle School was opened in Hackney in 1878, girls have been encouraged to think of others, and so began a strong tradition of fund-raising. In 2010, this generous tradition continued. For a number of years, the Seniors have raised over £10,000 annually for charities chosen by the Sixth Form-led Charity Committee. In the academic year 2009–10, they set themselves the very ambitious aim of raising £15,000 for a number of charities, including Street Child Africa. They also sent a sizeable donation to their link school,

Top: Fund-raising for charity – Junior Department girls with their contributions for a cake sale.

Left: Mr Budd, Geography teacher, takes his soaking in good part.

Nakanyonyi Girls' School (NGS) in Jinja, Uganda. The target was exceeded by £7,000.

LEH girls enjoy themselves whilst fund-raising, and the highlight each year is Charity Week. The theme in 2010 was fairytales and each house was allocated a day on which to hold an event. Tyrconnel held a quiz, 'Have I got fairytales for you?'; De Vere held its own 'LEH has talent'; Holles acted out a series of fairytales; and Fitzwilliam held a fairytale-themed dress-up race. One day in the week is given over to forms running stalls for the Charity Fair. 'Throwing the sponge at the teacher' proved to be one of the most successful stalls, with Mr Budd a popular victim. All in all it was an extremely

Right: Celebrating the links between LEH and Nakanyonyi Girls' School in Uganda.

Below: Suzie Zitter with NGS pupils in Uganda.

successful week, with over £3,000 raised for Street Child Africa. The Junior girls are also enthusiastic fund-raisers, and events in 2010 included a cake sale for Haiti, a mufti day to support UNICEF's Day for Change and, in May, sponsored aerobics for Baraka Community Partnerships, which raised £4,000.

Time out

There is also time at LEH just to 'hang out' and relax. For the Juniors, this might be playing with friends in the 'hedge homes', carrying on a tradition which goes back to when the school moved into its new buildings in Hampton in 1937. The 'hedge homes' provide, in the words of Jennifer Adams, Head of the Junior Department, 'opportunities for that kind of unstructured, imaginative, independent play that we are always hearing children don't get enough of today'.

Celebrations

Prize Giving is the formal occasion each year in which the successes of individuals and departments in all aspects of school life are celebrated. In November 2010, Jay Hunt, an alumna who is forging a distinguished career in broadcasting, gave out the prizes. She had just left her post as Controller of BBC One and was going on to take up the post of Chief Creative Officer at Channel 4 in January 2011. As a woman who has balanced a hugely successful career with the roles of wife and mother, she urged her audience to cherish the friendships made at school as ones that could be relied on in the future.

In 2010, celebration ceremonies to mark the achievements of every girl at the time of moving from the junior stage of education to the secondary, and from the Sixth Form to higher education, were added to the school year. These ceremonies both concluded a key stage in a girl's school career and looked forward to the next step.

The Junior Department held the first celebration afternoon in July 2010, to honour all the Upper II (UII) leavers, most of whom go on to the Senior Department, and their parents, and to thank them for their years in the Junior Department. Girls are sad to leave the warm, welcoming, family atmosphere, which all visitors to

Above: Jay Hunt, guest of honour at the 2010 Prize Giving with Mrs Low and the Head Girl and Deputies.

Left: Juniors enjoying the 'hedge homes'.

Girls in the Senior Department may spend a recess or lunch hour chatting with friends or lying out on the field on the sunniest days. The Lower Sixth has its Common Room and the Upper Sixth the Pavilion, with catering facilities, comfortable seating and beanbags, for those all-important chats about the latest trends, relationships and what was on television last night.

Each girl was invited to receive a Leavers' Certificate, which contained details of her academic qualifications and her key extra-curricular activities and achievements. Girls were also presented with their own alumna leaving badge. As girls received these items, a one-line citation was read about each girl, comments that the girls themselves had devised in collaboration with their form tutor, which ensured a light and celebratory feel to the whole occasion.

Above: Mrs Jennifer Adams (left), Head of the Junior Department with the Vice-Chair of Governors and Mr Philip Ward, handing out the prizes at the Junior Department celebration afternoon.

Right: Proud of their certificates at the Sixth Form Graduation Ceremony.

Burlington House comment on, but are looking forward to the new challenges of senior work.

Everyone in the UIIs received a book and a certificate showing their achievements, and a small number of subject cups were also awarded. The presentations were made by Mrs Marilyn Nagli, Vice-Chair of Governors, and this was followed by tea for UII parents, girls and staff.

The first Sixth Form Graduation Ceremony was also held in 2010. This was an opportunity for UVI pupils, their parents and relatives to recognise and celebrate girls' achievements throughout their Sixth Form career, and to bid them farewell and good luck for the next stage of their education. Mark Tompsett, Head of Sixth Form, explained how the event was organised.

A champagne reception in the Learning Resources Centre followed. This was a splendid send-off for the UVI. All the girls were going on to university, mostly to Russell Group universities, with 17 this year to Oxbridge, as well as pupils taking places at Yale and Harvard. After that? As can be seen from the answers given by a random selection of UVI in April 2010, there is no limit to the ambitions of the LEH girl. They will be represented well in the professions, many girls aiming to be doctors, lawyers or dentists. Journalism and broadcasting are attractive choices, while others aspire to careers in the arts world. At least one hoped to be prime minister!

Whatever their futures hold, girls are encouraged to keep in touch by joining the Alumnae Association.

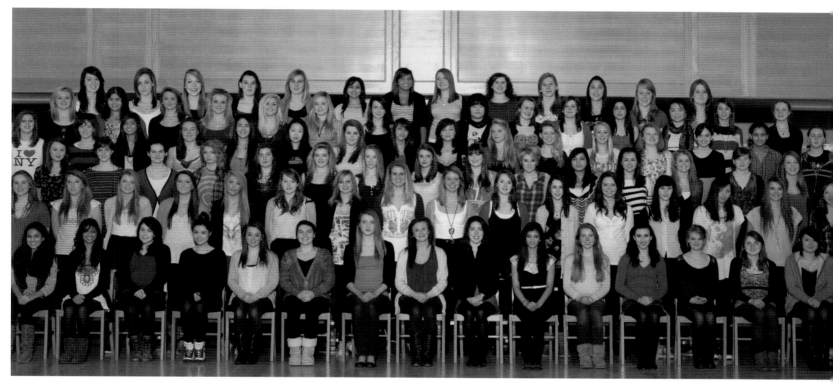

Alumnae

There has been an Old Girls' Association, the Holly Club, since the late nineteenth century. In December 1889, the Head Mistress at Mare Street, Miss Ruddle, reported to the Governors that an Old Pupils' Association had been formed 'to make all our girls feel that their school is to be a centre which shall always attract them and that a common bond of union connects them together'. The Governors expressed their pleasure at the formation of this association.[4]

All girls are encouraged to join the flourishing Alumnae Association, which developed out of the original Old Girls' Association, the Holly Club. One of the highlights is the annual lunch, which attracted 170 guests in 2010. As well as valuing those old girls who have always kept in touch, in keeping with the times and social networking LEH now has an official Facebook page called 'The Lady Eleanor Holles School Alumnae'.

A school career at LEH in the twenty-first century means that girls are well prepared for the many roles they may expect to have in their lives. How different from the world of the early eighteenth century! As today, the school then aimed to fit its pupils for the needs of society, but the society of the early eighteenth century was a vastly different place for women and the roles open to women were governed by the class into which they were born.

Top: UVI, 2009–10.

Left: Alumnae at the annual lunch.

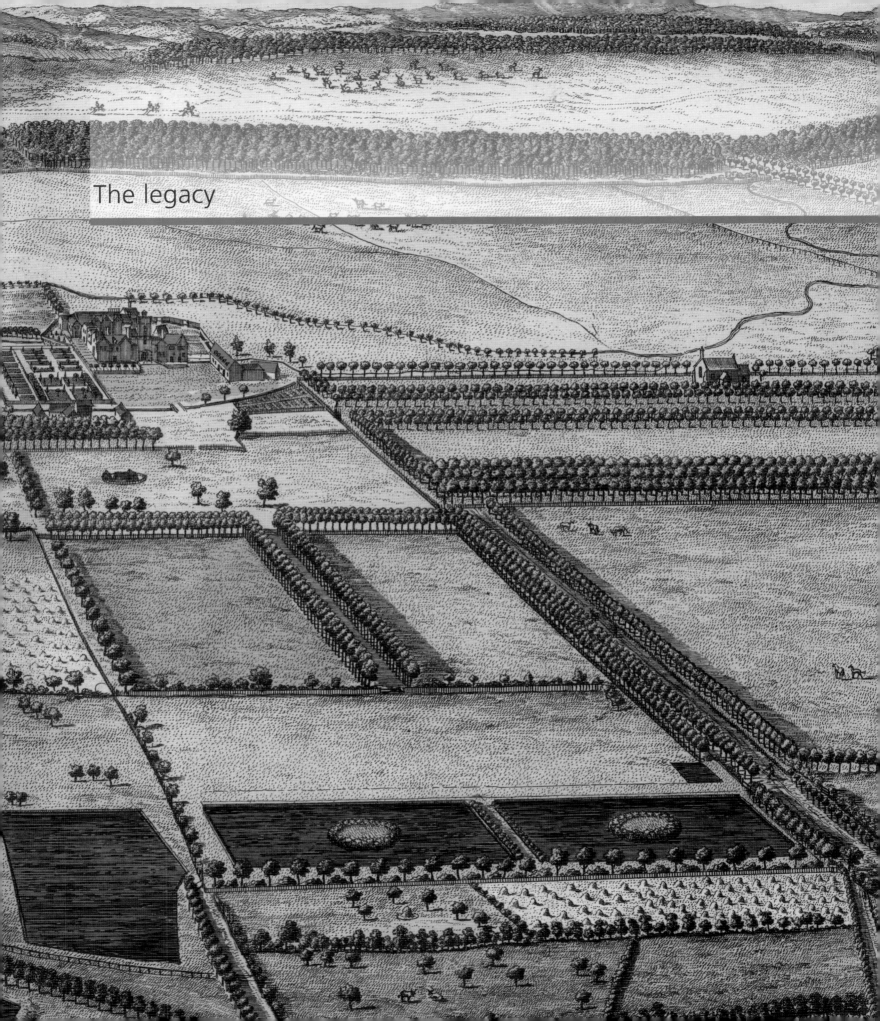

The benefactress: Lady Eleanor Holles

Eleanor's father, John Holles, 2nd Earl of Clare, noted that 'Ellenor' was born at Haughton on 'munday morning in Easter week the 18 of April 1636 at a quarter of an houre before one in the morning'. Eleanor was the sixth daughter of John Holles and Elizabeth Vere. In May the following year, when Eleanor's grandfather was writing to his son to tell him of the birth of yet another daughter, sister to Eleanor, he gave his own explanation of why the second Earl and his wife had so many daughters. He urged his son to 'give over your tobacco … else looke for more daughters'. As inheritance passed down through the male line, noble families looked for male issue, but although Eleanor's mother seems to have been pregnant almost every year between 1627 and 1647, miscarriages and deaths in early childhood meant that only one son and seven daughters reached adulthood. By the late seventeenth century, Eleanor's birthplace, Haughton Hall[5] in Nottinghamshire, was an impressive mansion, befitting the seat of the Earls of Clare, the title which Eleanor's grandfather purchased from James I of England. Haughton had been the Holles family seat since the early sixteenth century, when the manor was purchased by Sir William Holles, master of the Mercers' Company and Lord Mayor of London from 1539 to 1540. An engraving of the early eighteenth century reveals a substantial house surrounded by a moat, with a huge deer park of 900 acres stretching in front of the house. There was a separate chapel, the chapel of St James, and a burying place for the Holles family.

We know almost nothing of Eleanor's early life, although it seems likely that she was brought up at Haughton. Nor do we know why she was living in London in December 1707, when she wrote her will. She did not marry, but it is clear that she was a 'woman of quality', and a member of an influential and wealthy family. By the early part of the eighteenth century the Holles family had built up substantial property holdings in London, especially in and around the parish of St Clement Danes and around Drury Lane. According to Howell's *Londinopolis* of 1657, Eleanor's grandfather, John Holles, 1st Earl of Clare, lived in 'a princely mansion' adjacent to Clare Market, with the nearby street, house and market all bearing his name. The Rocque map of 1746 shows Clare Street leading to Clare Market and Holles, Vere and Haughton Streets, all reminders of the family connection with the area. Only Clare Market and Haughton (now Houghton) Street have survived to the present. Eleanor's nephew, John Holles, who became 4th Earl of Clare in 1689 and, on the death of his father-in-law, inherited the Newcastle estates and became, in addition, 3rd Duke of Newcastle, was, in the opinion of Bishop Burnet, 'the richest subject that had been in England for some ages'. As 3rd Duke of Newcastle, John Holles had immense wealth and influence. He became Lord Privy Seal, was trusted by Queen Anne and, when he died prematurely, after a fall from his horse whilst stag-hunting at Welbeck, was buried in Westminster Abbey. His daughter, Lady Henrietta Holles, married the son of Robert Harley, who was Lord Treasurer to Queen Anne.

However, the story that Eleanor was one of Queen Anne's ladies-in-waiting seems untrue.[6] The London season, when the royal family was in residence at court, ran from November to May, and this may explain Eleanor's presence in London. The season, with its balls, assemblies, plays, opera and promenades

Previous page: Haughton Hall, Nottinghamshire, an engraving by Knyff and Kip, 1707.

Right: John Holles, 2nd Earl of Clare, Eleanor's father (a miniature by Samuel Cooper, signed and dated 1656).

Opposite: Eleanor's mother, Elizabeth Vere, Countess of Clare (an oil painting attributed to Sir Peter Lely).

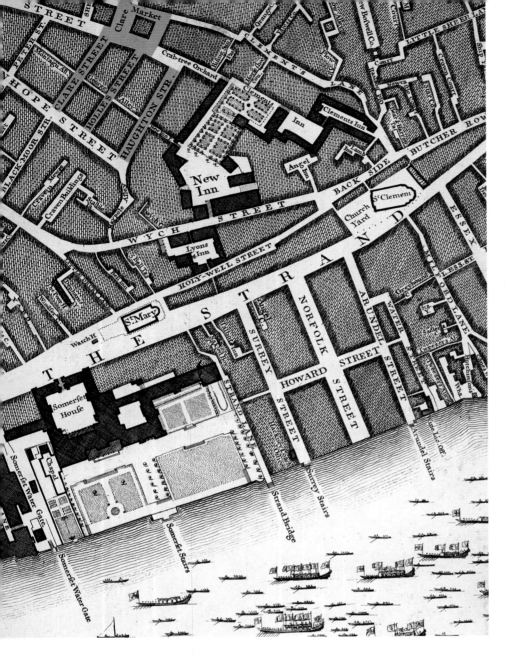

£2,000 in her original will, and the 'overplus' eventually amounted to almost £1,200 more. A codicil, added to the will in April 1708, revealed more of the well-to-do nature of her household. Her furnishings included a 'Jappan' (lacquered) cabinet, a 'China' jar and 'bason', which stood under her 'Jappan' cabinet, and a chest of drawers which became fashionable in the mid-seventeenth century. She owned several family portraits: one of her sister Anne, who married Lord Clinton; watercolour pictures of her Aunt Tyrconnell and her father; and pictures of 'Lord and Lady Clare'. Her will reveals that she had a considerable amount of personal silverware, which she bequeathed to her sisters, to their children and to her 'cozens', sisters, nieces and nephews of her executrix Anne Watson. Her most personal items, such as her silver egg cup and silver tumbler, went to her sisters, Lady Susannah Lort and Lady Diana Bridges. Visiting and taking tea played an important part in social interaction at the time, so it is no surprise that she had a silver teapot and two silver plates to leave

Rocque map of 1746 showing in the top left Clare, Holles and Haughton Streets and Clare Market.

Right: Portrait of Eleanor's aunt who married Oliver Fitzwilliam, 1st Earl of Tyrconnell. This portrait was for some years mistakenly believed to be that of Lady Eleanor Holles.

in the pleasure gardens of Vauxhall and Ranelagh, provided opportunities to see and be seen, and attendance was essential for those who aspired to make a 'good' marriage. It may well be that Eleanor had a role in chaperoning some of her younger female relatives, who are remembered in her will.

The little we know of Eleanor is gleaned from her will. In this she described herself as a parishioner of St Giles-in-the-Fields. This church was just a short walk from Greek Street, where she had her 'dwellinghouse', and was a church with which her family seems to have had connections. Her brother Gilbert, for example, was married there in 1655. By late 1707, when Eleanor wrote her will, she was a noblewoman of some means, with a household of at least three servants to whom she left sums of money and mourning clothes. As well as owning a 'dwellinghouse' in Greek Street, she bequeathed almost

A family taking tea in the early eighteenth century. This painting shows some of the 'equippage' associated with the preparation of tea which Eleanor referred to in her will.

to her niece, Lady Henrietta Holles, and 'my tea table and equippage to it', which was left to her niece, Susannah Cambell. Eleanor also made specific bequests of her personal jewellery, which included two rows of pearls, one with 50 pearls, the other with 49, a gold watch, a diamond bracelet and an emerald ring.

We also gain glimpses of her character from the will and its codicil. She shows particular concern to provide her sister Lady Diana Bridges with an independent income and to protect it from what might be a spendthrift, negligent or unkind husband. She instructs that the Honourable Thomas Wentworth, one of her cousins, be

given £1,000 to invest and that he should give the interest to Diana for the rest of her life. Her instructions add that, 'the said interest money shall be paid to the said Lady Bridges owne hands for her owne separate use and that her husband shall have nothing to doe with nor any powere to receive or dispose of the same'. She instructs the same cousin to sell her diamond bracelet 'and apply the money raised thereby to the separate use of my said sister the Lady Diana Bridges with none of which her husband is to intermedle'. Such explicit instructions were necessary, as otherwise all the property and money of a wife were at the disposal of her husband.

Above: St Giles-in-the-Fields where Eleanor was a parishioner. It is often assumed because the first school was in the parish of St Giles', Cripplegate that Eleanor lived in that parish. This is not the case. She lived two miles away in the parish of St Giles-in-the-Fields, which is now in the heart of the West End, close to Tottenham Court Road tube.

Right: Remains of the chapel at Haughton Hall.

Eleanor sounds to have a frugal nature, as she gives her niece, Lady Mary Boscawen, use of her house in Greek Street for two years, to live in or to let to a tenant, but warns her 'not to commit any Wast'. As was the custom, she also rewarded the loyalty of servants and meant to ensure that the proprieties should be observed after her death by providing mourning clothes for them.

Lady Eleanor Holles died in June 1708. Her funeral took place at St Giles-in-the-Fields, and the next month the parish register states that her body was removed to the 'country seat in Nottinghamshire'. This suggests that her resting place is at the burial ground next to the chapel of St James at Haughton.

It was then up to her executrix to carry out the many and varied instructions of the will.

The executrix: Anne Watson

Eleanor chose as her executrix Anne Watson, a woman she refers to in her will as 'cozen'. Anne was related to Eleanor through Eleanor's aunt, Arabella Holles. Arabella was the young and beautiful second wife of Thomas Wentworth, 1st Earl of Strafford. She had died in 1631 at the age of only 22, an early death which the Holles family blamed on Strafford. Arabella's three children from this marriage, William, Anne and Arabella Wentworth, were brought up at Haughton.

Anne Wentworth married Edward Watson, 2nd Lord Rockingham, in 1654, and it was their daughter Anne whom Eleanor chose as executrix. Eleanor seems to have had considerable affection for the Watson family, remembering many of Anne's brothers and sisters and their offspring with bequests. Although to date no portrait of Eleanor has been found, we do know what Anne Watson looked like. There is a beautiful oil painting, attributed to the circle of Godfrey Kneller, of the Honourable Anne Watson on display at Rockingham Castle in Northamptonshire. The National Portrait Gallery also has a picture of Anne Watson when she was somewhat older.

Lady Eleanor's will instructed that once Anne had paid and satisfied all debts, legacies and funeral charges, she should put the 'overplus' of her personal estate to 'such charitable uses' as my said Executrix shall approve of and think fit to dispose of the same'.

By 1709, it was anticipated that the 'overplus' would amount to around £1,500, as this was the amount mentioned in an old document, now lost, which was offered for 'the continual maintaining of a charity school for the teaching of 60 poor girls of the said parish, provided the parish will be at the charge of building a school for that purpose'. This offer persuaded the trustees of the boys' school in the parish of St Giles', Cripplegate, who were already making plans to build a new school on land they had purchased in Redcross Street, to include accommodation for the teaching of girls within the new building.

It is not known why Anne decided to use the 'overplus' for a school. At the end of the seventeenth century, the Church of England believed it was under

threat from nonconformity and irreligion, and that charity schools were a good way to foster the principles of the Church of England among the 'lower orders'. In 1698, an Anglican priest, Thomas Bray, had set up the Society for Promoting Christian Knowledge (SPCK), with the aim of encouraging the foundation of charity schools to educate the poor in the principles of the Church of England. As the purpose was to spread the ideas of the Church of England, it was necessary to educate girls as well as boys. The SPCK was remarkably successful, and it is reckoned that, by 1712, there were 117 such schools in London and Westminster. Anne's own parish in London, St James, Westminster, had one of the first charity schools in London. Anglican sermons in the early eighteenth century regularly reminded the wealthy that it was part of their responsibility to cherish and protect the poor. Educating the young in the principles of the Church of England was God's work and would preserve order in society. Queen Anne was a known supporter of charity schools, and the 1708 sermon preached at the anniversary meeting of the charity children was given by Robert Moss, DD, Chaplain in Ordinary to Queen Anne. Using the legacy from Lady Eleanor's will to establish a charity school for girls would certainly receive royal approval. Anne Watson herself seems to have had a genuine interest in the charity school movement, as when she wrote her own will in 1717, she left £600 towards a charity school 'to be erected at the discretion of my Executor'.

Top: The Hon. Anne Watson, Eleanor's executrix.

Left: Anne, Arabella and William Wentworth after Anthony van Dyck 1642.

ORDERS and RULES

For the Government of Lady *ELEANOR HOLLES*'s Charity School for Fifty poor Girls in the Parish of St. *Giles* without *Cripplegate, London*; Which said Orders and Rules were established and confirmed by a Decree of the High Court of *Chancery, Anno Dom.* 1710.

I. *Orders concerning the School-Mistress.*

THE Mistress to be chosen for this School shall be an unmarried Woman, and a Member of the Church of *England*, of a sober Life and Conversation: One that frequents the Holy Communion, and not under the Age of *Thirty Years:* One who understands well the Grounds and Principles of the *Christian Religion:* And one who can write a fair legible Hand, and cast Accounts.

2. She shall be chosen in for one Year only; and afterwards continue *School Mistress* only during Pleasure; and be removeable by the Trustees, or the greater Part of them, upon a Meeting to be summon'd for that Purpose, without assigning any Cause.

3. The Mistress shall constantly attend her proper Business in the School during the Hours appointed for Teaching, *viz.* from 7 to 11 in the Morning, and from 1 to 5 in the Evening, the *Summer* Half-Year; And from 8 to 11 in the Morning, and from 1 to 4 in the Evening, the *Winter* Half-Year.

4. To the End the chief Design of this School, *which is for the Education of poor Children in the Knowledge and Practice of the Christian Religion, as profess'd and taught in the Church of England,* may be promoted, the Mistress shall make it her chief Business to instruct the Children in the Principles thereof, as they are laid down in the *Church Catechism*; which she shall first teach them to pronounce distinctly and plainly, and then, in order to practise, shall explain it to the meanest Capacity by some good *Exposition* approved of by the Vicar of the said Parish for the Time being. And this shall be done constantly twice a Week, that every thing in the *Catechism* may be the more perfectly repeated and understood; and afterwards shall more largely inform them of their Duty, by the Help of the *Whole Duty of Man:* And when any Number of them can say the *Catechism*, she shall give Notice thereof to the Vicar, in order to their being Catechized in the Church.

5. The Mistress shall take particular Care of the Manners and Behaviours of the poor Children; and by all proper Methods shall discourage and correct the Beginnings of Vice, and particularly *Lying, Swearing, Cursing, taking God's Name in vain,* and the *Prophanation of the Lord's Day,* &c. At the same time minding them of such Parts of the *Holy Scriptures* and of the *Catechism*, where those Things are mentioned as forbidden by God, and the contrary Things as commanded.

6. The Mistress shall teach the Children the true Spelling of Words, and Distinction of Syllables, with the Points and Stops. And as soon as the Girls can read competently well, she shall teach them to knit their Stockings and Gloves, and to sew, mark, and mend their Cloaths, and to spin, and write, as the Trustees shall direct.

7. The Mistress shall bring the Children to Church twice every *Lord's-Day* and *Holy-Days*; and shall teach them to behave themselves with all Reverence while they are in the House of God, and to join in the Public Services of the Church. For which purpose they are always to have ready their Bibles, bound up with the Common-Prayer.

8. The Mistress shall use Prayers Morning and Evening in the School; and shall teach the Children to pray at Home, when they rise, and go to Bed, and to use Graces before, and after Meat. These Prayers to be collected out of the Public Prayers of the Church, or others to be approved by the Vicar of the Parish of St. *Giles Cripplegate* for the Time being. And in the general, the Mistress (in the Business of Religion) shall follow the Directions of the said Vicar.

9. The Names of the Children shall be called over every Morning and Afternoon, to know whether they come constantly at School-Hours: And if any be missing, their Names shall be put down with a Note for *Tardy*, and another for *Absent*. Great Faults, as *Swearing, Stealing,* &c. shall be noted down in Monthly or Weekly Bills, to be laid before the Trustees every Time they meet, in order to their Correction or Expulsion.

10. The Mistress may permit the Children to break-up three times in the Year; namely at the *usual Festivals*, but not oftner; and by no means during *Bartholomew Fair*, for Fear of any Harm by the ill Examples and Opportunities of Corruption at that Season.

11. This School being designed only for the Benefit of such Poor Children, whose Parents and Friends are not able to give them Learning, the Mistress shall not receive any Money or Gifts of the Childrens Friends at their Entry, or Breaking-up, or upon any other Pretence whatsoever: Nor shall the Mistress teach any other Children besides the poor Children of this School; but shall content herself with her Salary, upon Pain of being turn'd out.

II. *Orders to be given to the Parents, or Others, on the Admittance of their Children.*

1. THAT the Parents take Care to send their Children to School at the School-Hours, and keep them at Home on no Pretence whatsoever, except in case of Sickness. And that they send them clean wash'd and comb'd.

2. That they correct their Children for such Faults as they commit at Home, or inform their Mistress of them; Whereby the whole Behaviour of their Children may be the better ordered.

3. That the Children wear their Caps, Bands, Cloaths, and other Marks of Distinction, every Day; whereby it may be better seen what their Behaviour is Abroad.

4. That in Regard due Care will be taken that the Children shall suffer no Injuries by their Mistress's Correction, which is only design'd for their Good, the Parents shall freely submit their Children to undergo the Discipline of the School, when guilty of any Faults, and forbear coming thither on such Occasion: So that the Children may not be countenanced in their Faults, nor the Mistress discouraged in the Performance of her Duty.

5. That the Parents set their Children good Examples, and keep them in good Order when they are at Home, and call on them to say their Prayers Morning and Evening, and to use Graces before and after Meat.

6. And that this School may not only serve for the Instruction and Benefit of the Children, but also of their Parents, particularly of such who cannot read; They, for their own Sakes, as well as their Children's, are frequently to call on them at Home, to repeat their Catechism, and to read the Holy Scriptures, especially on the Lord's-Day, and to use Prayers Morning and Evening in their Family; so that all may be the better informed of their Duty, and by a constant and sincere Practice thereof procure the Blessing of God upon them.

7. If the Parents do not observe the said Orders, which they are to set up in their Houses, their Children are to be dismiss'd the School, and to forfeit their School Cloaths, and other Advantages of the School.

III. *Rules and Directions for the Trustees.*

1. THE Children to be taken into this School, shall be real Objects of the Charity: *Forty* of which shall be living in the said Parish of St. *Giles Cripplegate*, and *Ten* out of any other Parishes, as the major Part of the Trustees shall think fit; and be of the full Age of *Eight* Years, and not above the Age of *Twelve* Years. And before any Child is admitted, the Trustee presenting such Child, shall duly inform himself of the Condition of her Parents, and of her Age, &c. And moreover an Examination shall be made by the Treasurer and Trustees, or some of them, whether she be a real Object of the Charity, and also qualified to be admitted, in respect of Age, Habitation, &c.

II. That the Trustees meet at the School-House every first *Wednesday* after every Quarter Day: And what shall be agreed on at such Meetings, by the Majority of them met, so there be *Four* at the least then present, shall be observ'd; of which Meeting every Trustee shall have Notice. And that the Trustees present, do at every Meeting choose a Chairman, and he to have a casting Vote in case of an Equality.

III. A Treasurer out of the Trustees, that shall reside or live in the said Parish, shall be Annually chosen on *Wednesday* in *Easter-Week*, which Treasurer shall receive the Rents, and Profits of the trusted Premisses, and disburse the same for the Purposes of the said Charity; whereof he shall keep a fair Account, which shall be examined and made up once in the Year, on *Wednesday* in *Easter-Week* yearly; or oftner if required by the Trustees met at a Quarterly Meeting: At which Time all these Orders for the Government of the said Charity shall be read over, before the Business shall be enter'd on; Provided, that on the Death of any Treasurer, a new one shall be chose in his Room, as aforesaid; And upon an Audit-Day the Treasurer may expend upon the Trustees a Sum not exceeding *Twenty Shillings*.

IV. That such of the Trustees as cannot attend at any of the Meetings that shall be appointed, for the Electing of new Trustees, or a School-mistress, or Treasurer, or any other Matter wherein their Vote or Votes are necessary to be had, may, if they please, be at Liberty to Vote by a Proxy, to be appointed under the Hand of such Trustee or Trustees as cannot attend in Person.

V. That when the *Fourteen* Trustees hereunder first nam'd, shall be reduced to *Seven* or a less Number, then the Majority of the Trustees remaining shall choose so many new Trustees as will make up the Number *Fourteen*: And when the *Seven* Trustees herein last-named, who were Inhabitants of the said Parish of St. *Giles Cripplegate*, shall be reduced to *Four*, or a less Number, then the major Part of the Trustees shall choose so many new Trustees of the said Parish of St. *Giles Cripplegate*, as will make up the Number *Seven*.

VI. The Lord Bishop of *London* for the Time being is to be added to the above-mentioned Number of Trustees: And the Vicar of St. *Giles's Cripplegate* for the Time being is to be always a Trustee.

The Names of the present TRUSTEES chosen pursuant to the above mentioned Decree as they now stand, *A. D.* 1748.

'Orders and Rules' established by a decree in Chancery, which set out how the first Lady Eleanor Holles' School was to be run.

Extract from Lady Eleanor Holles' will, December 1707, asking her executrix, Anne Watson, to use any 'overplus' from her will for charitable purposes. – And I doe hereby constitute ordaine and appoint my said Cozen Mss. (Mistress) Anne Watson sole Executrix of this my last Will and Testament. And my will and mind is That after my said Executrix shall have paid and satisfyed all my Debts Legacies and funerall charges the Overplus of all my personall Estate shall be laid out by my said Executrix in such charitable uses as my said Executrix shall approve of and think fitt to dispose of the same ...

What happened next?

The next step was to obtain a decree in the Court of Chancery. This was a way of registering trusteeship arrangements for executors and seems to have been a regular practice when bequests were made for charitable purposes. On 17 April 1710, a decree of the Court of Chancery ordered that Anne should explain to a Master of the Court how she was proposing to spend the 'overplus', the nature of the charity she was proposing, who should be Trustees, and what rules and methods were to govern the charity. Master Gory reported that Anne Watson proposed to use the 'overplus' to purchase land and houses near the Old Artillery Ground, Spitalfields, and adjacent to a new street then called Fort Street. This estate would then be settled on named Trustees, including Eleanor's most senior male relative, John, 3rd Duke of Newcastle; Anne's closest male relatives, headed by Lewis, 3rd Lord Rockingham; and the Trustees from the parish of St Giles', Cripplegate, where the school was to be founded. The income from the properties would be used to maintain 50 girls and a schoolmistress, who would teach them to read and work, and instruct them in the knowledge and practice of the Christian religion as taught in the Church of England, according to rules agreed by the Master. The Master also examined and approved the land and houses that Anne was proposing to purchase, whose rents would provide the yearly income of £62 3s to maintain the girls' school. In the end, the cost of purchasing the houses came to £1,305 3s. There was a shortfall in the purchase money, as the 'overplus' of Lady Eleanor Holles' estate amounted to only £1,192 9s 7d, so the remaining £112 13s 5d was advanced by the parish Trustees. It took until the end of 1710 to complete the formal details and convey the properties to the Trustees. But, as can be seen from the treasurer's account book for the girls' school, which begins in 1710, girls were being taught from Lady Day 1710 (25 March 1710) and took part in the procession of charity children in Whitsun week 1710.

Below: Map showing in the top left the streets in which Anne Watson bought land and houses. The rents from this property were used to support the school.

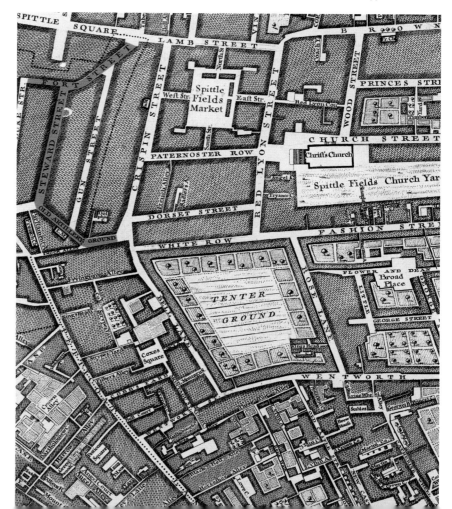

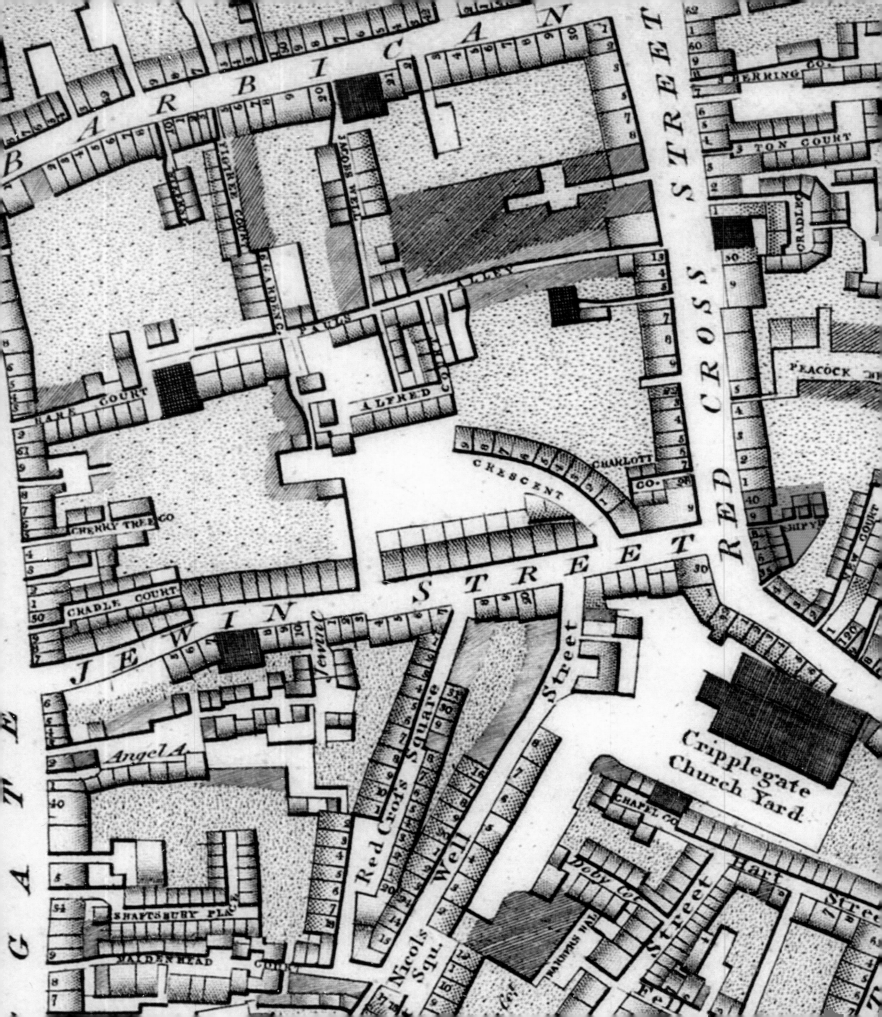

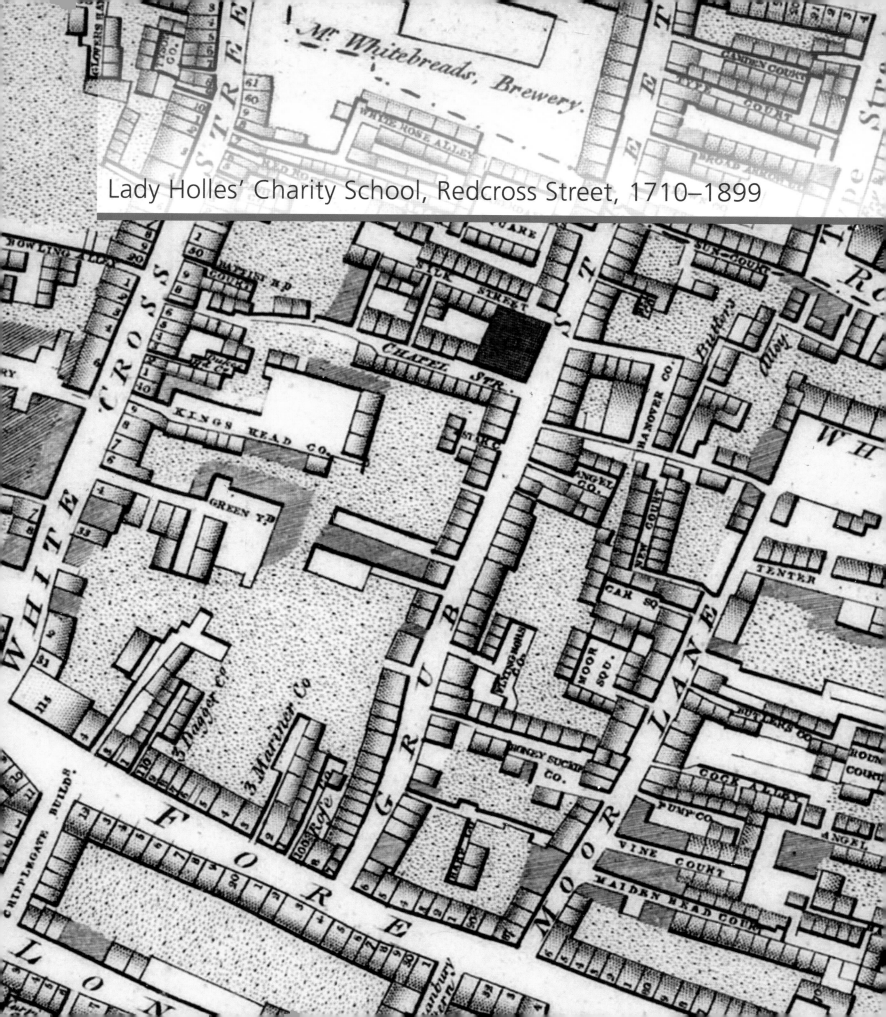

Lady Holles' Charity School, Redcross Street, 1710–1899

Redcross Street, Parish of St Giles' without Cripplegate

> " ... the chief Design of this school, which is for the Education of poor Children in the Knowledge and Practice of the Christian Religion, as profes'd and taught in the Church of England. "

From Orders and Rules established by a Decree of the High Court of Chancery, 1710

Overview, 1710–1899

The history of The Lady Eleanor Holles School began in Redcross Street in the parish of St Giles', Cripplegate, in the City of London. Redcross Street, which disappeared in the intensive bombing of the area in the Second World War, originally ran to the north of the church of St Giles', Cripplegate, linking Fore Street to the east with Golden Lane to the north.

In 1709, a Society, set up in 1690 to hear sermons and collect money for charitable purposes, and which had, from 1698, been running a school to educate and clothe 100 boys, was left a legacy by Mr Thomas Moore, a merchant. This money was used to buy a piece of land in Redcross Street. Voluntary subscriptions then raised the considerable, additional sum of £572 2s 9d needed to build a new school and apartments for two masters. This building also included

a large schoolroom up two pair of stairs with two ground rooms fronting Red Cross Street for an apartment for the

Mistress who teaches 50 girls maintained for some time by the Lady Eleanor Hollis's (sic) legacy of £62.10 per annum. This apartment for the mistress and the school Room up two pair of Stairs for the girls was let upon lease to Felix Feast Esq., Mr Henry Lowth and others of the girls trustees in 1709 at one shilling per annum they having consented and agreed to pay the half charges of all repairs belonging to the said school.

Although this extract from 'An Account of the Rise of the Red Cross Street Society'[7] may appear to suggest that Lady Holles' legacy had been maintaining 50 girls for some time, it is more likely suggesting that the legacy was to maintain the girls for some time into the future. The boys had moved into the new building by December 1709, and, as the Treasurer's account book for the girls' school begins in 1710 and records the paying of a mistress for the girls from Lady Day 1710, it seems that Lady Holles' School for Girls[8] began in the spring of 1710 (see extract from account book below).

The first Lady Holles' School was a simple affair of three rooms. The schoolmistress lived on the premises and had a parlour and kitchen. There was a schoolroom in which all 50 girls were taught together, and, apart from one table with a drawer and 12 Bibles, the only other equipment was eight benches for the girls to sit on.

By the 1830s, the number of girls attending had doubled and had outgrown the premises in the boys' school. The Trustees, as a result of their careful management of the finances of the school, were able to buy their own site and build a much larger school, just for the girls, on a site in Redcross Street facing Jewin Street. In the 1850s, this school was extended by buying tenements in Ship Yard,

Previous page: Horwood map (1792–9) showing numbers 35–38 Redcross Street and Ship Yard behind, the final site of the school in Redcross Street.

Opposite: St Giles' Cripplegate in the eighteenth century.

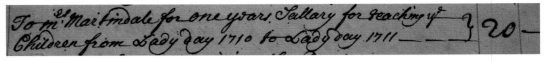

Extract from Trustees' account book: To Mistress Martindale for one years Sallary for teaching the Children from Lady day 1710 to Lady day 1711 £20.

which backed onto the schoolyard, and building an additional schoolhouse. This meant that the Trustees were able 'to extend the benefit of the charity' by increasing the numbers, and, in 1858, they opened an infants' school in addition to the girls' school. The final extension of the premises took place in the 1860s, when four adjoining houses in Redcross Street were pulled down and the site rebuilt.

By 1899, when the school in Redcross Street closed, Lady Holles' legacy was providing an elementary education for 350 girls and clothing about 100 of them.

The school in 1710

The decree of the High Court of Chancery in 1710, which established the school, included Orders and Rules setting out how the school was to be run. These, in outline, followed the model orders and rules published by the SPCK, which was formed in 1698 and encouraged the establishment of charity schools in the London and Westminster area, and elsewhere in the country. From the Orders and Rules a good deal can be learnt about the purpose of the school, how it was to be run and who should attend.

Lady Holles' School was set up to educate and clothe 50 girls between the ages of 8 and 12, who 'shall be real objects of Charity', 40 of whom should be living in the parish of St Giles', Cripplegate, and 10 from any other parish the Trustees should think fit. The Trustees were charged with inquiring into the family background of each girl, to make sure that girls qualified on all counts for admission to the school.

The school was to be overseen by two sets of Trustees. The first 14 named in the decree in Chancery were mostly male relatives of Lady Eleanor and the Honourable Anne Watson, including Lady Eleanor's nephew, John, 3rd Duke of Newcastle, and Anne Watson's brother, Lewis, 3rd Baron Rockingham.

As time went on, this 'out trust' came to be made up more of dignitaries from the City of London. Initially established so that the closest male relatives of the

Top: Eleanor's nephew, John Holles, 3rd Duke of Newcastle.

Right: Rockingham Castle, ancestral home of the Watson family.

deceased could ensure that a legacy, which would otherwise have gone to relatives, was properly used, the 'out trust' played little part in the regular management of the school. This was in the hands of seven Trustees who lived in the parish.[9] In 1710, these men would be considered of the 'middling sort', and included three brewers (one of whom was the memorably named Felix Feast), a distiller, a merchant, an upholsterer and a weaver. To these seven, the Orders added 'for the time being' the Lord Bishop of London, and said that the Vicar of St Giles', Cripplegate, was always to be a Trustee.

The Trustees were motivated by the view that it was the Christian duty of the better-off in society to offer help to the poor. By evangelising the poor, sponsors of charity schools also believed that they were helping to protect the Church of England at a time when it seemed under threat from dissenting groups, and in an age that seemed increasingly irreligious. In doing so, the Trustees would also gain standing in the community. The role of the parish Trustees was twofold: first, to manage the renting of the properties bought by the Honourable Anne Watson in Fort Street and Stewart Street in the Old Artillery Grounds in

List issued by the SPCK in the early eighteenth century of suitable books for charity schools.

'Spittle feilds' (Spitalfields), which provided the income for the school; second, they dealt with all aspects of the running of the school, from appointing the schoolmistress to deciding who could attend and what clothing should be provided. The original parish Trustees played a key role in establishing the school, as it is clear from the accounts that four of them gave loans to make up the purchase price of the properties whose rental would provide the yearly income for the school. The SPCK suggested that the cost of running a school in London for 50 girls 'cloathed' would be £62 3s per annum, 'including the charge of a school room, books and firing, the mistress's salary' and clothing for the pupils. In the early years, between 1713 and 1728, when the rents were not always enough to cover the school's expenses, the income of the school was supplemented by subscriptions from several of the parish Trustees.

Initially, the Trustees were to meet four times a year after the quarter days,[10] but in most years they held monthly meetings. A Treasurer was to be chosen annually from the resident Trustees, to 'receive the rents and profits of the trusted Premises, and disburse the same for the Purposes of the said Charity'. Accounts were to be audited once a year, and on audit day it was allowed that the Treasurer could spend 'a sum not exceeding twenty shillings' on the Trustees. For a number of years, this was spent on a dinner at the Albion Tavern.

The Trustees chose the schoolmistress, and the Orders and Rules gave precise details about the qualifications required. The mistress must be unmarried[11] and not under the age of 30. She should be a member of the Church of England, frequently take Holy Communion and understand well the 'grounds and principles of the Christian religion'. She should be 'of a sober life and conversation', and be able to write 'a fair legible hand, and cast accounts'. As the main purpose of the school was to educate poor girls in 'the knowledge and practice of the Christian religion, as profes'd and taught in the Church of England', it was of paramount importance to those encouraging the setting up of these charity schools that the mistress set a good example to her pupils. She was to be appointed for only a year at a time and was reappointed only at the 'pleasure of the trustees'.

In 1709, part of Samuel Bradford's sermon at the anniversary service of the charity children[12] made clear what Trustees were expecting from masters and mistresses. He said that they should:

give an example of all manner of piety and virtue, and that you should apply yourselves with much diligence and prudence to the forming the tempers and manners of the children committed to your care, as well as to the informing their understandings, attending your business not as those that would please men only, but would approve your selves in the sight of God. Teach them to be modest and humble, diligent and industrious, and above all perfectly true and just both in word and deed. Insinuate into them a sense of Almighty God and the apprehension of a future life. Endeavour to awaken their consciences in these their tender years, that they may act upon Principles all the days of their lives. Give them an early value for their Bibles, that they may ever look upon them as containing the great Rule of their Faith and Practice that Rule by which they are to live, and by which they shall be judged. In a word, manage them as Parents should do (for you are in the place of Parents to them) ...

Mistresses at Lady Holles' School were regularly reappointed, but had to earn their place each year by living up to these expectations.

[64]

Numb. III.

An ACCOUNT of the RATES of Cloathing Poor Children belonging to CHARITY-SCHOOLS.

The Charge of Cloathing a BOY.

	l.	s.	d.
A Yard and half-quarter of Grey *Yorkshire* Broad Cloth 6 quarters wide, makes a Coat	00	03	00
Making the Coat, with Pewter Buttons and all other Materials	00	01	00
A Waſtcoat of the fame Cloth lined	00	03	06
A pair of Breeches of Cloth or Leather lined	00	02	06
1 Knit Cap, with Tuft and String, of any Colour	00	00	10
1 Band	00	00	02
1 Shirt	00	01	06
1 Pair of Woollen Stockings	00	00	08
1 Pair of Shoes	00	01	10
1 Pair of Buckles	00	00	01
1 Pair of Knit or Waſh-Leather Gloves	00	00	07
The Total	00	15	08

The Charge of Cloathing a GIRL.

	l.	s.	d.
3 Yards and half of blue long Ells, about yard wide, at 16d. p. Yard, makes a Gown and Petticoat	00	04	08
Making thereof, Strings, Body-lining, and other Materials,	00	01	00
A Coif and Band of Scotch-Cloth with a Border	00	00	09
Ditto of fine Ghenting	00	01	00
A Shift	00	01	06
A White, Blue, or Checquer'd Apron	00	01	00
A pair of Leather Bodice and Stomacher	00	02	06
1 Pair of Woollen Stockings	00	00	08
1 Pair of Shoes	00	01	08
A Pair of Pattens	00	00	08
1 Pair of Buckles	00	00	01
1 Pair of Knit or Waſh-Leather Gloves	00	00	07
The Total	00	16	01

N. B. *The different Stature of Children is allowed for here; and 50 Children between the Ages of 7 and 12 (one with another) may be cloathed at thefe Rates.*
The Particulars abovementioned may be had at Mr. *R. Parker's* in *Queen's-Court* at St. *Katharines* by the *Tower.*

Numb. IV.

The SPCK list of suitable clothing for boys and girls at charity schools and what these items would cost. The list for a girl included a pair of 'pattens', overshoes for bad weather.

What do we know of the pupils?

The first pupils at the school were poor girls between the ages of 8 and 12, 'whose parents and friends are not able to give them learning'. Forty of the 50 girls selected were to come from the parish of St Giles', Cripplegate. The parish Trustees were expected to use their knowledge of the locality and its inhabitants to make sure that any girl recommended for admission was qualified in all respects. Girls were to be 'real objects of charity', and it was expected that before any Trustee recommended a girl for a place in the school, he would check 'the condition of her parents', to make sure that she was deserving of the 'advantages' that attendance would provide. In 1710, those

advantages included the provision of clothing for the girls, as well as being taught their catechism and how to read. Considerable emphasis was put on parents setting a good example to their children, keeping them in good order when they were at home and continuing the work of the school by asking them to repeat their catechism, reading the Scriptures and praying morning and evening. Through contact with the parents, 'particularly of such who cannot read', it was envisaged that the influence of the school would reach out into the community. Parents were to put up a copy of the Orders in their home, and were warned that if they did not keep to the rules, their children would be dismissed and the school clothes would be forfeited. It would seem that the first pupils came from poor but cooperative homes, with parents who would appreciate the advantages that the school was offering.

Clothing was a major advantage to the girls and consumed a considerable proportion of the income of the charity. The SPCK suggested that the yearly cost of 'cloathing' a girl with '2 coifs, 2 bands, 1 gown and petticoat, 1 pair of knit gloves, 1 pair of stockings and 1 pair of shoes' would be 16s and 1d. The girls were to wear their distinctive uniform, including 'caps, bands (collars)', every day, so that 'it may be better seen what their behaviour is abroad'. It was expected that girls receiving the advantages of the charity would distinguish themselves by their better behaviour and would be a credit to the Trustees and to the founder.

What were schooldays like in 1710?

As girls selected by Trustees began to gather for the beginning of the summer half-year in March 1710, they would climb the stairs to the schoolroom, ready for teaching to begin at 7am. The names of the girls were called and a note made of any who were absent or late. Prayers led by the Mistress were said and from then until 11am, when there was a two-hour break, the teaching of the catechism dominated. The main aim of the school was to ensure that girls had a sound knowledge of the beliefs of the Church of England and how good members of the Church should behave. Knowledge and beliefs were commonly taught at the time by learning the Anglican catechism, a series of questions and answers

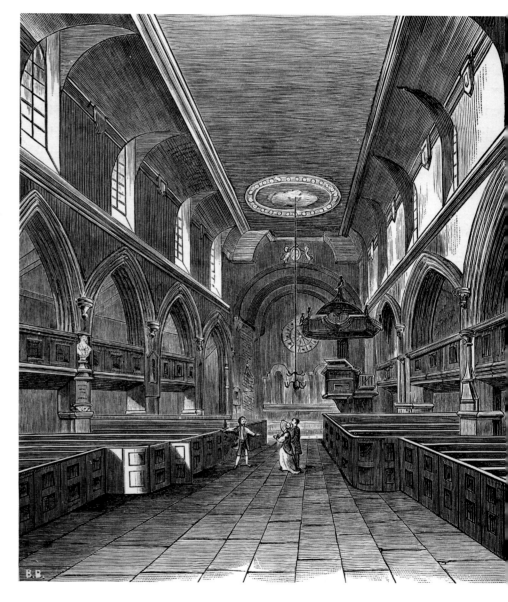

Inside St Giles', Cripplegate in the nineteenth century showing the galleries in which the boys and girls from the Redcross Street schools sat. Girls were expected to attend church regularly otherwise they would be dismissed from school.

which prepared children for confirmation. The catechism reminded them of the promises that had been made for them at baptism, taught them the articles of faith, went over the Ten Commandments and taught them what they should learn from these. Of particular interest to those who supported the charity school movement was the answer to the question, 'What is thy duty towards thy neighbour?' The answer made it clear that girls should 'order' themselves 'lowly and reverently to all my betters', and do their 'duty in that state of life, unto which it has pleased God to call them'. In other words, the Church taught the girls that their position in life was given to them by God and that they should do their best in that station in life. Girls who attended the school were destined to be domestic servants. The catechism encouraged them to accept this as their appointed lot in life, and prepared them to be honest, truthful and industrious servants and loyal members of the Church of England – a far cry from the ideas of the twenty-first century that talents and merit enable you to go as far as your ambition inspires you.

We may imagine the Mistress getting the girls to repeat the lines of the catechism after her, and then explaining until everything in the catechism could be repeated by the girls and was understood. Once a number of them could say the catechism, the Mistress was to tell the Vicar so that the girls could say their catechism at one of the two services they attended with the Mistress every Sunday. Girls were expected to attend church twice every Sunday and 'Holy-Day', when they sat in one of the galleries that then existed in St Giles' Church. It was another of the Mistress's responsibilities to teach the girls how to behave with 'reverence' in Church and how to join in the public services.

Afternoon school began at 1pm, with the names of the girls again being called, 'and if any be missing, their names shall be put down with a note for tardy, and another for absent'. Punctuality was especially prized as a virtue that should be encouraged in girls who were to be domestic servants – clearly the beginning of the modern register! In the summer half of the year, school went on until 5pm.

As soon as boys in charity schools could read 'competently well', they were taught to write 'a fair legible hand' and given some grounding in arithmetic, 'to fit them for Services and Apprenticeships', but the expectations for girls were different. After reading and spelling, knitting stockings and mittens, sewing, mending clothes and spinning took precedence over writing. It was not until 1770 that the Trustees first appointed a writing master for an hour a week to teach just 12 of the 50 girls. School ended with prayers, before the girls were dismissed into Redcross Street.

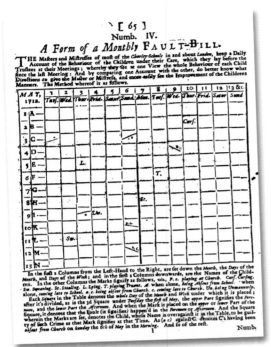

[65]
Numb. IV.
A Form of a Monthly FAULT-BILL.

THE Masters and Mistresses of most of the *Charity-Schools* in and about *London*, keep a Daily Account of the Behaviour of the Children under their Care, which they lay before the Trustees at their Meetings; whereby they see at one View the whole Behaviour of each Child since the last Meeting: And by comparing one Account with the other, do better know what Directions to give the Master or Mistress, and most easily see the Improvement of the Childrens Manners. The Method whereof is as follows.

The type of register which the school Mistress was expected to keep. This not only recorded lateness and absence from school and church but acted as an account of the behaviour of each child which the Mistress showed to the Trustees at their monthly meetings.

Particular emphasis was laid on 'the manners and behaviours of the poor children'. The Mistress was 'by all proper methods to discourage and correct the beginnings of Vice', such as lying, swearing, cursing and taking God's name in vain. Faults like these were to be recorded on a grid such as the one on the left, and shown to the Trustees at their regular meetings. Discipline in school was strict and certainly included corporal punishment. Parents were urged not to complain when their daughter was disciplined, as this was designed for her good.

By modern standards the curriculum was limited and monotonous, but was designed to fit girls for the lives they would lead, and the lives of poor girls in the early eighteenth century were harsh. However, there were more public and prestigious occasions to enjoy. Although the school was forbidden to have a holiday during the St Bartholomew's Fair, held nearby every August, to protect the girls from 'the ill examples and opportunities of corruption' provided by the acrobats, puppets, sideshows and wild animals on show, the girls took part every year in the annual procession of the charity children from schools in London and Westminster. On 1 June 1710, dressed in new sets of clothes for the occasion, accompanied by the Trustees, Mistress Martindale and the Parish Beadle, the girls joined boys from the boys' school, and almost 3,000 other charity school children, to process to St Sepulchre's Church in Giltspur Street. There, in the presence of some of those who supported the charity schools, they listened to a sermon given by a renowned preacher, George Smalridge, on the theme of 'The great charity of educating poor children'. In this he preached that what marked out 'men' as human was helping others. He argued that if humans harden their hearts against the distressed and are deaf to the needy, then they forfeit the title of men and 'degenerate into the rank of barbarous and cruel savages'. In his sermon he observed that the inclination towards 'acts of pity and compassion' is, generally speaking, 'most

strong and operative in Women'. He assured those who were sincerely charitable and who 'act upon noble and disinterested principles' that they could look forward 'to those more Glorious rewards, which are reserv'd for the Charitable at the great Day of Retribution'. Perhaps the Honourable Anne Watson and others of the noble trustees, her own male relatives and those of Lady Eleanor may have been present to hear Smalridge say that 'Acts of compassion and charity add a new lustre to persons eminent for their Rank and Dignity', and he referred to the example set by Queen Anne herself in supporting a charity school in Kensington.

The sermon makes clear the religious and social benefits that the ruling classes and the Church of England believed would result from supporting the establishment of charity schools. Smalridge talks of 'the pleasing spectacle' to men, Angels and God of the assembled children, who have been rescued from the 'hazards of body and soul', and of the blessings that will now instead come 'to themselves, to their families, to these populous cities, to the whole Kingdom, to the establish'd Church'. He sees the 'comely order' of the processions of the children and their 'decent and religious behaviour in the House of God' as evidence of the benefits of their education.

The children sang a hymn in unison and then returned to school for a celebratory dinner.

Right: The sideshows and frivolity of St Bartholomew's Fair from which the Trustees wanted to protect their girls.

56

The plaque which was ordered by the Trustees in 1857 to mark the building of the infants' school in Redcross Street. The right hand shield was later used as the Hackney badge.

Growth of the school, 1710–1875

Lady Holles' School prospered in Redcross Street for the next 165 years. Although, between 1713 and 1728, there were several occasions when, in order to cover the expenses, some of the Trustees had to help out with additional donations, they managed the income well. By the 1820s, they had built up a sufficient reserve to think of moving out of the school they still shared with the boys and into their own school. In 1831, they bought 39 and 40 Redcross Street and five tenements on the north side of Ship Yard, which were pulled down, and a new school building was erected in 1832. This was a two-storey building on Redcross Street, with a back door which opened onto Ship Yard. The schoolroom was on the first floor, with bedrooms and the closet for the girls' cloaks on the second floor. At ground-floor level there was an entrance hall, a committee room where the Trustees met almost every month, and a room for the Mistress. The kitchen and store rooms were in the basement.

By 1832, the charity was educating and clothing double the number provided for in the 1710 foundation. As the income from the trust had grown, the Trustees increased the numbers of pupils, so that by the time the new schoolhouse opened, 100 girls between the ages of 8 and 14 were being educated and clothed. By the mid-nineteenth century, numbers had risen again to 150.

Despite the costs of the new premises, the Trustees continued to have a good surplus each year, so, in the late 1840s, they began to consider what measures they could take to further extend and improve the school. They decided to establish an infants' school. In 1853, in

their application to the Charity Commissioners, who by then were regulating trusts such as Lady Eleanor's, the Trustees explained that the income of the said charity was now sufficient to enable them to extend its benefits. They proposed to do this by increasing the number of scholars, and they asked that power be given to them to admit to the school poor female children under the age of 8.

In 1849, the Trustees had already bought up more houses in Ship Yard, whose yard was shared with the school. In 1857, these houses were pulled down to provide the site for an additional schoolhouse for 120 children. This new schoolhouse, which connected with the schoolhouse built in 1832, enabled the Trustees to open an infants' school in April 1858. A Mistress was appointed to run the new infants' school, subject to the superintendence of the Mistress of the girls' school.

In 1861, the Trustees decided to expand the school again. They had bought the freehold to the adjoining tenements and shops of 35–38 Redcross Street in 1859. These premises were pulled down, enabling new buildings to be added to the existing school. Doorways connected the old and the new buildings. This provided the space for the Trustees to set up an Industrial School in 1867, initially for ten girls aged between 14 and 16. They seem to have built more space than was needed for the school, as it was decided to let out the ground floor and basement of the new buildings.

The houses in Redcross Street and Ship Yard which were used as the site for the school can be seen clearly on the Horwood map drawn at the end of the eighteenth century. The new schoolhouse, which opened in 1832, was

These were the wooden houses, 35–38 Redcross Street, which were demolished to extend the school. Tune the signwriter was at no. 38 and there was a greengrocer's shop at no. 36.

built where 39 and 40 Redcross Street had stood. Behind these houses you can see the tenements in Ship Yard, which were demolished to build the new infants' school, which opened in 1858. Adjoining 39 and 40 Redcross Street are numbers 35–38 Redcross Street, described as 'wooden erections' which provided the site for the final stage in the expansion of the school in the 1860s.

'Habits of order and industry', Archdeacon Hale

From the beginning, Lady Holles' School aimed to provide a Christian education, within the framework of the established Church of England, for poor girls who otherwise would not have access to any form of education. The Trustees maintained this aim throughout the eighteenth and nineteenth centuries. In addition, one of the purposes of the foundation was to train young women to 'habits of order and industry', and, as Archdeacon Hale, the Vicar of St Giles', Cripplegate, explained in a letter in the mid-nineteenth century, 'the first qualification which we should desire to impart to all the girls of the school' is that they should 'be able to read and write correctly, to understand the simple rules of arithmetic, and to give an account of the contents of Holy Scripture and of their faith and duty as explained and laid down in the formularies of our Church'. The school considered its job well done if a girl left with a 'good character', had found a situation as a domestic servant and remained in that position for at least 12 months.

That this education appealed to poorer parents in the parish of St Giles', Cripplegate, and nearby seems evident. Vacancies in the school were quickly filled, and the Trustees began to insist that parents must prove a girl's date of birth and show evidence of her baptism, as places were restricted to members of the Church of England.

How the school was organised

Until the late eighteenth century, one Mistress taught all the girls. But in 1782, as numbers began to rise, the Trustees appointed an Assistant Mistress, and by the beginning of the nineteenth century there were three staff in all. This way of organising the classes appeared to change in 1815, when the Trustees appointed Charlotte Clayton as Undermistress, provided she 'make herself perfect in the Madrass [sic] Plan of Education'. The Madras method of teaching large numbers of children, better known today as the monitorial system, was developed by Andrew Bell, a Church of England clergyman working as a missionary in Madras, as a way of teaching large numbers of orphans when there were few teachers available. In 1797, he published details of his system, in which a teacher taught monitors repetitive exercises, which they then repeated to the other children in the school. This was seen as an efficient and economical method of teaching large numbers of children and became the most popular method used in schools in the first half of the nineteenth century. The monitorial system spread rapidly under the National Society,[13] set up in 1811 to promote the education of the poor in the principles of the Church of England. It meant the Trustees could employ only one Mistress at Lady Holles' School, but that she must have training in how to use this method. Charlotte Clayton attended the National Society training school in London, to gain her certificate showing she was trained in the principles of the system.

Snapshot of 1846

For the most part, we have only hints from the records of how the school was organised. We get a rare, more detailed, glimpse in August 1846, during the time that this same Charlotte Clayton was Mistress. The Secretary to the Trustees, John Ellis, was responding to a letter from the Lord Mayor of London. The Lord Mayor had

The 'Madras' or monitorial system in which one school teacher taught a lesson to older pupils who then repeated the lesson to younger pupils.

written to say that a witness, Fanny Wettenhall, aged 12 years, who had been four years in Lady Holles' School, had appeared before him and 'when asked was unable to write'. Fanny's father had implied to the Lord Mayor that this was the fault of the school, as 'at one time the School had three persons appointed to instruct the children but that now only one infirm Woman of the age of 65 (Mistress Clayton) holds the situation of instructress to 150 children'. The Lord Mayor 'begs the Trustees will inform him if the Child's father has spoken what is correct', and continues, 'because if so his lordship will consider it his duty to make enquiries with regard to the management of the school'. The Trustees respond promptly and robustly to what they see as a slur on their management of the school. In his reply to the Lord Mayor, which was sent 'without delay', John Ellis gives us a succinct description of how the school was run. He tells the Lord Mayor that in 1846 there were 120 children attending the school, 110 of whom were provided with clothes, with 10 others admitted on probation. The children are educated 'upon the National System and divided into three distinct classes'. He goes on to say that, in accordance with a decree of Chancery, a Mistress is appointed and that she is assisted in educating the children by five teachers, and in addition there are five assistant teachers, 'selected from the first class scholars'. He is describing the monitorial system. He also makes it clear that writing and arithmetic are taught by 'a competent Master' only to selected pupils from the first and second class. John Ellis goes on to explain that, despite her time in the school, Fanny, 'from want of capacity and attention, did not make that progress in her Education

which the School is calculated to impart', so had not risen above the third class. In addition, he points out that her parents had withdrawn her two years before the appointed time of her leaving at 14.

The Trustees defend Mistress Clayton by saying that the school 'has always been under the management of One mistress', and that the present Mistress has conducted the school 'to the entire satisfaction of the Trustees for the last 22 years'. They defend themselves by making it clear that their management is 'hands-on', and point out they meet monthly to 'superintend' the affairs of the school.

The Lord Mayor's letter seems to have caused a considerable stir. Statements had appeared in the press and the Trustees decided that only a public examination of the children could refute the accusations circulating that they had been neglecting their instruction. This public examination, to which were invited Trustees, officiating clergy of the parish, many of the influential inhabitants of the parish, a representative from the National Society from Grantham and the Lord Mayor, was held on 3 September 1846. The Lord Mayor did not attend, but the Alderman for Cripplegate, Thomas Challis, who was Sheriff of London that year, chaired the events. All five classes were examined, and it was reported that even the youngest pupils, although some had been taught for only three months, could read and spell simple words. The writing books were examined and it was made clear that writing was taught only to those girls who 'distinguish themselves by their general application or evident ability'. More than half were able to read Scriptures and other books, 'not merely in the manner which usually prevails in Schools of

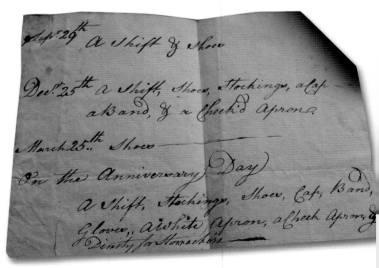

Model of a charity school girl. A pupil from the Redcross Street school remembered that, in the late nineteenth century, the model was kept on a landing in the school. Models such as these were often kept in niches on the front of charity schools to remind those passing of the need to be generous in their support.

a like description, but with care and feeling'. In the view of the Revd Jesson, MA, incumbent (Vicar) of Spittlegate, Grantham, who had himself had 'superintendence of more than 150 children', he had 'never found Children more ready and capable of answering the several questions put to them'.

The opinion of the meeting was that the examination had been 'highly satisfactory' and the Trustees and Mistress were vindicated.

Clothing

From the school's foundation the provision of clothing to all pupils must have been a considerable attraction for poor parents. In the early part of the nineteenth century, a probationary period was introduced, during which girls were not clothed, to ensure that pupils were suitable to benefit from the education and were not seeking admission just for the clothing. The Trustees were much more generous in their provision than the SPCK had envisaged at the beginning of the eighteenth century. By the beginning of the nineteenth century, over the course of a year, girls were provided with a gown; upper and lower petticoats; two shifts; a bodice; one stomacher; a girdle; buckle and lace; two aprons, one white and one coloured; one cap; one band; two pairs of stockings, one pair 'of their own knitting'; one pair of mittens, also knitted by the girl; three pairs of shoes and one pair of buckles; a hat; and, every two years, a cloak. In addition, a regular order was placed annually, about October, for 'patterns' (pattens), overshoes for the winter weather.

The cost of clothing the girls was a major expense in the running of the school, and tradespeople were asked to provide samples of the goods to be supplied before the orders were awarded each year. This gave the Trustees considerable powers of patronage in the area; supplying 100 pairs of shoes three times a year, for example, was a substantial order. Preference was always given to suppliers from within the parish of St Giles', Cripplegate, and the Trustees kept a careful eye on the quality provided. Suppliers were called to account if the Trustees felt that

goods provided had been of an inferior quality to the ones supplied as a sample. They had no qualms about changing a supplier if their goods were not up to the mark. The Trustees also made provision for cutting the girls' hair. Until 1851, this was done once a quarter, but was then increased to three times in the summer and twice in winter.

Clothing was given out four times a year, on the quarter days of Michaelmas, Christmas, Lady Day and on the Anniversary Day, which usually took place in Whitsun week. A complete set of new clothes was handed out for the anniversary service of the founding of the charity schools, so that the pupils' smart appearance would reflect well on their school and its Trustees. Mrs Louisa Hutchins, who had joined the school in 1866, when she was 4 years old, and attended for ten years, remembered that in her time girls had two identical sets of clothing, one for weekdays and one for Sundays. Girls had Wednesday afternoons off and went to school on Saturday mornings, which was when they collected their best clothes for church attendance on Sundays.

High days and holidays

In the early part of the eighteenth century, children from the charity schools across London and Westminster often took part in huge public occasions, such as the gathering of children in the Strand to celebrate the Treaty of Utrecht

Note from Treasurer's account book showing the clothing issued each quarter.

in 1713. The girls of Redcross Street were certainly there; a tiny contingent of 50 amidst the 4,000 charity school children singing hymns as part of the celebrations. The Treasurer's account book for 1713 refers to paying '10 and half the head' towards 'charg of seats for the children on the thanksgiving day'. The Treaty brought to an end war against France, waged since 1702 over who should succeed to the throne of Spain. One of Lady Eleanor's relatives, Thomas Wentworth, Lord Strafford, was one of the two British representatives at the Treaty talks.

Girls were also present when George I entered London on 30 September 1714, to become the new monarch. The charity children were seated in the churchyard of St Paul's and sang the 21st Psalm as the new King and his son passed in their coach. The Treasurer noted that he had 'paid for 50 seats for the children upon the kings comeing'. At least one of the royal party was impressed, as it was reported that 'His Royal Highness the Prince was pleased to say, that the charity children was one of the finest sights he had ever seen in his life'.

But the highlight of each year was the anniversary meeting of the charity children, which had begun in 1704 and was held every year until 1877. Girls were prepared, for months before, with extra coaching in psalmody given by the church organist of St Giles', Cripplegate. On the appointed day, usually Thursday in Whitsun week, the clergy of St Giles', the Trustees of the boys' and girls' schools and the children met to form their processional line. New clothes had been given out for the occasion and the girls carried nosegays. The event drew large crowds, so each year the Trustees paid for the Parish Beadle and at least one constable to protect the girls on the route. Children from each charity school in the London and Westminster area processed in lines to the service and entered the church in alphabetical order of parishes. From 1782, as the numbers had grown to upwards of 5,000, the anniversary service was held in St Paul's Cathedral. The route from Redcross Street took the procession down Jewin Street, along Aldersgate Street, through Paternoster Row, to the cathedral.

Charity children gathered in the Strand to celebrate the Treaty of Utrecht in 1713. Engraving by George Vertue, 1715.

imagined'. Some idea of the spectacle can be seen in this engraving of 1842.

By the mid-nineteenth century, the meeting of the charity school children had become a huge and moving public occasion, regularly reported in *The Times*. The singing of the charity children had an emotional impact on those who heard it. In June 1791, Joseph Haydn wrote in his 'London Notebook' after his visit to the service, 'No music ever moved me so deeply in my whole life'. In 1851, Hector Berlioz wrote to his sister after hearing the charity children in St Paul's, 'I have never *seen* or *heard* anything as moving in its immense grandeur than this gathering of poor children singing, arranged in a colossal amphitheatre'. It is reported that he was so impressed with the impact of the chorus of 6,500 children that he added a part for children's voices in his *Te Deum*.

By 1870, the anniversary gathering was a substantial musical event. The programme in 1870 began with the Hundredth Psalm, followed by prayers. Psalms were sung by the Cathedral Choir, with the children joining in the *Gloria Patri*. The *Te Deum* and *Jubilate* were sung together by the Choir and children. As *The Graphic* reported on 11 June 1870, 'The Coronation Anthem preceded the Prayer for the Queen and the well-known chorale from Mendelssohn's St Paul, "Sleepers, Awake", was given before the sermon, after which four verses of the 104th Psalm, and Handel's magnificent *Hallelujah Chorus* brought this impressive service to a conclusion'.

Whilst the girls may have enjoyed the grandeur of the occasion, once the service was over they may have looked forward even more to the dinner they were treated to back at school. By tradition, dinner on this occasion for the Holles' girls was roast veal, followed by 'plumb' puddings and buns, washed down with table beer. Cutlery, mugs and dinner plates seem to have been hired for the occasion.

In the nineteenth century, the girls also enjoyed other outings. In 1851, they visited the Great Exhibition in Hyde Park. After the Crystal Palace was moved to Sydenham, the girls went every year, sometimes to sing, taking a packed lunch of boiled beef sandwiches and biscuits. The girls travelled in horse-drawn vans and were accompanied by the Trustees, who travelled in style, in an open, full-sized carriage for six, with two horses and postilion.

Inside the cathedral, benches had been built in the shape of a Roman amphitheatre, rising in tiers to a considerable height, for the children to stand on. Spectators were seated in the centre of this amphitheatre and in the aisles. Banners displaying the names of the schools swayed in the air above the children's heads. The report in *The Graphic* of June 1870 remarked on the different colours of the children's uniforms and said, 'A prettier or more touching spectacle can hardly be

The Trustees

The preacher of the 1710 sermon, given at the celebration of the founding of the charity schools, in St Sepulchre's Church, spoke of the high standards expected of Trustees. In carrying out this 'good work' of 'nourishing, maintaining and instructing' the children, they should show diligence, 'unspotted integrity', 'prudent management' and 'disinterested intentions'. The record of the Lady Holles' Trustees from 1710 to 1875 seems to match up to these expectations. In 1819, the only fault the Commissioners inquiring into charities could report was that the income of the trust far exceeded the expenditure.

Between 1710 and 1875, the parish Trustees, all male and, apart from the Vicar, local businessmen, met regularly, usually once a month, at the schoolhouse. They managed the properties which had been in the original settlement from Anne Watson, an increasingly onerous task, as the Spitalfields area of London began to change in character and the properties began to show their age. Relying on the advice of an architect and surveyor, they met the challenges and continued to provide the charity with a good income. Their other task was the management of the school.

By the early nineteenth century, Trustee meetings had developed a regular pattern. Once the minutes of the previous meeting had been read and confirmed, girls were admitted either to the probationary list or, after a suitable period, to the school. To ensure that the benefits of the charity were given only to those qualified, Trustees continued to ask for evidence of age and baptism. In 1831, they also appointed a medical attendant, and decided, in 1844, that 'in future all children previous to their being admitted into the school shall be examined by the Surgeon and his certificate produced to the Mistress stating that such child is in a healthy state, and a fit and proper object to be admitted into the Establishment'.

Girls who had spent their full time in the school also attended Trustee meetings, 'to return thanks' for their time at the school and to receive the rewards provided by the Trustees on the recommendation of the Mistress. These rewards varied over the course of the eighteenth and nineteenth centuries. From 1776, the Trustees awarded extra clothing to a girl on leaving the school, provided she

School banner

The banners used by the two Cripplegate schools have survived and been restored. Although banners bearing the names of schools were used at the charity children's services in the eighteenth century, the first reference to a banner for Lady Holles' School is in 1850, when the Trustees ordered a banner of about 30 inches by 30 inches, with gold embroidery. It may be that they wanted a new banner to mark the fact that they had also decided that year to increase the number of pupils to 150. If, as seems likely, the banner was used only once a year for the anniversary service, this may explain why, even before restoration, the banner was in relatively good condition.

In the 1970s, the banner seems to have had a lucky escape. Stella Tomlins (then Wright) taught at LEH between 1965 and 1975. During that time, she ran the Naturalist Club and asked Chessington Zoo to bring an orang-utan to the club, which met after school. However, they arrived nearly 30 minutes early. Stella takes up the story.

I quickly thought to say put them into the small waiting room (where the banners from the boys' and girls' schools were on display). At 4.10pm I was greeted with the fact that the orang-utan had escaped, tearing one of the precious school banners that hung on the wall, and had made it along the corridor to the outside and was entertaining not only our girls, but boys playing cricket at Hampton Grammar School. Eventually, it was recaptured and carried, rather tired out, as it was quite a youngster, to the biology laboratory for my club members to meet. Chaos had reigned, but a bottle of school milk seemed to pacify the orang-utan and, of course, the event was a wow!

Stella had to face the Head Mistress the next day. It seems the damage was done to the boys' banner, as when the two banners were sent for repair in 2010, the repairer reported that the boys' banner had 'splits and tears' and had at some point been crudely repaired.

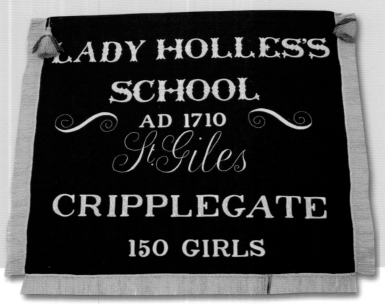

received a good recommendation from the Mistress. The warmth or otherwise of her recommendation determined how much was awarded. So, for example, in 1823, when Jane Elizabeth Beresford attended to return thanks on leaving the school, the Mistress having reported that her conduct had been very improper during her stay, the usual clothes were not ordered for her. Likewise, in September 1828, when Mary Ann Fish attended to return thanks on leaving the school, it was recorded that in consequence of 'general irregularity of Conduct it was considered prudent to mark the displeasure of the Trustees by Ordering Shoes and Stockings only'.

A place in service could mitigate an indifferent report, so, in 1822, although the Mistress gave Sarah Scarce only an indifferent character, as she had a job to go to the Trustees agreed that she should have the usual clothes. A star pupil such as Eunice Oats, in August 1838, received the usual clothes, ticket money earned by being punctual, a medal and had her needlework (probably a sampler) framed and glazed.

From 1851, all leavers received a Bible and prayer book. Ann Hearn, whose Bible is in the school archives, was one of the first recipients of this gift. She had originally asked permission to leave school before her time was up, as her parents had obtained 'a situation' for her. However, she was taken ill and her parents decided to send her into the country to recover. The Trustees decided that 'for her general good conduct during her time in the school' she should be awarded the usual clothing, her 'ticket money' and 'a superior bible and prayer book bound in Pearl Octavo'.

Favour from the Trustees could extend beyond your time in school. In 1836, it was decided that 'whenever a Girl after leaving this School shall continue in the same situation for the term of One year within the period of 18 months subsequent to her leaving it she shall receive a Gratuity of £1'. Girls, such as Jane Rhodes, who appeared at a Trustee meeting in 1839, with a note 'in testimony of her good conduct' from her employer, Mrs Stapleton of Clapham, regularly appear after 12 months in their situation to claim the money.

Girls left the school at 14 and the majority of them went into service. However, we have evidence of a few taking up other work. In 1853, Elizabeth Brightman was allowed to stay on as a teacher until she was 15. She was paid 3 shillings a week and provided with school clothing. She obviously did well, as the following year she was allowed to remain as a teacher and her salary was doubled.

Trustees had the final say in matters of discipline and dismissal of girls from the school. Parents were asked to attend meetings to explain their daughter's conduct and to promise improvement on pain of dismissal. The Trustees were keen to maintain standards and support the Mistress, as in the case of Louisa Thomas, for example, who was suspended in 1804 until her father called on the Treasurer to make apology for her mother's behaviour to the mistresses. There are other cases where they exercised compassion, based on their knowledge of the individuals, as in the example of a girl in 1817, who had frequently been absent from church and school. One of the Trustees promised to see the girl's father, whom he considered 'a sober industrious man', and said that the fault appeared to lay entirely with the mother, who 'stupifies [*sic*] herself with strong liquors constantly'. The girl was allowed to stay at school. In another case, in 1844, it was decided that, although a girl had served her full time in school and should leave, 'this child being an orphan and not provided with a situation the Trustees gave permission for her to remain in the school until further directives'.

It was not until the mid-nineteenth century that, apart from the Mistress, there was any involvement by women in the meetings. In 1868, the Trustees decided that the wife or daughter of each Trustee should form a Ladies' Committee. However, its remit was limited to recommending the clothing and materials needed for the children.

There is no doubt that the Trustees of Lady Holles' School took their responsibilities seriously and were conscientious, which could not be said of all such trusts. Parish Trustees often remained trustees until death, and a number of Trustees served for long periods. William King, who became a Trustee in 1834, was elected Treasurer and oversaw major changes in the development of the school before he resigned in 1868, is a good example. The pride he felt in the achievements of his 34 years as a Trustee is palpable in the letter he wrote to the Trustees when he resigned his post of Treasurer in 1868.

Elected a Trustee in 1834, the number of children amounted to 120 and in a short period were increased to 150 and the School house greatly enlarged. In the year 1854 I had the privilege of being elected Treasurer the entire revenue amounting to £1,313. From that period to the present time the number of children have been doubled and 12 of the Elder girls admitted and fully provided for as a commencement of an Industrial school. At the same time upwards of £10,000 have been expended in buildings and improvements of property, laying a sure foundation for the future benefit of the Institution without any addition to the endowment, whilst the average of the yearly income has not decreased the present year amounting to £1,437.

The Bible presented to Ann Hearn in 1851 in recognition of her 'good conduct'.

This photograph shows the last building in Redcross Street which housed Lady Holles' School. The final extension of the building had provided more room than was needed for the school so the ground floor was rented out to various businesses which can be seen on the right of the photograph. This photograph also raises a mystery. The inscription clearly reads 'Lady Holles's School for Girls Instituted AD 1702'. There is no other evidence at present which suggests that the school existed in 1702.

The Trustees decided to mark William King's retirement by buying and inscribing a piece of plate, 'not exceeding the value of 15 guineas', to be presented to him on his resigning the office of Treasurer, 'which he has held for so many years'. Another, Septimus Read, served for 30 years as Trustee and Treasurer, and it was recorded in the minutes of February 1873 that he had 'devoted his time and best energies to further the interests of the institution'. These two and many others clearly did feel the 'Satisfaction in their Own Consciences', which the 1710 sermon saw as one of the rewards of being a Trustee.

The end of an era

Between 1710 and the early nineteenth century, the Trustees, although always keeping in mind the terms of the decree set out in the High Court of Chancery, made their own decisions about the school. The nineteenth century brought other influences to bear.

As schools founded on the principles of the Church of England, it was not surprising that in 1823 the boys' school and Lady Holles' School were 'united' to the National Society. From 1811, this coordinated the efforts of the Church of England in education. In 1853, after investigations by the government into abuses in the way some charitable trusts were being managed had led to the passing of the Charitable Trusts Act, the Trustees became accountable to the Charity Commission. In 1869, the changing needs of society led to the introduction of the Endowed Schools Act, which allowed the terms of charitable trusts, such as that of Lady Holles' School, to be rewritten. This forced substantial changes onto the school. Determined to make sure that charitable trusts were true to the wishes of the founder, but also fitted in with the government's ideas about education, Trustees of schools such as Lady Holles' School had to discuss with the Commissioners a scheme for the future management of the school. Between 1869 and 1875, one of the Endowed School Commissioners, Mr JG Fitch, met the Trustees on several occasions, 'to confer with them on behalf of the Commissioners respecting the way in which this endowment may be most usefully applied for the future'. These discussions resulted in the scheme approved by Her Majesty in Council on 28 June 1875, which led to the

Redcross Street school becoming a public elementary school for girls on 9 August 1875.

In 1875, the school was about to move into a new era. The Trustees could look back with satisfaction at the contribution they had made to society in their part of the city. The mindset of the established Church in mid-Victorian times mirrored in many ways attitudes of the early eighteenth century about the inevitability of a class-structured society. The school had served to equip poor girls for their station in life and had fulfilled its aim well.

After 1875

The Endowed Schools Act 1869

In the mid-nineteenth century, three reports, the Clarendon, the Taunton and the Newcastle, dealt with educational provision for the different social classes into which Victorian society was divided. The Taunton Commission dealt with schooling for the middle classes and the Newcastle Commission with the working class. The Schools Inquiry Commission which produced the Taunton Report had looked at the provision for education for middle-class girls in particular. It found that there were only 13 schools for girls in the country. Evidence from leading advocates of better provision for girls, such as Dorothea Beale and Frances Buss, also made it clear that the education of middle-class girls was lacking in its scope and content. The 1869 Endowed Schools Act, a direct result of the Taunton Commission Report, provided for Commissioners to discuss with trusts, such as the one running Lady Holles' School, ways in which their endowments could be most usefully applied for the future. Trustees were invited to make their own suggestions for the consideration of the Commissioners.

The Endowed Schools Act had considerable implications for Lady Holles' School. The scheme finally approved by Queen Victoria in Council on 28 June 1875 took the charity well beyond the scheme originally proposed by the Trustees. In their initial proposal to the Commission, the Trustees had suggested that the charity should educate 150 infants at a day school, provide clothing and primary education for another 150 girls at a day school, and maintain and provide industrial training for 50 girls in the industrial school. The thinking of the

PUNCH'S ALMANACK FOR 1890.

MR. PUNCH'S FOUR PRIZE MIDDLE-CLASS WIVES.

MR. PUNCH LEFT MRS. JONES PLAYING LAWN-TENNIS WITH MR. JONES—THAT THE LITTLE JONES MIGHT BE SOUND IN WIND AND LIMB.

HE FOUND MADAME DUBOIS KEEPING MONSIEUR DUBOIS' BOOKS—IN ORDER THAT HE MAY PROSPER AND GROW RICH, AND SPARE AN EXTRA CLERK.

HE FOUND FRAU MÜLLER COOKING SAUERKRAUT AND SAUSAGES—THAT HERR MÜLLER SHOULD EAT OF THE BEST AND CHEAPEST AND MOST DIGESTIBLE.

HE FOUND MRS. VAN TRUMP READING BROWNING AND HERBERT SPENCER—TO BE AN INTELLECTUAL COMPANION FOR GEORGE P. VAN TRUMP, AND HIS ENGLISH FRIENDS.

Trustees lagged behind that of the government about the ways in which education for girls should develop. In particular, the Commissioners in Victoria Street made it clear that an industrial school was at odds 'with the general feeling of the times in the matter of elementary education', and that trusts must use their money 'to the advancement of education'. Thus the Trustees were advised that it was more conducive to the advancement of education that benefits such as clothing should be given only as 'rewards of merit' and not 'as matters of privilege or patronage'. Instead of spending large sums on clothing, the Commissioners suggested that the new scheme should come up with ways in which some of this money could be used to educate 'larger numbers in a more efficient and satisfactory way'. This led to the proposal in the new scheme that, as well as running an elementary school in the parish of St Giles', they should also establish a 'middle school', either in the parish of St Giles', Cripplegate, or elsewhere. This paved the way for the setting up of the Middle School in Mare Street, Hackney.

How did the 1875 scheme change the Redcross Street school?

When the Redcross Street school opened its doors again on 9 August 1875, after the summer holidays, it opened as a public elementary school for girls. Lady Holles' School became part of the national system of elementary education, which was introduced by the Elementary Education Act of 1870. This Act set up School Boards to build schools where none existed and to bring existing schools into a national system. Under the scheme approved by the Endowed Schools Commission for Lady Holles' School, the object of the foundation was 'to supply to girls a liberal and practical education in accordance with the doctrines of the Church of England in the parish of St Giles', Cripplegate and elsewhere'. Thirteen Governors replaced the Trustees and the scheme set out how these were to be selected. The Alderman of the Ward of Cripplegate, the Vicar and Churchwardens should be Governors by virtue of their office. There were to be six representative Governors, three elected by the Vestry and three by the School Board for London. In addition, there were three co-optative Governors. The scheme made the inclusion of women on the governing body compulsory. One was to be elected by the Vestry, another by the members of the School Board for London and the third was a co-optative Governor. The property held by the Trustees was now vested in the Official Trustee of Charity Lands, and all stock and other securities were transferred to Official Trustees of Charitable Funds. All dealings with property and income were now subject to the scrutiny of the Official Trustees of Charity Lands and Charitable Funds. Spending must now be authorised and kept within limits set by the Charity Commission.

For the first time, Lady Holles' School had women on the governing body. Although they were often concerned with the domestic side of school, and advice about appropriate materials for clothing was regularly delegated to them, they also had a more strategic role. The Ladies' Committee regularly inspected the schools before the Governors' meetings. Their opinions carried weight; for example, in 1883, not being satisfied with the management of the Girls' Department, they recommended to the rest of the governing body that the recently appointed Head Mistress should be asked to resign. The Governors promptly passed a resolution to this effect. Miss Price was called in, informed of the resolution and she handed in her resignation. On other occasions, one or other of the female Governors was prepared to challenge the male Governors.

In roles like these, many middle-class women, such as Mrs Gilbert, the wife of the Vicar, and Mrs Wood, the wife of a surgeon at King's College London, gained experience in management whilst women were still struggling to gain legal recognition. The disparity between the legal standing of the sexes in the last quarter of the nineteenth century is clear. Only male Governors discussed issues dealing with the properties owned and rented out by the charity; only male signatures were valid on leases. Under the new scheme, the London School Board appointed Governors, and it is at this time that Rosamund Davenport Hill, a member of a leading social reforming family, was one of the women appointed. As a social reformer, she was somewhat conservative, as, unlike some other female members of the London School Board, she supported practical training in domestic skills for working-class girls. She believed that domestic work and love of the home should be at the heart of their lives.

Religious instruction at the school was still to be in accordance with the doctrines of the Church of England, and the Governors decided that the first hour of the schoolday should be given over to religious instruction. However, the new scheme allowed parents to ask for a pupil to be withdrawn from attending prayers or religious worship. The rest of the curriculum was to be in line with

Needlework class. This late nineteenth-century classroom shows the double desks which were required in elementary schools. The desks were tiered so that in the large classes commonly taught, all pupils could see and be seen. Needlework was an important part of the curriculum for girls. Shown below is a miniature shirt made by a pupil in a London school in 1872.

what the 1870 Education Act required public elementary schools to teach.

Reading, writing, arithmetic, geography, grammar, needlework and singing were specified, and references to building a gallery and providing double desks indicate that the way in which teaching was to be conducted was also to be controlled. It was important that the schools met the requirements of the Act, as (another change from 1875) both the girls' school and the infants' school were inspected annually by Her Majesty's Inspector of Schools (HMI). The government laid down requirements for record-keeping and schools were expected to keep an admissions book, registers and a logbook. The inspection process lasted several days and government grants were awarded on the basis of the inspector's report. The size of the grants depended on regularity of attendance, 'upon which depends the standing and prosperity of the school', as HMI Revd T Sharpe noted in 1884; on the school providing the subjects required (from 1862 onwards, for example, failing to teach working-class girls needlework was one of the few offences for which a school could

lose its government grant); and on the number of girls who passed examinations in reading, writing and arithmetic.

The Head Mistresses of each school paid particular attention to keeping up attendance figures. It was suggested in the 1880s, for example, that attendance would improve if, instead of working on Saturday mornings, they worked on Wednesday afternoons. There was an element of self-interest in this, as each Head Mistress was given half of the grant earned as part of their salary.

A teacher's job also depended on the HMI's favourable report, and those found lacking were quickly dismissed. In 1881, for example, when the inspector commented that two of the younger assistants 'have not sufficient teaching power for this school', the Governors told the Head Mistress to submit names of other candidates for their posts.

The Clothworkers'
Company regularly
supported the
Redcross Street
school. In 1893, for
example, the Master
and Wardens of
the Clothworkers'
Company visited
the infants' school
to inspect the
summer clothing and
distribute prizes.

Another change was that girls attending LHS now had to pay school fees, set at 1 penny a week for those under ten, and 2 pence a week for the over tens, until elementary education was made free in 1891.

Clothing was, in future, only to be given to children as rewards for 'regularity of attendance, proficiency and good conduct and was restricted to not more than 120 scholars'. To mark the new era and to move away from clothing distinguishing the pupils as charity children, the Governors also decided to 'make the costume of the clothed children more in accordance with modern usage by the discontinuance of caps and tippets[14] as articles of dress'. As the new scheme also limited the amount Governors were allowed to spend on clothing and other rewards, the number of pupils given clothing was reduced still further, so that by 1886 fewer than half the pupils were receiving clothing. As a way of controlling costs, many of the garments were produced by the students. This may explain the recollection of Mrs Louisa Hutchins, who entered the infants' school in 1866 at the age of 4, and left in 1876, that they sewed every afternoon.

This sewing began to eat into time for other subjects and, in 1889, the Head Mistress of the girls' school asked for more assistance, saying, 'We have to compete in all subjects with other schools though our needlework is necessarily four times as much as is required in an ordinary school of the same number'. The practical suggestion of two of the lady Governors that two sewing machines should be bought was adopted. Eventually, in order to relieve the time spent on providing the clothing, it was decided in 1895 that they should get the clothing ready-made.

Why were the schools in Redcross Street closed?
Despite temporary problems, such as the serious illness of the Head Mistress, Maria Kavanagh, in 1882, the girls' and infants' schools, for the most part, did very well under the new regime. Although the resident population of the parish fell, from 14,361 in 1851 to 3,863 in 1881, and inhabited houses were replaced by warehouses and manufacturing, the schools were well supported, and annual inspection reports for both schools were good.

Between 1875 and 1899, when the schools were closed, well over 200 attended the girls' school, with an additional 100 in the infants' school. The infants' school, in particular, under the care of Alice Lydgate, Head Mistress for the last 15 years of its life, was regularly rated excellent by the inspectors and gained the highest grant possible.

However, it is clear that even at a time when the schools were doing well, there were difficulties. The Redcross Street school was running at a loss between 1889 and 1899, when the charity was under financial pressure as a result of the dilapidation of the properties in Fort Street and Spital Square, from which much of its income came. An additional financial pressure was the question of salaries. It was becoming increasingly difficult in the 1890s to attract sufficiently well-qualified staff. Staff were leaving to better their positions; advertisements for replacements either did not attract candidates or those who applied asked for higher salaries than those being offered. The Board Schools, which offered higher salaries and greater opportunities for promotion, were more attractive. In 1896, one of the inspectors regretted the effect staffing difficulties had had on the schools, and the Head Mistress reported that he 'greatly deplores the unsettled state of the Staff extending as it has over such a lengthened period and asks if we cannot offer higher salaries'.

The factor which proved decisive in the decision to close was the school inspectors' criticism of the existing buildings, suggesting they were overcrowded and not entirely well fitted for their purpose. As early as 1887, the Governors were discussing selling the site to build a 'more commodious school' on 'a less valuable site'. Despite rearranging the accommodation in the early 1890s, HMI inspections were still critical. In 1898, the Governors conceded that 'although suitable enough at the time it was built, [the building] is not now in accordance with modern requirements as laid down by the Education Department'. The site was a valuable one and, when an approach was made on behalf of London County Council (LCC), which was looking for a suitable location for a fire station after the

They trust your children have profited by their education and that you may be able to find them a school to attend directly after the holidays.
Yours truly,
WT Rainer (Clerk to the Governors)

The LCC demolished the school and built a fire station in its place.

Between July 1899 and April 1900, the Governors searched for a suitable site on which to open another school, and by March 1900 they had narrowed their choice to sites at Perry Vale, Forest Hill and Friern Barnet. However, a letter from the Charity Commission in April 1900 halted their search. This reminded them that 'the first object to which it would appear desirable that the funds now set free by the closing of the public elementary School of the Foundation should be applied would be the improvement of the existing Middle School'. This was the school established in 1878 in Mare Street, Hackney. The Commissioners went on to say that, after adequately providing funds for Hackney, they thought it doubtful there would be sufficient funds to open another school.

The Commissioners were right. A second school was never opened.

'great fire' in Cripplegate of November 1897, the Governors decided to sell, with the intention of reopening another elementary school in an area where land was less expensive. The site was sold to the LCC for £31,000.

The Redcross Street school closed on Tuesday 25 July 1899, with very little notice. The Clerk sent the following letter to parents:

Sir
I am directed by the Governors of this Trust to inform you that owing to these premises having been acquired by the London County Council the Redcross Street school must now be closed and will not be reopened after the holidays.

Far left: In November 1897 a fire started in a warehouse which totally destroyed 56 buildings, burnt out 15 and badly damaged 20 others, including St Giles', Cripplegate. Although the fire raged close to the school, the building was undamaged. However, the extent of the fire was so great it made national headlines and was remembered in this children's book.

Left: Redcross Street looking north from Fore Street with the LCC fire station on the right.

71

The Hackney years, 1878–1936

At the beginning

*Previous page:
Farewell photograph
in 1915 of Miss
Clarke, pupils
and staff taken at
the rear of the
Hackney school.*

*Opposite: The girls of
LHS waiting outside
school to greet Queen
Mary on her way
to open an extension
to a hospital in
Clapton, 1921.*

At 3pm on Friday 13 September 1878, a distinguished collection of guests, headed by the Lord Mayor of London, the Sheriffs of London and their ladies, gathered in a marquee erected on the lawn behind the newly built Lady Holles' Middle School at 182 Mare Street, Hackney. The opening ceremony was about to begin. This was a prestigious affair for 152 specially invited guests, including the Vicar and Churchwardens of St Giles', Cripplegate, and the Trustees of the Cripplegate Boys' School. After the Lord Mayor and his party were received, there were hymns, one from some of the children from the Redcross Street school, and speeches by the Chairman of Governors, Alderman Henry Knight and the Lord Mayor.

The guests were then led in procession to view the school, before 100 of them sat down in the large schoolroom to a 'dejeuner' of a 'cold collation', two hot soups with wines, 'including hock, sherry, claret, port and two champagnes'. The remaining guests were provided with sandwiches and other light refreshments at a buffet in the playground. This was to be a day of handsome celebration, as it was noted that 'any of the seated guests may, after the cloth has been removed obtain refreshments and wine at the buffet without additional charge'. The Governors spent £135 2s 11d on the day's celebrations, almost the annual salary of the second mistress, the majority of which was spent on refreshments.

There was a good deal to celebrate. As one of the Assistant Charity Commissioners was to say later, the opening of the Mare Street school was 'an important ... development of the Charity'. The building of Lady Holles' Middle School was a direct result of the recommendations of the Taunton Report produced in 1868 by the government's Schools Inquiry Commission. The Commission had investigated provision for secondary education as a whole, amidst fears that this was not keeping pace with Britain's industrial or democratic progress. It found that two-thirds of English towns had no secondary schools of any kind and that there were only 13 secondary schools for girls in the country. As part of its investigation, the Commission took evidence from Dorothea Beale, Principal of Cheltenham Ladies' College. She described the ignorance of middle- and upper-class girls who received the type of education typical for girls at the time, which focused on acquiring accomplishments such as playing the piano and needlework. In one example, she said that among a group of over 100 girls taking an entrance examination, not one had been familiar with the concept of fractions. Although Dorothea Beale did not believe that women should have the same kind of training as men, as their roles in life were different, she argued that the education of middle- and upper-class girls needed to improve. This would help them be better wives and mothers, and, for those who did not marry, would mean they could earn a living.

The Mare Street school, now part of the London College of Fashion, University of the Arts, London.

Head Mistresses of Lady Holles' School, Mare Street, Hackney, 1878–1936

Julia Maria Ruddle
1878–95

Ada Beatrice Clarke
1895–1915

Nora Nickalls
1915–36

Revd Philip Parker Gilbert, Vicar of St Giles', Cripplegate, 1857–86.

The Taunton Report recommended that a national system of secondary education be set up, based on the existing endowed schools. Secondary education was to be the preserve of the middle classes and three types of school were envisaged, one for the upper and upper-middle class, another for the middle of the middle class, and the third for the lower-middle class. The Endowed Schools Act of 1869 had given the Endowed Schools Commissioners power to negotiate with Trustees and draw up schemes of government for these schools. The scheme for Lady Holles' School, passed in 1875, proposed that, as well as continuing to run the elementary school in Redcross Street, the Governors should set up a school for the middle sector of the middle class, to provide for girls until the age of 16. The Trustees had considered, but rejected, the idea of sitting up a middle-class school in Cripplegate, probably because it was unlikely that the neighbourhood, which was turning from a residential area into one of offices, warehousing and manufacturing, would provide sufficient middle-class girls. So, on 5 January 1876, the Clerk to the Governors wrote to the Charity Commissioners to say they thought they would be able to build a middle-class school for 250 girls, and 'that they would be glad if the Commissioners would inform them in what locality such a school is most required'.

Following their advice, an advertisement was inserted in *The Times* and the *Daily Telegraph*:

> *Site wanted from 4,000 to 6,000 square feet of freehold land for the purposes of a Public Building in a district bounded by the following streets: Essex Road and Balls Pond Road northwards Kingsland Road eastward Old Street Road and City Road southward and Shepherdess Walk and Packington St westward.*

The Governors visited sites in Islington and Hoxton, before paying 3,000 guineas for 'the house and premises known as the Manor House, 182 Mare Street Hackney'. This site was brought to the attention of the Governors by the Vicar of Cripplegate, Revd PP Gilbert. At first, the Governors hoped to adapt the original building, but, after discussions between their surveyor and the Education Department about what must be provided in the building, it was decided to demolish the Manor House, sell the materials and start afresh.

1878–1895: Julia Maria Ruddle

The original school built during 1877 was much smaller than the building that can still be seen today at 182 Mare Street. There was a large schoolroom on the ground floor, 55 by 20 feet, for 96 pupils, and three more classrooms for 24 children each. There were more classrooms on the first floor, as the school was built for 264 pupils. Ideas about teaching were changing, and the Education Department had insisted that the plans include more small classrooms than the surveyor had originally planned. The building included a residence for a Head Mistress. The expenditure for the building and plans had to be approved by the Charity Commission, which set a ceiling of £6,800 for the building.

All aspects of the management of the new school were governed by the 1875 scheme. Although there was a conscience clause allowing pupils to be exempt from religious instruction and worship, the constitution of the governing body ensured that a majority of its members were members of the Church of England. For the whole of its time in Hackney, there was a very strong relationship between the Church of England and the school, with the Bishop of London and other leading clergy regularly presenting school prizes.

Under the 1875 scheme, the Head Mistress had to be a member of the Church of England, and to attract the best candidates, the Governors were required to advertise the post. In April 1878, Julia Maria Ruddle, Head Mistress since 1874 of Loughborough High School, the first girls' grammar school in England, was selected from 71 candidates. She was to be paid £100 per year, plus a capitation allowance, referred to in the scheme as 'head money', of between 10s and 30s yearly per girl, so there was an incentive to keep up the numbers. The Governors fixed her capitation fee at £1 per pupil, so if the school was full the head money accounted for more than 70 per cent of her salary.

Lady Holles' Middle School in Hackney was a fee-paying school for girls, aged between 8 and 16, 'who are of good character and sufficient health'. Girls were admitted by entrance examination, which took place the day before term began, each term; the scheme set the minimum standard as reading easy narrative, small-text handwriting and knowing the first two rules of arithmetic. The fees varied by age, and in 1880 were £4 a year for children under 11, £5 for those between 11 and 13, and £6, the maximum allowed under the scheme, for those above 13. (At a similar period, the fees for North London Collegiate School (NLCS) in Camden Town were 19 guineas a year.[15]) The opening of the school was advertised in local newspapers, such as the *Hackney and Kingsland Gazette*, and 5,000 prospectuses were printed and distributed in the neighbourhood of the school and in St Giles', Cripplegate. The result was that, when the school opened in September 1878, 126 pupils were admitted. Encouraged by further advertisements in the local papers and at railway stations, and by circulars sent round the neighbourhood, pupil numbers rose steadily, and by 1880 the school was full.

The curriculum was laid down in the scheme. Girls were to be taught religious instruction in accordance with the doctrines of the Church of England, reading, writing, arithmetic, English grammar, composition and literature, geography, history, French or Latin or both, one or more

Julia Maria Ruddle (seated centre) with her staff. Ada Beatrice Clarke is seated on Miss Ruddle's left.

The girls of Lady Holles' School, in white dresses, waiting outside the school to see the Duke and Duchess of York (the future King George V and Queen Mary) on their way to open Hackney Library c. 1908.

branches of natural science, elementary mathematics, domestic economy, needlework, drawing and vocal music. German and piano instruction were available as extras. This curriculum followed that established by the North London Collegiate School, which had been set up by Frances Mary Buss in 1850.

As well as offering a broad curriculum, girls were encouraged to enter the local examinations of Oxford and Cambridge, which would prepare them to go on to higher education or into the Civil Service. As a way of checking the efficiency of the school, the scheme also required that once a year there had to be 'an examination of the scholars by an Examiner or Examiners appointed for that purpose by the Governors and paid by them, but otherwise

unconnected with the School. The examiners shall report to the Governors on the proficiency of the scholars, and on the position of the School as regards instruction and discipline, as shown by the results of the examination'. In the early years at Hackney, this examination was regularly carried out by the College of Preceptors.

Success in the 1880s

Lady Holles' Middle School soon established itself in the neighbourhood and between 1880 and 1890 was usually full. By 1884, the Governors were even considering increasing the number of children. The Assistant Charity Commissioner who inspected the school in 1884 expressed himself delighted with the Mare Street school, 'as an

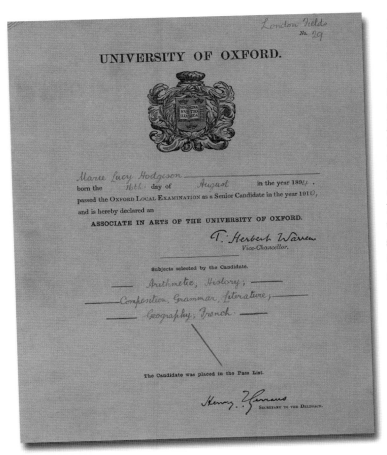

UNIVERSITY OF OXFORD.

Marie Lucy Hodgeson
born the 16th day of August in the year 1894,
passed the OXFORD LOCAL EXAMINATION as a Senior Candidate in the year 1910,
and is hereby declared an
ASSOCIATE IN ARTS OF THE UNIVERSITY OF OXFORD.

T. Herbert Warren
Vice-Chancellor.

Subjects selected by the Candidate.

Arithmetic, History;
Compostion, Grammar, Literature;
Geography; French.

The Candidate was placed in the Pass List.

Henry
SECRETARY TO THE DELEGACY.

Left: Certificate awarded in 1910 to Marie Hodgeson for her success in the Oxford Senior Local Examination.

has for some time been a very low one', increasing numbers took external examinations, such as those set by the College of Preceptors and the more demanding and prestigious Cambridge and Oxford Junior Local examinations. In September 1884, Miss Ruddle reported the success of the seven pupils who had taken the Oxford Junior Local, saying that only six girls had been placed in the First Division, and 'of these three were ours'. The Governors recorded their satisfaction with this success. Miss Ruddle went on to suggest that the Governors could encourage girls to sit the university examinations by offering incentives, for example, 'to those who pass with 1st class honours free tuition for one year in the school, 2nd free tuition for 2 terms, 3rd free tuition for 1 term and a pass the return of the exam fee'. She said that something of the same kind was done in the Grocers' Company's School in Hackney Downs, which the brothers of many of the girls attended. The Governors accepted her suggestions and this continued throughout the school's time at Hackney. By December 1891, more than 30 pupils had given in their parents' wish that they should be entered for the Oxford Local Examination to be held the following July. This was a sufficiently large number for the school to ask the Oxford Secretary to make Mare Street an examination centre.

Problems for the Mare Street school

Although by 1890 the school was well established and had a good reputation in the area, there were signs its position was being weakened by financial constraints; the limitation of the scheme, which insisted girls had to leave at 16; the opening of schools in areas from which girls had previously travelled to the Mare Street school; and the changing nature of the neighbourhood.

From its earliest days, the Governors had been concerned about the costs of running the Mare Street school. In 1880, the auditors noted, 'we strongly impress upon the governors the necessity of so arranging the expenditure that it may be met by the annual income of the school and that the Head Mistress be instructed that in recommending outlay to the governors she especially keep this fact in mind'. They were concerned that all the costs of the Mare Street school should be paid for from its fee income.

important and successful development of the Charity'. The College of Preceptors' annual reports were favourable and the Governors regularly sent their congratulations to the staff. In 1890, for example, the Clerk was directed to express to the Head Mistress, 'The approval and gratification of the Governors at the successes achieved', and, again, in 1891, the Governors resolved that 'an expression of entire satisfaction with the school work at Mare Street be sent to the Head Mistress'. In 1888, the Governors had been so pleased with the report of the examiners that they had wanted to have a summary printed and sent to the parents, but discovered that the conditions of the College of Preceptors meant they could not publish anything short of the entire report.

Also, despite Miss Ruddle's concern, in 1883, that 'The standard of attainment reached by candidates on entrance

Gertie Watkins, 11 years old on her way to LHS Hackney (left) and at 19 years old (right).

regretted this news, as 'The loss to the school will be well nigh irreparable. Really good teachers are born, not made, they are very scarce and difficult to meet with, and it would be worth any effort to retain their services'.

The Governors listened to her pleas and offered the additional salaries hoped for!

Miss Ruddle did her best in the circumstances and, in her yearly reports, looked for ways to save on costs whilst keeping good standards in the school. In 1882, she proposed that as the French master had given notice, he should be replaced 'by a lady who being cheaper can also provide more'. She argued:

It has long been my wish to have French conversation and composition cultivated in the school. This has not been the case, and cannot be done to any great extent with a master because of the greater money value set on his time. For about the same sum we could procure a lady who spending nine hours here could be very useful in promoting colloquial French, facility of expression in writing and a good pronunciation from the commencement of the language.

A sharp reminder to the modern reader of the gender differences of the time!

By such means, the school's budget was sufficient until other factors intervened and the number of pupils dropped. One of the pressures on numbers, even in the 1880s, was that parents who were prepared to pay fees to educate their daughters often wished them to go on to higher education. However, places at training or other colleges were not available until the age of 18, but according to Clause 56 of the scheme governing Lady Holles' Middle School, girls had to leave at 16. This meant that pupils whose parents wished them to go on to higher education had to transfer to another school. Almost from the first, this was an issue. In 1881, Miss Ruddle reported, 'We lose each term, a number of girls whose parents would be glad for them to continue at least another year. This acts as a constant drain upon the school and deprives us of some of our best scholars'. In 1882 and again in 1883, parents petitioned the Governors over the issue of the leaving age, saying, 'We respectfully venture to submit that in many cases this restriction takes

Unfortunately, this constraint had an impact on the recruitment and retention of qualified staff. As Miss Ruddle reported in 1882, she was having difficulty finding a new assistant teacher, as the school was offering only £50 a year and all the ladies she had seen and heard from were asking for salaries from £75 to £100 per annum. The candidate Miss Ruddle had considered best fitted for the post had declined, 'in consequence of the salary. The other accepted, but the stipend, being less than she asked for, undertook also an evening class, did not throw her energies into the work and could not be retained. I have engaged no one in her place'. These problems were ongoing. In 1884, she noted, 'Well-educated teachers able to teach and keep in good discipline large classes cannot be obtained unless good salaries can be offered'. In 1885, what Miss Ruddle described as 'two of our best and most popular teachers, throwing their whole hearts into their work and exercising an excellent influence over their pupils' had resigned; Miss Eggar, because the governors had refused her request for a £20 rise, and Miss Walmesley, 'to seek for a more lucrative appointment'. Miss Ruddle

Until the leaving age at LHS was changed in 1889 from 16 to 18, girls who wished to go on to higher education had to transfer to another school. A number of girls, including Ada Beatrice Clarke, transferred to North London Collegiate School for Girls, then based in Camden.

effect when the pupil is in the midst of the benefits to be derived from the liberal education imparted at the school and the pupil is compelled to resign at a time when the advantages of the preparatory training of the previous years is about to be realised'. They went on to say they believed 'that an extension of the age limit will conduce to the more complete education of the pupils and that their proficiency will still further raise the high reputation your school has already gained'.

However, until 1888, the Governors rejected these pleas. Miss Ruddle had argued throughout that the

limit should be lifted, pointing out again in 1885, 'We are constantly losing girls, whose parents would gladly continue to send them, but cannot because of the limit of age: this also prevents many from entering. No such limit exists in Government Schools and a large "Higher Grade" is to be opened in the neighbourhood'. When she was asked to comment in 1888, as the Governors were considering the matter again, she made clear her view that the age limit had been damaging the school. 'It has been a great drawback to the popularity and efficiency of the School. About 30 pupils have had to leave yearly from this cause, many of whom would certainly have remained one or two years longer by the wish of their parents. Training Colleges and female Clerkships in the Post Office are only open to girls of 18.' Finally, the Governors applied to the Charity Commission to raise the leaving age and this was agreed in August 1889.

Unfortunately, just at the point that this might have benefited Mare Street, the opening of other schools, in areas from which girls had previously travelled to Lady Holles' Middle School, provided some with alternative and more convenient schools. In February 1890, Miss Ruddle reported that 'partly perhaps from the prevalence of influenza and partly perhaps chiefly from the opening of a public school at Walthamstow[16] and the expectation of one at Stamford Hill[17] our numbers have fallen from 243 to 225'. In addition, a Higher Grade Board School was opened in Victoria Park. Miss Ruddle continued her report to the Governors by saying:

> Parents naturally prefer a school at their own doors when they can afford to pay the fees. The area from which we shall in future draw our supplies will be much contracted ... The Stamford Hill School will probably deprive us of nearly all our pupils of a better class. Your secretary can no doubt give you statistics shewing [sic] that our supply from the immediate surroundings of the school has always been a limited one.

It was likely that these new fee-paying schools would attract the parents of the 40 girls from Stoke Newington, Stamford Hill and Walthamstow who had previously travelled to Mare Street. In addition, the opening of the Higher Grade Board School in Victoria Park offered a similar curriculum to that provided at Mare Street.

Miss Ruddle concluded her report by saying, 'I trust that we may still do good work though on a smaller scale'. However, the fall in numbers came at a difficult time for the Charity. The endowment funds were dwindling as the result of a decline in the Spitalfields area, where the properties from whose rents the charity gained its funds remained. Many of the properties in Fort Street and Spital Square needed extensive refurbishment and rebuilding, and the Governors were negotiating with the Charity

Where pupils came from in 1890

Place of residence	Numbers
Clapton	27
Dalston	34
Hackney and Victoria Park	96
Stoke Newington and Stamford Hill	32
Bethnal Green and Mile End	9
Spitalfields, Aldgate and Houndsditch	9
Walthamstow	8
Homerton	4
Wood Green	2
Hampstead and Finchley	2
Finsbury Park and Enfield	2
Total	**225**

Commissioners to borrow to carry out these works. From 1891, the Mare Street school began to run at a deficit of between £500 and more than £600 a year, just at the point that the endowment funds were not in a good position to cover the shortfall.

Nor was it likely that the immediate vicinity of the school would provide additional pupils. In her annual reports since the late 1880s, Miss Ruddle had been pointing out the changes in the neighbourhood. 'Hackney as a neighbourhood is not increasing in wealth', and this was already having some impact on the school. In 1889 she pointed out, 'It must be remembered however that we get now a different class of girls to those who first entered the School. The immediate neighbourhood is going down and people of a better position prefer sending their children to schools that they think are more select. Many of our girls become Pupil Teachers in Board Schools at 14 or go into business houses. Only a very few wish now to go in for advanced study'.

Again, in 1890, she reported, 'The immediate neighbourhood of Mare Street is not at all what it was when this school opened; rents have gone down, houses are let out in flats. Board schools have multiplied, the rates are heavy and many people now send their children to

The opening of The Skinners' Company's School for Girls in Stamford Hill in 1890 meant that many girls from that area who had previously travelled to Lady Holles' Middle School no longer did so.

them until they think they require a "finish" when they are passed on to us for merely a short time'.

Numbers at Mare Street began to decline sharply. In 1889, there were 243 girls in the school, but numbers had dropped to an average of 207 in 1891–2 and 206 in 1892–3. In 1893, the Governors began to discuss the idea of closing Mare Street and disposing of the property. Unfortunately for the school, this became known as a result of a letter written by one of the Governors to a local paper. This had an even greater impact on numbers, as, fearing the school was to close at Christmas, only 137 girls returned in September 1893. In the Bryce Commission Report of 1895, the Charity Commissioners had acknowledged the problems caused to schools such as Mare Street by the setting up of Higher Grade elementary schools, supported by rates and parliamentary grants, charging fees so low that it was impossible for secondary schools, third grade or second grade, to compete with them. These Higher Grade schools provided education in secondary subjects, which, they concluded, 'threatens to interfere seriously with the prosperity even of second grade schools'.[18] Pressures such as those being felt at Mare Street from these Higher Grade Board Schools led to the outlawing of School Board help to these schools, and to the 1902 Education Act. However, without the intervention of the Charity Commissioners it would have been too late for Mare Street.

Charity Commission saves Mare Street

At a special meeting in May 1895, the Governors decided to close Mare Street at the end of the summer term, and sent notice of this to parents on 24 June 1895. However, closure required the approval of the Charity Commission. A letter sent from the Charity Commission to the Clerk to the Governors, WT Rainer, complained that the Governors were taking steps to close the school, 'without authority from the Commissioners, and without the pressure of any palpable necessity'. The Commission made it clear that consent would not be forthcoming and the Governors were informed, in no uncertain terms, that they must withdraw the notices of closure and provide for the school to continue, otherwise the matter would be referred to the Attorney General.

After discussion, the Governors received promises from the Charity Commission that they would be given the necessary help to continue the school. So, in a special meeting on 23 July, the Governors decided that Mare Street would 'be reopened after the vacation on Sept 10 and that a circular be forthwith sent out to that effect to parents and guardians and every publicity be given'.

All the staff at Mare Street, including the Head Mistress, had already been given notice. Now five of the assistant mistresses were asked to remain on the staff and Ada Beatrice Clarke was appointed Head Mistress at £100 per year and 10s per head capitation fees.

From pupil to Head Mistress: the early career of Ada Beatrice Clarke

Ada Beatrice Clarke's career began as a pupil at Lady Holles' Middle School. As the leaving age was 16, girls who wanted to go on to a high school or college had to go to another establishment. The Governors awarded some exhibitions each year to enable girls to do this. In 1883, Ada was awarded an exhibition of £20 for two years to go to North London Collegiate School, then based in Camden, to continue her education.

Ada worked as an unpaid student teacher at Mare Street from September to December 1883, before she took up her exhibition, and, according to Miss Ruddle, showed 'powers of class management'. She entered the senior department of NLCS in January 1884, and matriculated at London University in January 1886. Miss Ruddle then asked permission from the Governors for her to work at Mare Street as an unpaid teacher for the rest of the summer term 1886, when Miss Clarke 'would then be willing to commence in September at a salary of £40 p.a.'.

Miss Clarke did well at Mare Street. In February 1887, Miss Ruddle reported that Miss Clarke 'is taking great pains with her class'. Between October 1889, when Miss Clarke was the second 'mathematical' teacher, and 1894, Miss Ruddle asked the Governors several times to raise her salary, describing her as one of 'our really valuable teachers'. In November of that year, recommending another salary increase, Miss Ruddle explained, 'She is not only Mathematical Mistress but one of the best teachers we possess and has now been with us for a number of years. She is highly popular with the girls and fully deserves an increase. It would come with especial grace just now as her father an old inhabitant of Hackney is in a very critical state of health'. The Governors agreed.

By March 1895, when the position of second mistress became vacant, Miss Ruddle suggested that Ada was the obvious choice. Later in the same year, when the Governors were instructed by the Charity Commission to reopen a much smaller school, she was well placed to be offered the post of Head Mistress.

1895–1902: finding its way

The reorganised school was opened in September 1895, with a reduced permanent staff of five, including Ada Beatrice Clarke, and 87 pupils. There were visiting staff for piano, French, Swedish drill, singing and drawing. It is clear that the Charity Commissioners had concerns about the behaviour of the Governors and were determined to keep a closer eye on events. In October 1895, one of the Commissioners, JE White, wrote to the Governors about a meeting to discuss the future administration of Mare Street, and concluded in his letter, 'I may add that in the opinion of the Commissioners recent events seem to point to the need of some changes to secure the stability of the School in future'.

The new Head Mistress, Ada Beatrice Clarke, had been a pupil at Mare Street and returned as a mathematics mistress. She was highly regarded by Miss Ruddle, who, on several occasions, had praised her qualities to the Governors. The slimmed-down school of 1895 was less costly to run, and Miss Clarke's salary as Head Mistress, for example, was less than the salary that had been paid to Miss Ruddle. The basic salary of £100 per year was the same, but the capitation fee was reduced to 10s per head, which meant that in 1896–7, as the average number of pupils was 104, her salary was £152 in total. It was agreed that the capitation fees would increase if the school proved successful, but numbers increased only slowly. In March 1897, when the numbers had risen to 112, she acknowledged:

> Although I do not seem to be able to make very great strides, as I should wish, yet the numbers have gone on steadily increasing since I accepted the post of Head Mistress at your school and that in the face of considerable difficulties and I think a certain amount of ill feeling. I think I have thus shown my capability of managing the School and also of teaching the highest form since _all_ the girls _I sent_ in for the Oxford Local last year passed and two with distinction.

Between 1895 and 1901, the pressures on Mare Street continued. Competition from Higher Grade Board Schools made it more difficult to attract pupils and the school ran at a loss, putting pressure on the endowment funds.

Ada Beatrice Clarke (second row, third from left) with pupils.

Competition from Higher Grade Board Schools continued to have an impact on numbers. In September 1898, Miss Clarke noted her disappointment that only eight pupils presented themselves for the examination for new pupils. 'The number is disappointly [*sic*] small and I can think of no explanation except that a higher grade school has been opened in South Hackney which will no doubt prevent us getting any more girls from that neighbourhood.'

Extensive discussions began between the Charity Commissioners and the Governors about the best way to use the endowments and the way forward for the school. The Charity Commission suggested, for example, that the Technical Education Board might help with some grants. A report, in 1896, from the Secretary to the Technical School Board made it clear that Mare Street should be retained, as it was the only public secondary school in South Hackney, but that it needed to be made more attractive if it was to compete with schools such as the Skinners' School at Stamford Hill. He suggested this could be done by building a gymnasium and a combined laboratory and arts and crafts room. The Technical Education Board could make a liberal grant to the latter if the Governors could pay for the gym.

The pressure on the endowment funds eased after the 1899 sale of the Redcross Street site. Although the

Governors had been planning to use this money to open another school, the Charity Commission reminded them in 1900 that the Governors' first priority should be to use some of the funds to improve the Mare Street school. Their letter suggested money should be used 'to improve and maintain the buildings, to strengthen the teaching staff and to provide entrance scholarships for children from public elementary schools'.

The Governors took this advice and decided to concentrate on improvements to Mare Street and to postpone building a second girls' school until the financial position was better. As we know, a second school was never built.

Ada Beatrice Clarke welcomed the opportunities extra money could provide. She pressed for the building of a gymnasium and the Governors also agreed to build a laboratory. The laboratory meant the school would be able to offer higher-level work and girls could prepare for the London Matriculation examination. Additional funding also meant that higher salaries could be offered to employ better qualified staff, though Miss Clarke warned that they should look to appoint those with experience as well as degrees. 'Degrees without experience are practically valueless as I have known mistresses with the best certificates who have no more idea of teaching and

This drawing of the gymnasium and apparatus at NLCS illustrates the type of Swedish gymnasium which Julia Maria Ruddle recommended the Governors should visit when they were considering plans for a gymnasium at LHS in 1889. Plans were shelved at the end of that year for financial reasons.

discipline (and this latter is most essential in a School of this kind) than a child.'

In 1895, the same year that the school was reorganised, the Royal Commission on Secondary Education (Bryce Commission) had reviewed the progress towards secondary education since the Endowed Schools Act of 1869. In twenty-first-century Britain, where secondary education for all until 16 is the norm, it comes as a shock to realise that only as little as 115 years ago, the expectations were quite different. The recommendations are a sharp reminder of the class-conscious nature of Victorian society. Access to more than a basic level of education and life expectations were governed, for the most part, not by merit, but by class. The Bryce Commission recommended that secondary education should be available to only ten out of 1,000 of the population. They retained the idea of three grades of secondary school and recommended that only two out of the ten should be educated in first- and second-grade schools. This would mean only 64,000 pupils in a population of 4 million. The Commission believed that these 'distinctions' corresponded roughly to the 'graduations of society'. This report led to the 1902 Education Act, which abolished School Boards, set up Local Education Authorities and made provision for secondary education.

It seems clear that the Head Mistress and Governors were positioning Mare Street to earn its place as a first-grade secondary school. Already, in 1897, when Miss Clarke was discussing the issue of a new prospectus for

Mare Street, she suggested dropping the word 'Middle' from the name of the school.

> *The education given here is exactly the same as at any High Class School and I think to call it a 'Middle School' is injurious to its well being. This term a gentleman called to see me, his girls are at a High School and he intends taking them away and sending them here but he said his girls did not like the idea of going to a Middle School after having been at a High School. It certainly can do no harm in having the word omitted and may do much good and I prefer the school being known as Lady Holles' School for Girls, Hackney.*

A new scheme for the management of the school was approved in March 1902 by the Board of Education, which had taken over supervision of educational work from the Charity Commission. This scheme allowed girls to stay at school to the age of 17, and to 18 with special permission. It also provided for no fewer than ten Cripplegate Scholarships, which covered tuition fees and a yearly sum of between £5 and £10, 'since these Scholarships will be substantially now that the Elementary School of the Foundation is closed the only provision by way of regard for the original trusts in favour of the poor of Cripplegate'. These scholarships were to be awarded to the daughters of persons resident or having their occupation in the ancient parish of St Giles, including the parish of St Luke. The scheme also gave permission for a kindergarten for boys and girls between the ages of 5 and 8.

Finally, in October 1902, when Miss Clarke reported that numbers had risen from 140 to 160, she suggested that, instead of having the Annual Examination held by the College of Preceptors, the school should be examined by London University. She admitted this would be more expensive, but it included inspection of the regular school teaching and work. She said that if the Governors approved, 'it would read well and give a high class tone to the school if in the new Prospectus you would add a clause to the effect that the school is inspected and examined annually by the London University'. Mare Street was moving up in the educational world.

Original cover design for the school magazine started in 1902.

'A Public Secondary school for girls as day scholars': 1902–15

The 1902 Education Act reorganised the administration of education. As well as abolishing School Boards and putting newly created Local Education Authorities (LEAs) in charge of elementary schools, the Act made significant provision for secondary education. The Act encouraged Councils to subsidise existing secondary schools and to provide free places for working-class children. In 1904, as a result of the closure of the Cripplegate Boys' School in 1903, a new scheme set out by the Board of Education provided for the sale of the Boys' School buildings, amalgamated the Boys' and Girls' Trusts and created the Cripplegate Schools Foundation. The boys' funds provided a scholarship fund for boys to attend other schools, and the girls' funds were to maintain and provide scholarships to Lady Holles' School, which was now to be a public 'secondary school for girls as day scholars'.

Girls continued to be admitted by entrance examination and paid an entrance fee of not more than 10s, with tuition fees to be fixed by the Governors between £4 and £8 a year. The 1904 scheme also provided for a number of scholarships and exhibitions. Foundation scholarships, 'not more than one for every ten girls in the School', were awarded on the result of either the entrance examination or, to girls already in the school, the yearly examination. In addition, no fewer than ten Cripplegate Scholarships were to be awarded. These scholarships recognised that even free places might have to be turned down because parents could not afford the extra costs. Cripplegate Scholarships could be awarded only to girls who had attended a public elementary school for at least three years and who were the daughters of people resident or working in the parish of St Giles', Cripplegate. As the scheme said, these scholarships had 'the double object of attracting good scholars to the School and advancing education at Public Elementary Schools'. In this way, it was now possible for girls from some families who could not previously have aspired to a secondary education to receive one. The admissions registers for Mare Street from 1902 include details of the father's occupation, and we can see that girls with fathers who were post office sorters, plasterers, bricklayers, decorators, salesmen and train drivers were now being educated alongside the daughters of businessmen, doctors, accountants, clergymen, headmasters and other professionals. Scholarships made this possible and began to erode social and class barriers. In this way, the 1902 Act provided an 'educational ladder' for a few. Governors were also to spend not less than £100 a year in providing exhibitions of between £30 and £50 a year, to allow girls who had been at the school for at least three years to attend for up to four years at any university or institution of higher education the Governors approved.

Lady Holles' School was recognised by the Board of Education as 'an efficient secondary school', and, with a kindergarten for boys and girls added in 1903, the school now provided for girls and boys until 8, and for girls from 8 to 17. Nora Nickalls, who became Head Mistress in 1915, credits Ada Beatrice Clarke with understanding 'with the whole of her rigorous personality and clear-headed appreciation of how the school community might be developed', and says that while 'Miss Clarke was fortunate in the era of educational expansion during which she built up the school, the Governors were quite as fortunate in having a headmistress who could and did show them how those opportunities might be used'.

Girls in the gymnasium built in 1902.

School life: 'going up in the world'

The Revd WE Andrews, Rector of St Paul's, Homerton, in his speech before the presentation of prizes at Sports Day, July 1902, encouraged the girls to have pride in their school, 'especially as they belonged to one that was going up in the world'. Revd Andrews knew the school well, as he had been, for a number of years, one of the examiners for the Oxford Local Examinations. In 1902, the school was full of energy and purpose, led by a Head Mistress determined that the school and its pupils should excel. A school laboratory had been fitted for 22 students for physics and chemistry. Finally, a gymnasium, equipped with apparatus designed 'to cultivate the elasticity of the body and stimulate courage', with a stage at one end, was being built in the garden. This was the type of Swedish gymnasium which, years earlier, Julia Maria Ruddle had recommended to the Governors, but which lack of funds had prevented. In 1902, the school had 162 pupils in a school designed for 200, but by 1904 the school was full and the Governors were seriously considering expansion.

The annual report on the educational work of Lady Holles' School made in 1906 by the University of London has survived. The inspectors describe the school in glowing terms and pay particular tribute to the fact that it has maintained 'the high tone and excellent work', despite the building operations which might have proved an unsettling factor. The Governors had extended the school by adding an art studio, a domestic economy department and new classrooms.

The inspectors commented that 'the accommodation has been so generously and so judiciously improved that the buildings may challenge comparison with those of any girls' school in London'. Better rooms and more convenient arrangements 'conduce to the still higher efficiency of what is already an exceptional school'. The school magazine, *Our Magazine*, reported that the opening of the new wing, on the evening of 22 February 1906, by Sir Arthur Rucker, Principal of London University, had caused great excitement in school. 'It was an event to which we had all been looking forward for some time, and when the eventful evening came all the girls dressed in their white frocks,[19] were assembled in the various classrooms awaiting the arrival of the distinguished company.'

In 1906, 284 pupils attended the main school in 11 forms, with an additional 34 boys and girls in the kindergarten. This was a large increase from the previous year, when there had been 208 in the school proper and 28 in the kindergarten.

Scripture, English, history, geography, French, Latin, mathematics and science formed the basic curriculum, with singing for the most junior forms. There were constructive comments for all subjects and ones that a modern teacher would be well pleased to receive. In English, for example, the inspectors commented that, 'The teachers render even the grammar lessons interesting, and in the literature lessons they succeed in inspiring a love of good books which is certain to have a lasting effect on the girls'. Pupils in school today might smile wryly at the comment from the inspectors on some pupils in mathematics that 'at present they are too apt to call in the aid of the mistress as soon as a difficulty presents itself', and their encouragement to the mistresses that, 'By giving them frequent opportunities of grappling with difficulties for themselves, the girls should be taught self-reliance'.

Science for girls in the lower forms meant natural history, studied 'by means of living and stuffed animals', and botany. Once girls reached the IVs there was a four-year course in physics and chemistry.

The summary of the report concludes with praise for every section of the school: 'in every department the work is of high quality'.

The staff … consists of exceptionally zealous and capable teachers; the tone of the school is excellent, the pupils acquiring not merely good habits of work, but a healthy outlook on life, and the right equipment for its struggles; the headmistress possesses organising power, tact and sympathy to an unusual degree; and the governing body have spared no pains to ensure that the conditions in which the work is carried on shall be as favourable as possible.

Their final verdict is that 'It is an unmixed blessing for the whole district from which the pupils are drawn; and there is little doubt that the girls and their parents realise how great a debt they owe to Lady Holles' School'.

Cover design for the school magazine used from 1908.

The school magazine, begun in 1902 on Ada Beatrice Clarke's initiative, and published initially twice yearly, shows us the pattern of the school years and what else the school offered in 1906 – what the school of 2010 calls 'the other half'.

Highlights of the school year

The school usually held a harvest festival in the autumn term. However, in the autumn of 1905 this was prevented by building work. Instead, girls brought in money to buy hampers of groceries to be distributed to the poor in East End parishes. Letters of thanks were received from the Corpus Christi College, Cambridge Mission in New Cross Road, St Michael's Vicarage in London Fields and the United Synagogue, East London.

Our Magazine.

President:
Miss A. B. CLARKE.

Editor:
Miss CLARE SMITH.

Committee:
M. BARTLETT.
N. GABB.
R. GOVEY.
E. HIBBERD.
P. MONTAG.
D. MOSS.

M. ROBEY.
B. SKIPPER.
E. STUBINGTON.
N. STUBINGTON
E. ZERFASS.

NUMBER 9.]   MAY, 1906.   [PRICE 6d.

PRIZE DISTRIBUTION AND OPENING OF
NEW WING.

GREAT excitement prevailed at the School on Wednesday,
February 22nd, when the new wing and enlarged classrooms were inspected by Sir Arthur Rucker, Principal of the
London University; Sir Henry Knight, Chairman; and other
Members of the Governing Body, and the Head Mistress. It was
an event to which we had all been looking forward for some time,
and when the eventful evening came all the girls, dressed in their
white frocks, were assembled in the various class rooms awaiting

Extract from the school magazine, originally published twice a year.

Above right: Girls with form mistress c.1909.

Far right: Princess Marie Louise was the guest of honour at Prize Giving in 1913.

Prize Giving was usually held in December, but the Prize Giving for the end of 1905 had been held over to be combined with the opening of the new wing in February 1906. We can see from descriptions of Prize Distributions, as they were called, that it was usual to include not just, as today, a report from the Head Mistress and the Chair of Governors, but also a full-scale entertainment. In December 1906, the girls performed Dr Somervell's operetta, *King Thrushbeard*, libretto by Mr Claude Apeling. It was reported that 'notwithstanding an unfortunate epidemic of coughs and colds, the work was performed in most creditable style'. Hilda Denney (1908–17), a pupil who later became a member of staff, at both Hackney and Hampton, remembered the Prize Giving in 1913 well, because she received a prize, and royalty was to present it.

In 1913 HRH Princess Marie Louise came to present the prizes. I had a prize for History… and so formed one of a double line of prize-winners stretching from the stairs leading to the stage to the back door of the hall, through which the Princess was to pass. We all wore white dresses, black stockings and shoes and gloves.

Much rehearsal had been held to achieve perfection. We were to curtsey as the Princess passed. This involved beginning the curtsey when she was two girls away from us, and finishing it when she was two girls past us. On the platform, as well as the usual curtsey given to all distinguished visitors on these occasions, we were to leave walking backwards! With Miss Clarke's eyes upon us, all went well. Nobody fell over or barged into the many guests seated on the platform.

Towards the end of term in December, the lower school, including the kindergarten, was invited to a party, complete with Christmas tree, given by Miss Clarke and the Governors. The party began with musical chairs, which, in 1905, 'resulted in a good many tumbles, the floor having

Left: Dress rehearsal for a school production.

Below left: Costume design for a school play.

There was an annual Fancy Dress Dance given for the older girls by the Chairman, Governors and Head Mistress. Nora Gabb, in the Vth form, gave a full description of the dance held in December 1906 in the school magazine. She described the School Hall filled with 'Holly fairies' in 'brightly coloured dresses … whilst ferns decorated the stage, and the electric light cast a soft glow over all characters, real and fictitious'. She recalled one of the tallest girls was 'attired as a baby brought up on Mellin's Food' and wrote that 'though perhaps it was bad for her baby ideas, she danced with a Suffragette escaped from prison!'

Her article continued:

Towards the end of the evening, all the girls joined in the dance, 'Les Carillons'. Then, after a short speech, Sir Henry Knight (Chairman of Governors) awarded the prizes, which were voted for by the visitors, as follows: for the best dress costing less than two and sixpence, to Elsa Vanderlinde, who represented a Silver Bell; for the best dress costing over two and sixpence, to Edith Stubington, dressed as a Dutch peasant; and for the most original dress, to Nora Gabb, as a Suffragette.

been previously polished for the elder girls' dance'. Tea followed, more games, and at about 6.30 'the distribution of presents from the lovely Xmas tree. It was beautifully dressed with all kinds of toys, and illuminated with tiny candles'. The children lined up to be presented with toys by Miss Clarke, and two of the kindergarten children later wrote of their enjoyment in the school magazine.

In the era before the First World War, pupils in the magazines regularly referred to themselves as 'Holly fairies', with Miss Clarke as Queen, and to the school as 'Hollyland'. Readers today may smile at this, but what was clearly being encouraged was a sense of community, which, in different ways and language, is encouraged in the school today.

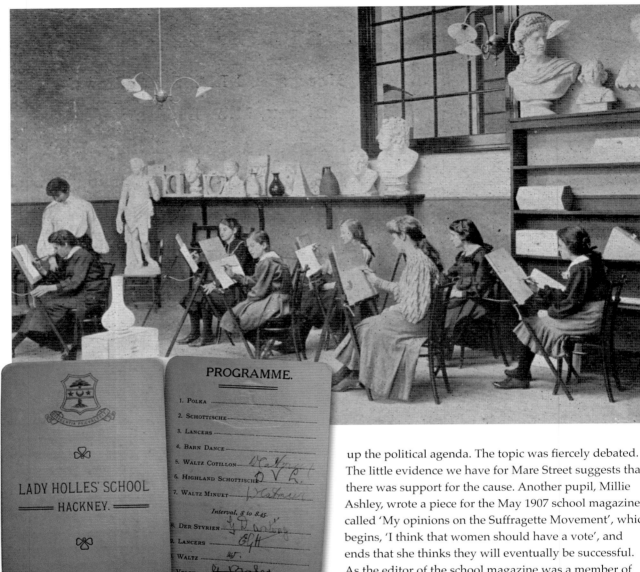

Above: Art class.

Right: Dance card for the annual dance for the senior girls, 1905.

PROGRAMME.

1. POLKA
2. SCHOTTISCHE
3. LANCERS
4. BARN DANCE
5. WALTZ COTILLON
6. HIGHLAND SCHOTTISCHE
7. WALTZ MINUET

Interval, 8 to 8.45.

8. DER STYRIEN
9. LANCERS
10. WALTZ
11. VELETA
12. LES CARILLONS

LADY HOLLES' SCHOOL
HACKNEY.

December 20, 1905.

It was common practice at dances at the time for female guests to be given dance cards. The gentlemen at the dance asked for the pleasure of a dance, and initials were placed against the dance they had engaged. A dance card for the 1905 dance has survived, though in the case of the Lady Holles' School dances, girls took the part of gentlemen.

Nora's choice of costume reminds us that the cause of votes for women was receiving a good deal of attention in this period. Following the formation of the Women's Social and Political Union in 1903, and their adoption of tactics such as disrupting political meetings and being arrested, the question of votes for women had moved up the political agenda. The topic was fiercely debated. The little evidence we have for Mare Street suggests that there was support for the cause. Another pupil, Millie Ashley, wrote a piece for the May 1907 school magazine, called 'My opinions on the Suffragette Movement', which begins, 'I think that women should have a vote', and ends that she thinks they will eventually be successful. As the editor of the school magazine was a member of staff, and the president of the editorial team was the Head Mistress herself, the inclusion of this article implies that there was some sympathy for the cause, if not the methods. In Barbara Megson's account of the school in 1947, she remembers being told that some of the staff wore Suffragette buttons in their colours of purple, white and green. Hilda Denney, who was a pupil at Hackney before the First World War, also remembered: 'Many of us supported Votes for Women and we listened avidly to what we could overhear about their demonstrations.'

In the autumn and spring terms, hockey was the main competitive sport, with First and Second Eleven fixtures against neighbouring schools, such as Skinners', Tottenham High School and Mile End Pupil Teachers. Inter-form hockey, introduced for the first time in 1906, was won by the VI form, who were awarded 'a handsome silver shield' to

hang on their form-room wall, presented by Mr Stubington, father of one of the VI form girls. The hockey captain, Millie Vanderlinde, reminds us that, at the time, games such as hockey were introduced as much for character-building and developing loyalty to the school as for exercise.

Hockey particularly is a splendid find for schools. A girl to play Hockey well must do something more than hit hard; she must be keen of sight and quick in action, and more than all she must be unselfish, by sometimes playing so that another may take the credit. Enthusiasm,

so strong in a school girl, will be felt amongst all those who are players; not only enthusiasm for the game, but for the School.

In the summer term, tennis replaced hockey and the girls also played badminton, cricket, croquet, netball and basketball. Bull board, an indoor game for wet days, was also introduced. Swimming does not appear to have been added to the list of sports until 1910, when girls went to Hackney Baths and an article in the school magazine explained why swimming should be encouraged:

Additional land bought for the school in 1908 provided space for three tennis courts, including this grass court.

K. Portlock, swimming championship, 1922.

It is good that this most valuable of physical exercises should be encouraged, for not only is a girl made strong and active by indulgence therein but there is the decided gain in the fact that she can should occasion arise, save her own life from boat accident or ship-wreck; and, too, she has the power, be she a good swimmer, of saving the lives of others. Again, surely there is no other occupation out of school time which is so great a help to children in developing their courage and powers of endurance. Every child, boy or girl, should be taught to swim, as a matter of necessity, as it is taught the facts of history and the details of geography.

The annual Gymnastic Display, given over four days in front of Governors, parents and friends, took place in the spring term. The exercises on various pieces of apparatus,

ropes, ribstools and vaulting horse were designed to show agility, 'suppleness of the spine' and 'general fearlessness'. Figure marching showed off 'erect carriage', and 'movements on the double bar made it plain that girls, as well as boys, can develop muscular strength, and combine it with grace of movement'. Girls wore a special costume designed by Miss Clarke when the gymnasium opened in 1902. The April 1906 display included work by both senior and junior girls, including, towards the end, jumping, 'which showed elasticity of body and the rope was cleared on several occasions at the height of four feet six inches. The display was concluded by a maze in which the little ones valiantly tried to keep up with the steps of their elder sisters and succeeded very well'.

The summer term was largely given over to examinations and the annual inspection. However, there were the school sports to enjoy and end-of-term school visits rounded off the year. In June 1906, the Kindergarten Sports were combined with a concert and described in the magazine. The programme began with choruses and recitations of nursery rhymes, such as Little Miss Muffet and Humpty Dumpty, 'and last, but not least, that old favourite, "Hey-diddle-diddle" was delivered by a small boy with a piping childish treble'.

Edith Hyde, one of the older pupils, described the senior girls' enjoyment of their Sports Day, which went on into the evening and usually finished about 8pm. 'Early in the afternoon almost all the girls of the School,

Sports Day, clockwise from top left: Scooter race; Netball shooting competition; Slow Cycle race; Kindergarten Sports, waiting for the last competitor to get into line for the egg and spoon race.

and most of the mistresses were assembled in the garden. Those who were entering the lists were conspicuous in their blue gymnastic costumes, their eager faces promising well for the spirit in which the competitors undertook their contests'. Despite the cloudy weather and a shower, which 'was not so severe as to interrupt the all-important tugs-of-war which were at the time demanding every one's attention', competitors and spectators followed the programme enthusiastically. Of the many races, Edith tells us, 'The sack and obstacle races were great sources of merriment, calling forth much laughter both from the competitors and the spectators'. Tea followed the heats and then came the final contests. 'By this time many friends of the girls had arrived to witness the final races,

and in addition, Sir Henry Knight and other members of the governing body were present. The excitement was now very great, reaching its highest pitch during the jumping competition, which concluded the sports. This finished, Sir Henry Knight presented the prizes to the many victors.' After 'vigorous cheers, the garden was deserted gradually by the many folk who had spent such a very enjoyable time there'.

Right: Violet Rudd's school report for July 1906.

Below right: The cot at the children's hospital in Bethnal Green supported by LHS.

'The other half'

Compared with the choice on offer in the twenty-first-century school, there was a limited range of clubs. But girls could join, amongst others, clubs for sketching, history, French, swimming and games. There were also occasional visits arranged to the theatre or to lectures.

Lady Holles' girls were encouraged to be generous. There was often a Christmas appeal for warm clothing to be sent to the poor in East End parishes and the school regularly supported a cot at The Queen's Hospital for Children in Bethnal Green. As well as regular support for some causes, one-off donations were made, for example to the Children's Country Holiday Fund, which still exists today, and the Fresh Air Fund. During the First World War, girls directed their energies into knitting and supporting relief funds for Belgian, Polish and Serbian refugees.

It seems that races were altered to be topical, as Elsa Vanderlinde wrote that for Sports Day 1909, 'As aviation and Polar discoveries are the topics of the day, we of course had to be up-to-date. So in the obstacle race we had to fly in balloons, make parachutes and reach the North Pole, where we had to defend ourselves by shooting down a poor little white Teddy Bear'.

The summer ended with a number of visits. The V and VI formers were invited to look round St Paul's Cathedral by one of the Governors, the Revd Prebendary Barff. Their visit was followed by tea in the Vicarage of St Giles', Cripplegate. Others visited Kew Gardens, where at least some of the 1906 school girls were no more virtuous than their twenty-first-century counterparts, as Edith Zerfass noted: 'Having been told at what time we should meet at the gate, we divided into several groups and went our various ways, some of us being on pleasure bent and others, with praiseworthy zeal, entering the houses to examine the specimens of floral beauty with which they were filled.' The rest of the school was not left out; the UIV and LIV forms went for a picnic and games in Chingford, and form II visited the zoo.

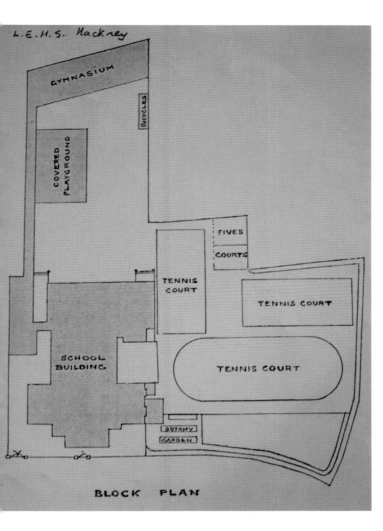

Maintaining momentum

Described in 1902 as a school on the way up, it was clear, by 1906, that Lady Holles' School, Mare Street, Hackney, had arrived. The job now was to keep the school at the top. The popularity of the school meant that there was competition for places. The Governors continued to expand the facilities, and in 1908 provided the school with greatly enlarged grounds. They bought the adjacent house, with its large garden, and seven cottages up to Saxony Avenue, pulled down the buildings to provide two asphalt tennis courts, one grass court, two fives' courts, beds especially reserved for the botany girls and a greenhouse. In 1911, an additional wing provided a library and six new classrooms in place of four old ones. Two of these classrooms were used for botany and geography. The geography room was fitted with the latest technology, an electric lantern to show pictures. It was during this rebuilding that the grand terrace, with its row of new white columns, was added, along with a roof garden. The school prospectus for 1913 shows the extended school.

Prospectus from 1913 showing from top left: layout of the school; Botany room; Geography room with electric lantern.

Above: A group of friends at LHS in 1909. Three went on to train as teachers, one went to a Domestic Economy Training college and another went to university.

Above right: Monitor's badge from Hackney.

Jobs for the girls

By the beginning of the twentieth century, it had become more common for women from all parts of the middle classes to work and to go on to higher education. However, the range of work available to them was limited. The Hackney registers[20] show the types of work available to lower- and middle-class women at the start of the twentieth century. Out of a sample of 170 girls who left Lady Holles' School between 1908 and 1911, 23 went on to be clerks or take up shorthand and typing; others went on to Clark's College in Chancery Lane, to prepare for positions in the Civil Service or to be clerks in business; 23 left to be student or pupil teachers at colleges like Avery Hill and Fulham training college; 5 became telephone operators; and others left to take up millinery, dressmaking or tailoring. One girl, Kate Sturrock, after gaining her certificate at the Apothecaries Hall in 1902, became Assistant Dispenser at Tottenham Hospital, and then private dispenser to two Tottenham doctors. In an article for *Our Magazine* in March 1904, she explained why this work might appeal. Articles appeared on a regular basis in *Our Magazine* from girls who had gone on to Pitman's School of Shorthand or to college, or who had

spent a term elsewhere as part of pupil teacher training. These articles gave girls an insight into what life after school might offer.

One of the ways into higher education was to pass the London Matriculation Examination, a school leaving examination. In 1904, the first pupils matriculated directly from Lady Holles' School. Lena Mendoza and Dorothy Catmur were the successful candidates that year and both went on to study science. Dorothy was one of eight Catmur children, including two boys, who attended the school between 1895 and 1917. Dorothy's brother, Keith, recalled his eldest sister's career in 1986. 'Dorothy … took Matric at the age of 15 and was an early Head Girl soon after Miss Clarke was appointed Headmistress. She later returned as the first "qualified" Maths teacher. She was also the first girl to obtain an MA in the University of London, having trained at East London College.'

From then on, a steadily increasing number of girls matriculated. Lena Mendoza went on to earn a BSc with first class honours in psychology. Many other girls went to the East London College, now part of Queen Mary's College, to follow university courses. Once advanced courses were offered at Mare Street, others, such as Hilda Denney, could do the advanced work there. Hilda went from Mare Street to Somerville College, Oxford, between 1917 and 1920. London University, unlike Oxford and Cambridge, admitted women to its degrees from 1878, and the school magazines regularly reported successes of old girls achieving BAs or BScs at London University.

However, for some parents, education up to secondary level was considered sufficient for a girl, and of the 170 in the sample, 20 left to stay at home.

End of an era

When Ada Beatrice Clarke announced that she would be resigning to marry Edwin Percy Haslam in July 1915[21] she was leaving the school at a pinnacle of success. As Miss Nickalls recalled in her speech at the Prize Distribution of December 1915, the last year of Miss Clarke's career, 1914–5 was 'perhaps the most brilliant year'. Of a total of 15 candidates, 14 matriculated in the London Senior

Left: A farewell
photograph of Ada
Beatrice Clarke with
her staff in 1915.

Below: Frontispiece
from an illuminated
testimonial presented
to Miss Clarke by the
Governors in 1915.

School Examination and 10 girls gained Intermediate
Scholarships from London County Council, double the
number gained in any previous year. Of the senior girls
who left in the summer, 11 went on to a university course
and 4 of those were studying medicine, 'with a view to
help supply the shortage of doctors caused by the war'.

The inspectors from the University of London, at the
start of their report in March 1917, also paid tribute to Miss
Clarke's work. They acclaimed her as a Head Mistress
'who by her strong personality and conspicuous ability
had raised this School from insignificance to a proud
position among London Girls' Schools'.

Miss Clarke's leadership was a major factor in the
success of the school, as Edith Kimpton, one of the staff,
recalled when Miss Clarke left.

*Everything about the school had to be of the best, from
gymnastic displays and prize-givings to the prefects'
badges, the curtains on the stage, and the girls' hair-
ribbons. If we had a gymnastic display, it must be the
best any school had ever known; if there was a dramatic
entertainment, it must be the best any school had ever
staged; our prize-giving must, of course, go without a
hitch. And lo! It was so. Everything did go smoothly.
She believed that staff and girls could do whatever tasks
she gave them, so we all said gladly and meekly, 'Yes,
Miss Clarke', and did them.*

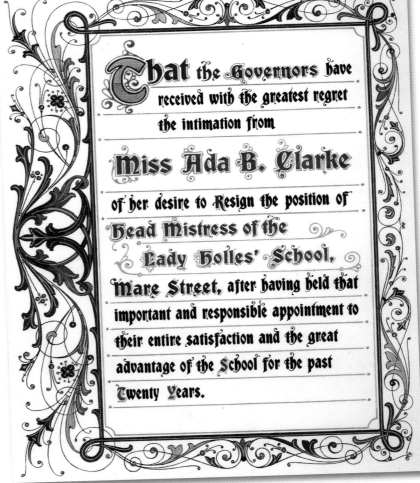

That the Governors have
received with the greatest regret
the intimation from

Miss Ada B. Clarke

of her desire to Resign the position of
Head Mistress of the
Lady Holles' School,
Mare Street, after having held that
important and responsible appointment to
their entire satisfaction and the great
advantage of the School for the past
Twenty Years.

Nora Nickalls (middle row, fourth from left) with the staff.

Marjorie Goldston, a pupil since 1912, left in September 1917, 'on account of the air raids', and moved to St Winifred's Convent, Swansea to continue her education.

Mare Street under Nora Nickalls: 1915–36

Although the character of Hackney was changing in the years during and after the First World War, Lady Holles' School survived to celebrate its Jubilee in 1928 and for eight more years. When Nora Nickalls took over as Head Mistress in September 1915, the standing of the school was very high. Miss Nickalls told the story that, on her appointment, Her Majesty's Inspector for Kent had written to congratulate her, saying he had heard it was one of the plums of the profession. She took over as Head Mistress a year into the First World War, and, writing later, she recalled the stresses of those early days. As well as 'food coupons to complicate school dinners, fuel and light restrictions', 'the school was in a direct line from Woolwich to Enfield and Gothas came over nightly. The Cuffley Zepp[22] was seen both sides of the "school house" at once'.

She had unofficial notice of air raids from two parents and another friend, and recalled:

> *After the first daylight raid when, to shelter*
> *the girls from possible falling of glass, school*
> *dinner was served under the desks, procedure*
> *became one of routine. Nine rooms to clear at*
> *the 'first' warning, gas and electricity to be*
> *turned off, a substitute for gas masks[23] kept*
> *in every form-room cupboards and everyone*
> *kept at school and given something to do*
> *or think about till the 'All Clear' signal*
> *had arrived.*

Stoicism was the order of the day, according to Sybil Long, who was at the school from 1916 to 1923. 'I missed the first daylight raid at school, but was told by my form that the mistress taking the lesson had promptly ordered the girls to put their heads under the lids of their desks, and had then continued reading.' After this, air-raid drill was a regular event, with the girls 'lying on our fronts with our heads towards the wall, having been told that the investigation of bombed buildings showed that the fire place wall often remained standing when the rest of the building was demolished'.

There was some disruption to school life, as people moved out of the district to avoid the bombing. The war created other strains on the school too. There were plenty of opportunities during the war for girls to gain employment, so it seems there was pressure on some to leave to take a job. At Prize Distribution in December 1915, Miss Nickalls urged parents 'to make every effort to give their girls a sound and sufficiently long education followed by proper training' and to let their 'school girls grow up normally'.

However, it was clear from the inspection of 1917 that the school was thriving. The school had increased considerably in size since 1906 and now had 368 pupils, with another 42 in the kindergarten, 16 of whom were boys.

Miss Nickalls recalled, in 1947, that 'The burning question when I came was that of a post-matriculation Sixth Form', in other words, whether the school should begin to offer advanced courses, what we know today as sixth form work, as preparation for university entrance. This had been recommended at the inspection in 1914 and, shortly after taking up her post, Nora Nickalls recalled seeking the advice of an inspector. Mr Urwick told her, 'After five years the school will lose its reputation if it is

not undertaken'. The decision was taken to go ahead, and, in their report of 1917, the University of London inspectors commented favourably on how post-matriculation work was developing. In 1917, there were 14 post-matriculation students, 7 taking an arts course and 7 taking science.

Elsie Mitchell (née Collier 1916–23) remembers, 'We had a very small Sixth Form when I was there, so small that we did not have a form room, we used the library for our work. I think there were only 8 girls. Higher School Certificate, which was the same as A levels, more or less, was introduced rather late in my time, in fact mine was only the third form which took it'.

However, the inspectors noted that expansion was hampered by lack of accommodation. They suggested extending the buildings for the seniors and that a separate block be built for the juniors and the kindergarten. They recommended that the juniors become a separate department of the school, to include girls under 11, subject to the overall supervision of the Head Mistress.

The inspectors' overall conclusion was 'The tone of the school is excellent, and the behaviour of the girls again made a very favourable impression'.

As is evident from the subject reports the level of teaching capacity in the staff is high and good work is being done in every department. The mistresses are zealous and happy in their work, they preserve discipline without obvious effort, and the girls respond readily to their appeal. All are maintaining the deservedly high reputation of the School, which under the new Head Mistress bids fair to be even enhanced, for she is alive to all possibilities of development, and has considerable experience to guide her in all she undertakes.

The school continued to do well academically. In 1917, three pupils had gone to Somerville College, Oxford, one as Senior Clothworkers' Scholar and another with an exhibition. In 1918, the school received its first Advanced Course grant in modern studies, followed, in 1920, by a similar grant in mathematics and science, which continued until 1935. Marjorie Emery (1922–30), who went on to Cambridge to study natural sciences, recognised the importance of her grounding in science at Mare Street in the 1920s.

Miss Nora Nickalls was very wise. She had studied History at Oxford and, accepting that she knew little science herself, asked advice of Mr Westaway, one of His Majesty's Inspectors. He recommended having good Mathematics, Physics and Chemistry as the basic sciences if the school could not cover the full spectrum. This was rather hard on the Biologists but it gave them a good foundation for their future work.

Top: Mare Street in the 1920s with the school on the right.

Bottom: Cookery.

Marjorie particularly remembered the impact of her physics teacher, 'As a Physicist, I must pay tribute to our Physics mistress, Miss Mary Beach', whom she describes as 'a most thorough teacher and gave us a good grounding'. There were visits and lectures of scientific interest too. Girls went to North Yorkshire to see the total eclipse of the sun in 1927, and Marjorie recalled a trip to Selfridges to see Baird's first

Above: The Lord Mayor of London (one of the Governors) and his Sheriffs arriving to open the temporary building, constructed out of two very large Army huts, which provided separate accommodation for the Junior Department.

Far right: Miss Nickalls at the Annual Conference of the Head Mistresses' Association, which was held at the school in June 1922.

Cripplegate Schools Foundation.

THE
LADY ELEANOR HOLLES SCHOOL
(FOUNDED 1710)

Jubilee Souvenir

IN HACKNEY

1878–1928.

public display of television: 'Here we really were seeing something that made history and we caught the excitement of pioneer science.'

By 1922, the Governors had acted on the recommendation of the inspectors and a separate temporary building was opened for the Junior Department. The same year also saw the Annual Conference of the Head Mistresses' Association held at the school.

In 1928, The Lady Eleanor Holles School[24] celebrated its Jubilee, the 50th anniversary of its foundation in Hackney. There were celebrations at the school and a Jubilee service held at St John-at-Hackney on St Luke's Day, 18 October 1928. The Jubilee programme celebrated some of the successes of its old girls, including one who had been appointed a house surgeon and another who became a medical missionary. It was fitting that this celebration took place in the same year in which women gained the vote on the same terms as men at the age of 21. In its 50 years in Hackney, the school had played its part in enabling girls, who were by no means from privileged backgrounds, to gain an education which enabled them to take up responsible and professional jobs in society. Hilda Denney, previously a pupil and then a member of staff (1926–59), remembered the social mix at Hackney: 'There were fee-payers and the cream of the local elementary school; varying from tram-drivers' daughters, local shopkeepers' and the children of the local doctors and clergy. A good mix.' According to her, they were resilient girls. 'They were sturdy creatures. If they wept, the tears were probably of rage, they stood up firmly for themselves and this pleased me.'

What was the school like in this era?

There were no school magazines produced between 1917 and 1935, so we have to rely on the memories of old girls to give us a glimpse into school life.

Elsie Mitchell left Mare Street in 1923 with a leaving exhibition to go to university. She recalled some aspects of school life in a letter, in 1978, to a pupil who was writing a project about the school. Elsie's memories of the school uniform may convince the modern school girl never to complain about uniform again. She remembered what the uniform was like in 1916: 'Navy blue gym slips (dreadful things with box pleats, made of serge or some other thick and heavy material), pale blue blouses, thick black woollen gym stockings which we wore all the time and I think this persisted until I left, straw hats like boaters only more oval in shape, with a hatband of striped navy and pale blue petersham ribbon with the crest in front.'[25]

And to comfort those whose uniform is perhaps more roomy than they would like, Elsie goes on to recall: 'We all wore navy blue bloomers all the time, and, since it was wartime and then, and for some time afterwards, materials were expensive and in short supply, all our mothers bought underwear and everything else larger than needed at the moment, so new bloomers were like pantaloons!'

She remembers that school rules were strict, since the aim of the school was to produce ladylike and God-

Souvenir programme celebrating 50 years in Hackney, 1878–1928.

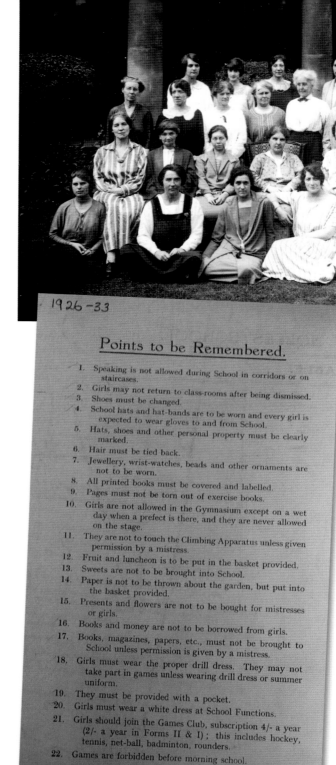

fearing girls. She gave some examples. 'I knew Miss Nickalls throughout my time at the school, and she was feared very much as being very strict on discipline in and out of the school, for example we were not allowed to walk in the street without gloves and we were reprimanded, often in front of the school, if we were seen "eating" in the street. It was a great temptation to buy buns or sweets on the way home.'

Florence Nicholson (1925–31) also remembered the importance attached to wearing gloves and found the habit became ingrained: 'The thing that sticks in my mind was the fact that we were always supposed to either wear or carry gloves. Failure to do so could result in a "Signature", strangely, this habit was so instilled on me, that it has really stuck all my life. My husband was always amused, because even in a car, I would sit with my gloves on my lap!'

On the right is the full set of rules when Miss Nickalls was Head Mistress. Rules were enforced with the signature system. It seems to have taken Elsie some time to get used to this.

Our punishment took the form of 'signatures' – the mistress in charge would call out 'Elsie Collier, take a signature'. Each form was allowed a certain number of signatures, I mean each girl in the form. The first year I was there it was, I think, 12 for the term, and I disgraced myself by getting 39! If any form had no one in it who exceeded the allowed number that form went on to the Golden List, which hung on a board in the gymnasium, which was used as a hall for assembly, prize-givings etc. It was an attempt to teach some sort of social responsibility, not to let down your fellow pupils.

The system survived into the 1930s, though it seems to have had modifications, as Doris Faris (1927–32) remembered it.

Above: Staff c.1920.

Far left: Mare Street pupil c.1912.

Left: School rules in Nora Nickalls' time at Hackney.

1926–33

Points to be Remembered.

1. Speaking is not allowed during School in corridors or on staircases.
2. Girls may not return to class-rooms after being dismissed.
3. Shoes must be changed.
4. School hats and hat-bands are to be worn and every girl is expected to wear gloves to and from School.
5. Hats, shoes and other personal property must be clearly marked.
6. Hair must be tied back.
7. Jewellery, wrist-watches, beads and other ornaments are not to be worn.
8. All printed books must be covered and labelled.
9. Pages must not be torn out of exercise books.
10. Girls are not allowed in the Gymnasium except on a wet day when a prefect is there, and they are never allowed on the stage.
11. They are not to touch the Climbing Apparatus unless given permission by a mistress.
12. Fruit and luncheon is to be put in the basket provided.
13. Sweets are not to be brought into School.
14. Paper is not to be thrown about the garden, but put into the basket provided.
15. Presents and flowers are not to be bought for mistresses or girls.
16. Books and money are not to be borrowed from girls.
17. Books, magazines, papers, etc., must not be brought to School unless permission is given by a mistress.
18. Girls must wear the proper drill dress. They may not take part in games unless wearing drill dress or summer uniform.
19. They must be provided with a pocket.
20. Girls must wear a white dress at School Functions.
21. Girls should join the Games Club, subscription 4/- a year (2/- a year in Forms II & I); this includes hockey, tennis, net-ball, badminton, rounders.
22. Games are forbidden before morning school.

N. NICKALLS, M.A. (Oxon.),
Head Mistress.

The punishment for 'crimes' such as talking in class was a signature. At the beginning of each term every form appeared on a board in the gym headed the 'Golden List'. In the lower forms each pupil was allowed eight signatures during the term but if any one member of the form exceeded this number, the form's name was removed from the Golden List. The number of signatures

Above right: Lower VA 1924–5 Miss Malkin and form with Kathleen Keilich, third from left, on front row. The two Keilich girls, Dorothy and Kathleen, generously remembered the school in their wills.

Right: Marjorie Dodd (right) with friend on Geography expedition, 1930s.

decreased as one moved up to the higher forms and we all prayed that we would not be the one responsible for the ultimate disgrace of removal of our form from the Golden List. At the end of each day we had to report on signatures received, from whom and for what offence, and our 'crimes' were recorded by our form mistress.

Elsie Mitchell also remembered Miss Nickalls for passing on an important message to her pupils about women, at a time when there was still debate about whether women should have the vote and on what terms. She 'certainly managed to pass on the message to some of us that women's brains were as good as men's, which was not even then a common belief'.

Miss Nickalls had been one of the first women to receive a degree at Oxford. Women had been allowed to study at Oxford and take the examinations, but were not allowed to receive degrees until 1920. When she went back to Oxford to receive her degree in 1925, she took the School Captain, Barbara Atthill, and a Senior Prefect, May Wyatt, with her.

The decision to leave Hackney

At Prize Giving in March 1935, Sir William Baddeley, Chairman of Governors, announced that The Lady

Eleanor Holles School would move in September 1936 to Hampton. He explained that, whereas it used to be thought that the best size for an efficient and economic secondary school was 300 pupils, the increased costs of schools and specialisation in the upper forms now meant that the Board of Education recommended units of at least 450. Hackney was increasingly an industrial rather than a residential area. Hilda Denney, first a pupil and then a member of staff, recalled that 'Hackney had become a very different place from the days of my youth. The houses opposite the school had given place to a large factory and more had sprung up round about'. The Board of Education inspection of 1929 had already pointed out that The Lady Eleanor Holles School was one of three schools (the others were Dalston and Clapton) in a district where two schools of about 450 each would be sufficient. It had gone on to suggest that two of these schools should be merged.

The Governors had been considering the situation for some time, and, in 1934, a special committee of the Cripplegate Schools Foundation was set up to consider the future of the school. They had before them a table illustrating the fortunes of the school between 1924 and 1934. This showed 'continuously increasing cost to the Foundation and a continuous diminishing number of pupils'. There had been 349 pupils at the school's last inspection in 1929, but numbers had been dropping. The committee reported, 'it considers the immediate removal of the school from Mare Street as advisable'. In July 1934, the Governors accepted this recommendation and resolved that as 'the present school maintained by the Governors at Mare Street Hackney cannot be usefully and economically carried on', the school should be closed, its buildings and ground disposed of and 'that a new school to be maintained by the Foundation and to be known as Lady Eleanor Holles School … should be established in the County of Middlesex'.

As the *Hackney Gazette* reported on 29 March 1935, the decision was received 'with regret'. It went on to say, 'The proposed re-building of the Dalston Secondary School for Girls on a new site and the merging of the traditions of the two schools into one will not compensate Hackney for its loss'. The editorial made clear the high regard in which the school was held, and continued, 'as the octopus

of industrialism spreads its tentacles in our direction … Hackney's sacrifice will be others' gain'.

Once the decision was taken, arrangements were made for most of the senior pupils to transfer to Dalston Secondary School. Some staff remained with the junior forms at Mare Street until Dalston's new buildings were ready in 1939. Miss Nickalls praised the Head Mistress of Dalston, Miss Griffith, and her staff, 'for all their help at a difficult time and their kindness to the girls we left behind to join Dalston. She became a Vice-President of the Holly Club and I of the Dalston Old Girls' Club during the years that any of the LEH girls were still at school'. Miss Nickalls regretted leaving Hackney, especially leaving the older pupils, but she concluded, 'it is infinitely better for them to be transferred to a larger and a living school with more opportunities and interests than are possible here'.

The Mare Street buildings remain, having served in their time as a technical institute, belonged to the Cordwainers' Company and now form part of the London College of Fashion, University of the Arts, London. The Hackney badge and Cripplegate symbol placed there when Lady Holles' School was built are a visible reminder of its origins.

The removal from Hackney was recalled in the school magazine in December 1936.

We had finished all examinations, and behind the scenes books were being separated from books and maps from maps. Then we tore down pictures and blackboards, tossed desks to the furniture repairers and removers, and labelled the rest. We hurried these with all speed into two hundred or so packing cases. The sound of the hammer was heard everywhere. They packed up the laboratories, a delicate task; they packed up the kitchen, glass and china; they packed up two thousand volumes in the Library. The scene of desolation beggared description as we surveyed it with aching limbs.

Then it was time to go. 'We said good-bye to Mare Street, Hackney.'

Above: The badge used at Redcross Street and at Hackney on the facade of the Mare Street school.

Far left: Some of the pupils who remained at Hackney.

Move to Hampton, 1936–40

Why Hampton?

Once the decision to move had been made, the Governors considered a number of locations, in Northwood, Pinner and Cockfosters, before concluding that Hampton was most suitable. Why was this? The site itself, 18 acres, part of Rectory Farm, owned by the Trustees of Hampton Grammar School Foundation, and next to land on which the Grammar School was planning to build its own new school, was attractive. As the Clerk to the Foundation, J Woodman-Smith, reported to the Governors in November 1934, the Trustees would be willing to sell a portion of the land for a girls' secondary school, 'complementary to the Boys' Grammar School'. Part of the attraction of the area was that a senior elementary school, then called Rectory Farm, now Hampton Academy, had already been built along the same road, and it was considered 'that the conjunction of the elementary, boys' secondary and girls' secondary schools should form a convenient and attractive educational unit'.

In his report, the Clerk argued that there were good road and rail links to enable girls from Teddington, Twickenham, Whitton, Feltham, Hanworth and Kingston to reach the school, and that the district surrounding the school was being developed with houses 'of a class which will bring a population requiring, in a large number of cases, unassisted secondary education'. The deciding factor was whether there would be sufficient demand for largely fee-paying education. The only provision for girls' secondary education in the neighbourhood, at Twickenham, was 'already over-crowded', and the Clerk to Middlesex County Council had pointed out that 'in any case a considerable proportion of the population, rather than avail themselves of a school under the secondary education system of Middlesex, send their daughters to school in Kingston as fee-payers'. The conclusion was drawn that 'in all probability there will not be the slightest difficulty in filling, in that area, a three-form entry Secondary School and that a considerable proportion of entrants should be fee-payers rather than assisted places'.

So the Governors agreed with Middlesex County Council to build, equip and maintain from their endowments a three-form entry girls' secondary school for 450, and to contribute £26,000 towards acquiring the site and the cost of building, on condition that Middlesex County Council meet the difference between £26,000 and the total cost. The new school would be a direct grant-aided, fee-paying school, in which the Governors would provide up to 25 per cent of free places for Middlesex scholars.

The original intention was that the new school would open in September 1936, but a dispute over the value of the site meant that the sale of the land was not completed until December 1936. As arrangements had been made to leave Hackney at the end of the summer term, 1936, the school took over a small private school and its pupils in Teddington, and used the building as its temporary home while the new school was built in Hampton.

Summerleigh

On 29 September 1936, The Lady Eleanor Holles School opened in its temporary home, Summerleigh, Hampton Road, Teddington. There were 67 pupils, including some, like Barbara Megson, who had been pupils at the private school run there for many years by Madame Mottu, who was retiring. There had been a great deal to do to prepare Summerleigh for its new residents. The school magazine of December 1936 made this clear.

Immediately preceding that beginning were three weeks of concentrated hustle. While plumbers and painters were dealing with drains and decorating and maids were scrubbing floors, moving-men were unloading furniture from seven large lorries, and places had to be found for the many cupboards, chairs and tables brought amongst other things from the much larger Hackney building … Staining floors, laying carpets, changing a large room into six curtained cubicles for dormitory, stowing superfluous things into the roomy attic, hanging

Previous page: LEH in 1937.

Opposite: Playing tennis on the Middle lawn at Summerleigh, LEH's temporary home in Teddington, 1936–7.

Summerleigh was cramped after Hackney. One of the LV girls, writing in the school magazine of December 1936, praised the staff for adapting to the changed circumstances. 'One of the things that surprised me most was the way in which the School has managed to run so smoothly in such small premises when the Staff has been used to a great deal more space. There seems to be very little difference in the day's curriculum.' However, it is clear, from the editorial in the school magazine of July 1937, that staff looked forward to their new premises: 'We shall not be sorry to reach a home where one room has one function! Here double, triple, nay quadruple uses have been required.'

In the gardens at Summerleigh. Left to right seated, Betty Stoodley, Dulcie Pyne, Joan Blythe, and Joyce Ward standing.

pictures, interviewing men who called about gas, water, electric light, and every other conceivable household item, snatching lunch in relays at a local cafe, endless unpacking of domestic crockery and school-books, these were but a few of the pleasures that filled those busy days.

As the school assembled in the gymnasium, with 'its neat rows of chairs, grand piano and platform', for prayers on the first morning, it seemed unbelievable that so much had been accomplished in such a short space of time.

Miss Nickalls had agreed with the Governors that she would mastermind the move and had brought five staff with her from Hackney. Six of the Hackney pupils, including Muriel Tuffill, Peggy Morris (née Clark 1924–39) and Joan Blythe (1932–38), also transferred and became weekly boarders. Peggy had been a pupil since 1924 and Joan since 1932. Joan had a Cripplegate Scholarship which could only be used at the school, so she had little choice but to follow the school to Hampton, though she never regretted having done so. The six who had been day girls at Hackney now found themselves weekly boarders, sharing the dormitory which had been hurriedly prepared for them.

MAGAZINE

THE LADY ELEANOR HOLLES SCHOOL

SPES ADJUVAT AUDACEM

DECEMBER, 1936

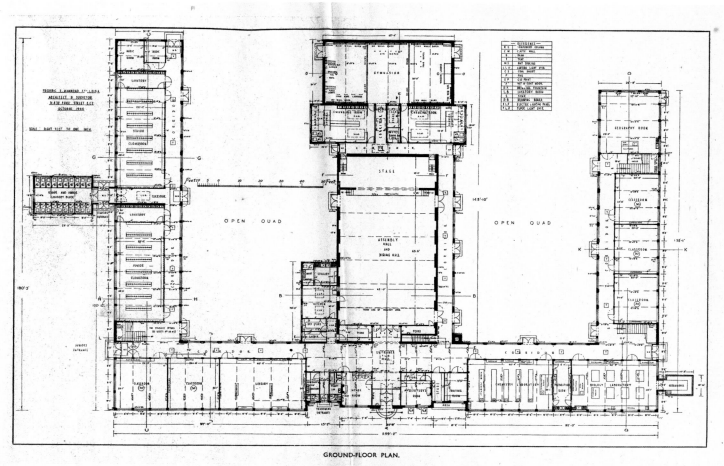

GROUND-FLOOR PLAN.

MR. F. S. HAMMOND, L.R.I.B.A. (HAMMOND, JACK AND AUSTIN), ARCHITECT.

Relocation

> We have bright hopes for a fuller sphere of usefulness in Hampton where a good girls' school has long been needed and which it seems likely that all classes will attend.
>
> **Miss Nickalls' last report to the Governors from the schoolhouse at Hackney, July 1936**

The new buildings, designed by Colonel FS Hammond, whose father had designed the Hackney school,[26] were in the shape of an E. The central block contained a large Assembly Hall, seating 544 on the ground floor and 120 in the balcony, with a stage, dressing rooms and a fine gymnasium. The right wing and adjoining part of the front block included the geography room, main staffroom, classrooms and Science Department. The left wing included all the cloakrooms and lavatories and the art room, whilst the main building between the left wing and the tower contained the library, housecraft room and remaining classrooms and administrative offices.

The foundation stone of the new building was laid on 16 September 1936 by Sir William Baddeley, Chairman of the Cripplegate Schools' Foundation. Under the foundation stone were a copy of Lady Eleanor's will, a badge of the school at Cripplegate, a prefect's badge of the school at Hackney and a new postage stamp. Girls moved into the new buildings to start the autumn term on 21 September 1937. In her history of the school published in 1947, Barbara Megson recalls the initial delight of moving into the new buildings, with their airy classrooms, and how impressive the Hall seemed on that first morning at prayers. On that first day, as forms were taken on a tour of the school by their tutors, they were warned not to run or slide on 'the beautiful polished parquet floors'

Ground floor architect's plan of The Lady Eleanor Holles School, Hampton, 1936.

Clockwise from above: 1937 library; 1937 domestic science room; gymnasium.

(mostly gone now, except in a few classrooms), and some wondered why there were little windows cut into form-room doors. Barbara remembers that the gym mistress soon found her own use for them. 'She inaugurated "Position Marks" for bad posture sitting, walking or standing, and found these windows admirable for taking girls unawares and making a fine haul of position marks!'

The school was officially opened on 7 December 1937 by HRH The Duchess of Gloucester. The formal opening was preceded by weeks of meticulous preparation, to greet not only the Lord Mayor of London, Sir Harry Twyford (Alderman of Cripplegate and Governor of the School), and the Lady Mayoress, the Sheriffs of London and their ladies, but also local dignitaries, the Lord Lieutenant of Middlesex and the guest of honour, Her Royal Highness, The Duchess of Gloucester.

Peggy Brandon (1936–8) in the UV described the opening day in the March 1938 school magazine. 'Tuesday, December 7th dawned cold and rather foggy but bad weather did not damp the spirits of the nearly two hundred girls who were lined up outside the School just after two o'clock in the afternoon to welcome HRH the Duchess of Gloucester.' A film of the opening shows girls in black velour hats and school coats jumping up and down to keep warm while they waited for the Duchess's car to appear.

Sighs of disappointment greeted each car which did not slow down at the main gates. Suddenly, however, there was a burst of cheering from the crowd lining the

roadway, and a police car came sweeping through the gate, followed by a magnificent Rolls Royce limousine. From inside, the Duchess looking perfectly charming, smiled at the excited school.

After the ceremony and the Duchess's tour of the school, she walked the length of the driveway to greet the thousand or so schoolchildren from neighbouring schools who had been invited to cheer her goodbye.

Putting down roots

The March 1938 school magazine referred to the school as a 'transplant into new soil'. Now the pomp and ceremony were over, the real business of ensuring that the 'transplant' would flourish and that the school would establish itself firmly in the area began. The new start in Hampton was signified not only by new buildings, but also by a new badge, motto and uniform. Miss Nickalls had consulted the College of Heralds about a new badge that would incorporate elements of the school's history. Barbara Megson explained how the changes in the badge decided the colours for the new uniform. 'The shield of Lady Eleanor Holles combines two black piles with ermine on silver. It was therefore decided that the uniform should be grey to represent the silver, and that a black hat should symbolise the ermine. The hat-bands are "Lord Mayor's Red", as a sign of the school's connections with the City.'

So the blue of Hackney was abandoned, along with the tunics, and, from 1936, the Senior Department girls wore a uniform of grey blazer and skirt, with a white blouse, and a red, silver and black striped tie. UII and below wore grey kilts and grey jumpers, with red and black stripes. Both juniors and seniors wore similar black hats, with Lord Mayor's red hatbands.

The Hackney motto of *Diligentia Praevalebit* ('Diligence will prevail', or, as Miss Nickalls explained it once, 'It's dogged as does it') was replaced with the Holles family motto, *Spes Audacem Adjuvat* ('Hope favours the bold').

Beginning with 67 pupils at Summerleigh, the Governors' expectation that there was a need for a new girls' secondary school in the Hampton area seemed to be borne out by steadily increasing numbers. At the opening ceremony in December 1937, Miss Nickalls explained that the school's aim was 'to afford a sound moral education without overstrain, such as will lead to preparation for some definite career and to a right use of leisure'. This seemed to appeal, as numbers began to build. Girls were admitted at all ages, though the intake was greatest from 11-year-olds. In the autumn of 1937, 175 pupils started, but there was only one girl in the VI form, CIC Reilly, who was also School Captain. The UV had eight girls and there were nine in the LV. Numbers were larger lower down the school, with 23 in UIV and 27 in LIV. There was a two-form entry in the IIIs, with 19 in IIIX and 23 in IIIY. The

The Duchess of Gloucester opened the school officially on 7 December 1937.

113

The school badge, crest and motto

It is not clear exactly when the school first began to use a badge and crest. But in September 1857, as the Trustees were building the Infants' School in Redcross Street, there is a reference in the minutes to their resolution 'that a tablet with the crest and arms of Lady Eleanor Holles' and the date of the building should be placed in the wall of the new schoolhouse. Part of this tablet has survived, and above the date, 1857, and the name, Lady Holles' School, can clearly be seen two coats of arms, the one on the left with ermine and the other with an oak tree, stars and a crescent moon. The ermine was part of the coat of arms of the Holles family and the other symbols were thought to be from the coat of arms of the Watson family.

The coat of arms with the oak tree, stars and crescent moon also appears prominently on the facade of the Mare Street buildings, placed there to mark the date of building in 1877. By 1902, the school badge at Mare Street was navy and silver, with an oak tree, stars and a crescent moon. It was always understood that these symbols had been chosen to honour the Honourable Anne Watson, who had used the money left from Lady Eleanor's estate to fund the original girls' school. However, in 1976, it was discovered that these symbols came from the coat of arms of an unrelated Watson family. It is not known how this mistake occurred. The crest included a representation of the old city gate of Cripplegate and the school motto at Hackney, *Diligentia Praevalebit* ('Diligence will prevail').

When the school moved to Hampton, Miss Nickalls, after consultation with the College of Heralds, introduced a new badge, crest and motto. This badge included the shield of the City of London, and the ermine of the Holles family with the gate of Cripplegate, whose Aldermen were frequently Governors of the school. The new crest included the name of the founder and the Holles family motto. The school took the Holles family motto of *Spes Audacem Adjuvat* ('Hope favours the bold') for its own.

In 1976, during Miss Smalley's time as Head Mistress, it was found that the badges used at Hackney and Hampton were both heraldically incorrect. According to Wing Commander Kenneth Newman MBE DFC, the Bursar at the time, the Vice-Chairman of Governors, Mr Charles Higgins, had taken the badges to the College of Arms, where this was discovered. The Governors had the badge and crest redesigned and approved by the College. The badge now in use includes ermine representing the arms of the Holles family, the sword of St Paul, remembering the school's links with the City, and the gate of Cripplegate as the original school was in that parish. The crest shows an arm and hand grasping a holly branch, which is a variation of the crest originally granted to Sir William Holles[27] in 1539, when he became Lord Mayor of London. His success marked the start of the Holles family's rise to fortune.

Redesigned badge and crest, 1976.

junior forms, Preparatory, I, LII and UII were also filling up well, with 69 pupils. By the end of the first full year in the new buildings, there were 223 girls in the school, about half the number the school planned to accommodate when it was full.

The autumn term of 1938 opened with 308 pupils. This was more than expected, so four extra staff were appointed. At the end of the second academic year, in July 1939, numbers were still growing, and school life was developing a similar rhythm to that of Hackney. In December 1938, the first school dance in Hampton had been held. An Inter-form Gymnastics Competition took place in March 1939, for which Colonel Hammond presented a cup, and school clubs and societies began at the end of the spring term 1939. Sports were already well established, with tennis and netball matches organised against Thames Valley County School and Twickenham County. The Badminton Captain relished their victory over

the City of London School, 'our old friend the enemy', against whom they had played at Hackney. Lacrosse was still in its infancy. According to Isabel Markham's (née Davis 1938–46) recollections, lacrosse was introduced as the winter game instead of hockey, because 'hockey encouraged the dreaded round shoulders' and lacrosse was considered better for posture. Peggy Clark, who wrote lacrosse reports for the school magazine, listed a number of improvements, such as more tackling and dodging needed in each year group's play, and concluded, in 1938, that 'the games had not yet reached a very good standard'. However, inter-form lacrosse matches improved the standard, and by the autumn and spring of 1941–2, the First XII felt strong enough to play their first matches against Haberdashers and Drayton Manor. Unfortunately, as the school magazine reported, all three matches were lost, but the report put a brave face on defeat and reassured readers that 'they were very well-fought games',

Above: Lacrosse was introduced as the main winter sport at Hampton.

Above left: In 1937 LEH had a preparatory intake. This photo of Preparatory pupils in summer 1938 was taken after an entertainment which explains why the boy second from the right in the front row is wearing a ruff. In 1938 there were three boys in the class, all of whom had older sisters in school.

LEH had just begun to establish itself in Hampton when the Second World War was declared on 3 September 1939.

and the teams that they 'should do well next season'. From such small beginnings!

Excursions and fund-raising events, such as a Country Fair with entertainments and stalls, including one selling beautifully knitted scarves in school colours, began to emerge on the school calendar. Miss Nickalls was keen to keep up links with Cripplegate, and some girls accompanied her to the Harvest Festival at St Giles', Cripplegate.

However, just as it seemed that the school was becoming well established, and as girls were about to return in September for the beginning of the school's third year at Hampton, the Second World War broke out. Miss Nickalls was to recall in November, 'Nor can we be glad enough that the move took place when it did and that we were firmly established in a permanent home in a neutral area two years before the war broke out'. But the

outbreak of war had an impact on numbers. Some parents heeded the government's advice to evacuate their children from the area. In September 1939, 420 pupils had been expected, but by November there were only 333 at school. However, numbers crept up again in the New Year, so that by the time of the full inspection by Board of Education inspectors in May 1940 there were 373 pupils, almost one-third of whom were ex-public elementary school pupils.

One of the reasons girls may have returned to school was that, after the initial movement in September 1939 of mothers and children away from areas in which bombing was expected, many returned to their home areas. This 'phoney war' period lasted until May 1940, and ended with the invasion of Holland and Belgium on 10 May 1940. This coincided with the last day of a four-day full inspection of the school. Miss Nickalls recalled listening with one of the

Pupils outside the main entrance, late 1940s.

inspectors to the 10.30am news bulletin and hearing that the Germans had invaded Holland and Belgium.

May 1940: 'a promising start'

How successful had the relocation been? The inspectors congratulated the Cripplegate Schools Foundation on acquiring, with the help of Middlesex County Council, 'an excellent modern school with 18 acres of playing fields', 'a happy result on which all concerned may be heartily congratulated'. At this stage, the boarding house, Burlington House, was privately owned and provided accommodation for the Head Mistress and five assistant teachers, as well as the boarders. In May 1940, there were 373 pupils in the school, including 115 in the Junior Department and 12 boarders. Although there were individual cases of pupils who came from as

far north as Hounslow, as far east as Wimbledon and as far west as Staines, 70 per cent of pupils came from the immediate areas of Hampton, Hampton Hill, Teddington and Twickenham. Many of these, until the outbreak of war, went home for lunch. Of the annual entry into the Senior Department, 25 per cent of places were reserved for Middlesex Scholarship holders, as agreed between the Governors and Middlesex County Council before the school moved to Hampton. Another 14 per cent came from across the river in Surrey, with a sizeable group of 27 pupils coming from Esher and Claygate. Local girls walked to school, with bicycle or bus being the usual options for others. The inspectors considered that the school was not too easily accessible, being about an eight-minute walk from the nearest main bus route, and that some girls living further afield had awkward journeys.

Burlington House.

The inspectors had particular praise for the Junior Department, with its 115 children, including a few boys, in four forms. Since the outbreak of war, the two lowest forms of the Junior Department had used a hall adjoining the boarding house and the drawing room of the boarding house as classrooms. The inspectors suggested that, as numbers grew in the Senior Department, this arrangement should be continued, leading to the Junior Department being permanently based in Burlington House. They felt that the children were following an appropriate curriculum, with 'interesting, yet suitably exacting' work, and were 'happy and well-cared for'.

However, the inspectors were very aware of the difficulties caused to the Senior Department by the removal of the school and the outbreak of war. They felt it was early days and that the need to fill places had led to the admission of some girls perhaps not best suited

to benefit to the full from the type of education on offer. At the time of the inspection, there were three III forms, three LIV forms, two UIV forms, one LV and one UV. The UV School Certificate form had only ten pupils, and there were only three girls in the VI form. The inspectors suggested that 'really high standards of work cannot be looked for until a settled organisation is functioning smoothly'. Their report focused on giving advice about the development of the school, so that a strong VI form would emerge when the current middle school pupils had reached that age. So they urged that staff appointed in the future should be able to teach their subjects beyond the level of the Higher School Certificate. Some of this advice gives an interesting insight into what was considered appropriate at the time to be included in the curriculum for all girls. They urged that a continuous course of cookery and needlework be provided for all girls, saying

Assembly Hall in 1937, later known as the Nora Nickalls Hall.

that this was usual in a school of the size, as well as a course to examination standard, to make sure that all pupils had a background knowledge of housecraft. However, this was not just so that homemakers would have this knowledge, but because, as a result of the food situation created by the war, and 'the growing interest in dietary matters and the acknowledgement of the effect of right feeding on development and health', there would be a need for trained workers in future. They saw school 'dinners' as an important opportunity not just to provide proper nourishment in wartime, but also 'for spreading the knowledge of right feeding'. They seem to have been taken aback to find that meals were being served in the corridors as the school did not have a dining room. They had obviously made it clear that this was not an acceptable arrangement, noting in their report, 'It is hoped that the use of the school hall (Assembly Hall), which would ensure that the school meal is served under proper conditions, is by now the usual procedure'. The inspectors also took it for granted that one of the physical education teachers would collaborate with the school doctor to do remedial work to build up girls' health, and that posture classes were a regular feature.

Overall, the inspectors were impressed with the appearance, manners and general behaviour of the pupils, and concluded that 'it is to the credit of all concerned that, in spite of everything, a promising start has been made

and that the School has been so readily "adopted" by the neighbourhood'.

The foundations having been 'well and truly laid', the school, despite the additional difficulties of war in the next four years, built up its strength in the community.

Production of Murder in the Cathedral in the Nora Nickalls Hall, 1956.

Preparations for a possible outbreak of war had been made during the Munich Crisis of late September 1938. Trenches had been dug in what remained of the orchard, and Peggy Morris recalls cutting up hessian to make sandbags. Heather Vit (née Watson 1937–44) remembered that slit trenches had been dug in the orchard where the Great Hall now stands, but were not used as shelters, as the water table was so high that they were too damp. So when war was finally declared on 3 September 1939, expecting widespread bombing of cities and the use of gas, the Governors, the architect and the Head Mistress reassessed the air-raid precaution measures for the school. They decided that providing shelter inside the building instead of outside would be more suitable. The corridors were converted into shelters, described by Nora Nickalls in the school magazine of February 1940.

Though our spacious airy corridors now look like the B or C deck of a liner complete with bulkhead doors and the ground floor of the building is disfigured, we are thankful the Governors of the school decided on indoor protection. Rather possible bombardment than probable pneumonia, so no one is allowed at school without gas mask, and we are in our stations in under two minutes.

Heather Vit recalled how the corridors became shelters by shoring up the outside windows, stacking sandbags against them and criss-crossing the windows with brown gummed paper to minimise flying glass. In addition, windows were fitted with blackout blinds. She remembered the drill during the daylight raids of 1940–1.

Every girl was allocated a peg in the corridor and there she hung a cushion. En route to her class room each morning, she had to add her hat and her gas-mask. When the air-raid siren sounded, girls filed downstairs to their allotted places and lessons continued in the shelters until the all-clear was heard. We also had our individual tins of iron-rations in case we were confined there for hours on end.

'Iron rations' were variously described as sweets, biscuits, raisins and chocolate, which girls were often tempted to nibble even when there was no hint of a raid. Jeanette Twidle (née Harbutt 1939–47) got into trouble at home because she so often ate her emergency rations.

Pamela Gidney (née Hornsby 1939–44) remembered that the roof of the school was camouflaged, as were the roofs of Hampton Grammar School (opened on the Hanworth Road site in 1939) and Rectory Farm, because from the air the buildings looked like three large factories. Part of the school library was turned into a first-aid post to be used in case of emergency.

The return to school in 1939 was staggered, with UV and VI forms returning first on 19 September, and full term beginning for everyone on 9 October. There were about 100 fewer pupils than had been expected, as a result of evacuation, though, as the expected raids on Britain

one of Miss Denney's history lessons – and was not reprimanded!

Once at school, the schoolday was often interrupted. After the Battle of Britain in September 1940, when the Germans turned to daylight bombing, girls became used to filing down to the shelters and having their lessons in the protected corridors. As one of the UII wrote in the school magazine, in the autumn of 1940, 'we were popping in and out of the shelters the whole day'. As tactics changed, there were fewer daytime raids, but, increasingly, nights were disturbed by raids. A rota of staff, three staff for three 'watches' every evening, were on fire-watch duty. Ruby Davies, a member of staff, recalled, 'Very few liked the second watch as it was quite eerie to walk along the dark corridors, with the aid of a black-out torch'.

The realities of war had already come home to the school community when they received the news of the

Above: At home or at school pupils practised air-raid drill and needed to remember their gas mask at all times.

Right: The SS City of Benares was carrying 90 child evacuees en route to Canada when the ship was torpedoed.

did not materialise in the autumn of 1939, some girls returned to the area. Miss Nickalls had decided to alter the schoolday, so that the bulk of teaching would be done in six 35-minute periods in the morning, with what the inspectors had described as 'an elastic afternoon time-table', with optional afternoons for domestic science, art, library periods or games.

This 'elasticity' helped to cope with the additional difficulties of getting to school once air raids began in the autumn of 1940. Transport was scarce, so cycling or walking became the norm, but the journey might well be interrupted. Pamela Gidney remembered:

We often had to 'take cover' in a friendly house or air-raid shelter on our way to and from school, and if we arrived without our gas masks we were sent back home to get them. During the bad night-time raids we often arrived at school late, having walked four or so miles because the buses and trolleybuses were out of action. On one memorable day a friend actually fell asleep during

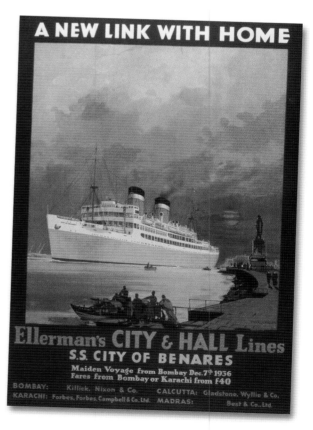

A NEW LINK WITH HOME

Ellerman's CITY & HALL Lines
S.S. CITY OF BENARES
Maiden Voyage from Bombay Dec.7th 1936
Fares from Bombay or Karachi from £40

BOMBAY: Killick, Nixon & Co. CALCUTTA: Gladstone, Wyllie & Co.
KARACHI: Forbes, Forbes, Campbell & Co. Ltd. MADRAS: Best & Co. Ltd.

death of Barbara Fairhead, one of the child evacuees on the SS *City of Benares,* sunk on 17 September 1940. Nora Nickalls remembered her as 'a bonny bairn ten years of age, pulsating with life and expectation of a happy home with an aunt and cousins when she came with her parents to say good-bye the previous Friday morning'. Seventy pupils from the school had prepared to take part in the Overseas Evacuation Scheme. Four were among the first to start in July and early August, one to Canada, one to the US and two to Australia. However, after the sinking of the *Benares*, sailings stopped. The neighbourhood of the school also suffered damage and casualties, and later in 1940, another pupil, Barbara Liddiard, who had been at the school for only two months, was killed with her parents and brother in a direct hit on their home in a night-time raid.

There were other difficulties as the war went on. Some staff, both teaching and domestic, went into war work. In 1943, Nora Nickalls wrote that one member of staff was at the Foreign Office, another at the Treasury, a third had joined the Wrens (Women's Royal Naval Service) and another was in the Auxiliary Territorial Service. It was difficult to find replacements, but Miss Nickalls was resourceful in trying to fill the gaps by calling on contacts made earlier in her career. These appointments were not always a success. Isabel Markham recalled that a 'young and popular' classics mistress who left to join the Wrens was replaced by a lady 'long retired and with rather strict and bizarre discipline methods'. Jeanette Twidle, Jean Deacon (née Bulley 1941–6) and Iris Hawkes (1936–40, 1941–5) remembered that one way Miss Nickalls got round the shortage of domestic help was by using the home economics groups to clean Burlington House!

Wartime restrictions also meant that the school could not be heated adequately. Eve Turner (1938–45) describes 'the bitter cold of some of the wartime winters when heating fuel had to be conserved', and the physics mistress's remedy. 'During double Physics, we had to stop and do physical jerks to keep warm, encouraged by the rotund, cheery Miss Emery.'

Food rationing meant extra administration for Miss Nickalls, who became 'quite expert at filling up forms which are altered about once a fortnight'. The school also

Signing up for the Auxiliary Territorial Service.

made its contribution to the 'Dig for Victory' campaign. Six acres of the school grounds were used to grow fruit and vegetables. In May 1941, Miss Nickalls reported that Mr Rainer, groundsman, and subsequently caretaker from January 1942, helped by a member of staff and some of the girls, had grown sufficient vegetables so that between July 1940 and January 1941 the school had no greengrocer's bill, 'and even since then we have only bought potatoes'. Later, they also had the help of two land girls. Miss Nickalls showed her usual resourcefulness in adding to

Right: Several acres of the school grounds were turned over to food production in response to the 'Dig for Victory' campaign.

Far right: Goats provided milk for the boarders.

the school's supply of food. She went on to say, 'Further, last August with sugar allowed by the "surplus fruit committee" we made more than 450lbs of jam and bottled about as much fruit then and in the autumn'. She had also experimented with beans put down in salt, and hoped that 'if crocks [containers] can be found they may have some for the school'. Her efforts were not always well appreciated, to judge from Isabel Markham's recollections. 'A glut of runner beans in the summer of one year was to provide the main meal served frequently in the autumn. These beans were salted in huge crocks, but they needed careful washing before use; this did not always happen and the main meal of beans covered with mashed potato was truly horrible.'

Another of Miss Nickalls' wartime appointments to the boarding house in Burlington House brought some goats with her, and rabbits and hens were also kept. At least one of the boarders remembers porridge with goat's milk for breakfast. Some of the girls and staff continued to do their bit for food production during the school holidays. Isabel Markham remembers the agricultural camps set up by the government to provide labour at harvest time.

The patriotic thing to do was to give up your annual holiday to work on a farm. In 1944 Miss Lacey helped to organise a party of sixth formers to join the scheme. The first was to Laleham not too far away, and we joined the scheme again in 1945 and 1946 when we went to Broxbourne in Herts and to Tenterden in Kent. We were issued with railway warrants and slept under canvas, we were also paid £1 to 30 shillings a week. The average pocket money would have been 5 shillings a week so we felt well rewarded.'

The school magazine of December 1945 described a typical day at the Harvest Camp in Tenterden. Whilst the description might well have provided the storyboard for a feature designed to keep up morale in one of the newsreels of the time, it reflects the spirit of the time.

A typical day began at six-thirty when we were aroused by 'Wakey, wakey, rise and shine' in the raucous tones of the camp handyman. Then for the first time during the night our straw mattresses felt comfortable! Some minutes later we crawled out of our tents and rushed

Vaughan Williams.

others, Twickenham County, Rectory Farm (now Hampton Academy) and Tiffin, and in the spring of 1942 the first lacrosse matches were held. The always generous nature of the girls was now channelled into charities supporting the war effort. Traditional school collections continued and each form made penny per week collections, which were sent to the Red Cross and the Polish Relief Fund, for example. Gloves, socks and scarves were knitted for seamen in the Navy and on trawlers; clothing was collected for those who had been bombed out of their homes in the local area; crayons, paint boxes and painting books were sent to Hackney schools that had been evacuated. A National Savings group started in 1940, and in 1943 the school began to support a cot in the children's

to get ready in time for breakfast at 7am. The food was good, though murmurs about the frequent appearance of cheese and kippers on the menu were occasionally heard.

We were taken to and from work by lorry, and the tail board seats were in great demand, but we all enjoyed singing lustily even though we could not see the view! Our work included stooking and carting corn, gathering pea crops grown from seed, and windfall apples, but the greater part of the time we spent picking plums. We had great fun in the orchards balancing on precarious ladders in all sorts of weather.

Despite the difficulties, the staff tried to make sure that life went on as normally as possible. Lessons continued and school terms followed the pattern of peacetime. A particular highlight in July 1943 was the annual South-West Middlesex Music Festival, visited by Vaughan Williams, who conducted his *Fantasia on Greensleeves*. The school clubs, art, French and German, history, literary, music and science, started in 1940, went from strength to strength, with competitions, outside speakers, concerts, visits and, on one occasion, 'a demonstration of spectacular chemical reactions' given by Miss Lacey to the Science Club. Matches continued against, amongst

National Savings poster 1940.

Below: Bomb damage to St Giles', Cripplegate.

Right: School choir singing at St Giles', Cripplegate, 1940s.

ward of Hampton Cottage Hospital. Always keen to maintain its links with the original home of the school, in September 1943 the school choir visited the City to sing at a lunchtime service in the ruins of the bombed church of St Giles', Cripplegate. Even Prize Givings continued, though, as Miss Nickalls noted, they had to be arranged with an eye on the international situation, and were 'always about a year late as only in the summer can we be home by daylight afterwards'.

In 1942, General Dwight Eisenhower had made Bushy Park, Teddington, the Supreme Headquarters Allied Expeditionary Force centre for planning Operation Overlord, the D-Day landings. Iris Hawkes remembered all the girls being taken into the Assembly Hall to listen to Eisenhower's broadcast to the people of Western Europe, telling them that a landing had been made on the coast of France on 6 June. Their excitement over this was short-lived, as a new enemy threat emerged a few days later, when the Germans launched the V1s, the flying bombs commonly known as the 'doodlebugs'. Miss Nickalls' letter to parents, written just nine days after the first flying bomb landed in Britain, is full of the straightforward good sense for which she was renowned.

THE LADY ELEANOR HOLLES SCHOOL,
HANWORTH ROAD,
HAMPTON, MIDDLESEX.
22nd June, 1944.

Dear Sir or Madam,

So many of the parents have asked my personal opinion about school attendance at the moment that I have decided to send a note. My opinion may be judged by the fact that I have sent away the two remaining boarders, aged 16 and 12 years, to an area out of reach of pilotless planes. The girls are often more nervous when they do not admit it, and they are tired, and, even when here conditions are not conducive to good work. School examinations will be postponed until further notice.

Every allowance will be made for time lost in passing into upper forms. This allowance has always been made even with outside pupils who have missed or changed school. The school can deal with the girl who has missed work provided her nerves are in a good state when she begins again, but neither school nor parents can do much with the children in a nervous state. The school is open and some staff always here, and every care will be taken, but we do not expect girls to set out for school during a period of alert, and I have told the staff too that they are not to run unnecessary risks on journeys here during an alert.

Pilotless planes may fall anywhere and I think dispersal of population is the right policy, and where possible parents will prefer to have their children with them. It is a pity to have large groups concentrated anywhere. I think the danger period is not likely to be lengthy, but long or short, life and spirit are of more value than work. Many of the upper school have taken books home.

The decision of what is best in each individula case lies with the parents, and I am not prepared to offer any advice, but phone calls asking my opinion are so frequent, at a time when the phone should be spared, that I send this letter.

Yours sincerely,

N.Nickalls.
Head Mistress.

The flying bombs badly disrupted school life, as Cynthia Reynolds (1940–5) remembered.

When Hitler launched his pilotless planes known as doodlebugs, these tended to come over in waves and we spent a lot of time in the specially reinforced ground floor corridors instead of in the classrooms. There was a period when only the pupils whose work for examinations would be otherwise seriously hindered were attending school on a full time basis. By then I was cycling to and from school and I can remember we felt we had a better chance of survival on our bikes rather than sitting in a trolleybus which might be under a doodlebug as it fell, once its engine had cut out.

At school, Ruby Davies recalls that 'staff volunteered to stand outside the school and listen for the moment when the engine cut out, and we all knew that the bomb was on its way down. There was just enough time for the "Look outs" to rush for shelter and give a warning'.

All excursions and games fixtures were cancelled, and desks were brought down into the corridor shelters for those sitting their State examinations. Pamela Gidney remembered what it was like.

We took School Certificate, as it was called in those days, our desks spaced out alternately on either side of the downstairs corridors, so that we

Above: Nora Nickalls' advice to parents about school attendance during the 'doodlebug' attacks.

Left: A V1 pilotless bomb on its way down.

were already in the 'shelters' should there be an air-raid. And there were many. I still have my exam papers, on which I had written '3 air-raids' or '4 air-raids' – all in the space of 2½ or 3 hours! It was 'doodlebug time', and when the engines of the diabolical rockets cut out, the doodlebug would plummet to the ground and explode. Whenever one cut out in the vicinity, the invigilating teacher would call out, 'Under your desks girls!' and we would dive under them until the explosion came, and then climb back onto our chairs and resume our examination.

Miss Nickalls retired at the end of the autumn term 1944, before the war ended in Europe in May 1945. She could look back with justifiable satisfaction on her role in the successful transplanting of The Lady Eleanor Holles School from Hackney to Hampton. In November 1944, the main school was fuller than it had ever been; the Junior Department had been moved to Burlington House; the VI form numbered 37; and she was delighted to report that 'our first Hampton girl is now at Oxford, Maude Eburne, at St. Anne's with a School Leaving Exhibition'. She paid tribute to the Hackney members of the Holly Club and the school staff, saying it was owing to them 'that the welding of the new took place, that this is not a new school, but an old one transferred to "fresh woods and pastures new", with a continuity of life which must be seen to be believed and the Hampton girls with the old traditions behind them'. The Governors, staff and girls acknowledged Miss Nickalls' many qualities in their tributes. The Chairman of Governors, Mr S Wilfred Geard, summed up the admiration of many when he said, 'I regard Miss Nickalls as the perfect type of Head Mistress, combining the capacity for management with a human sympathy that makes it easy to smooth out difficulties which, without such understanding, might easily be exaggerated into mountains rather than molehills'.

In Miss Nickalls' last letter to the school as Head Mistress (school magazine, December 1944), she referred to 'the new era' and the problems this might bring for the school. Once again, as in 1869 and 1902, national legislation, this time the Butler Education Act of 1944, was to change the course of the school's history.

Windows in the Biology laboratory prepared for war.

> What better place to start than with the sight of a black gowned figure striding along the corridor, often bringing terror to the wrong-doer, 'Old Nick' as she was affectionately known. Miss Nora Nickalls, that remarkable and indefatigable woman, who was headmistress from 1915 to 1944, and who guided the school through two world wars. I consider myself privileged to have been at the school during her lifetime, and to appreciate her high standards, compassion and humour.

Nora Nickalls remembered by Eve M Turner (1938–45)

Nora Nickalls MA (Oxon) (1877–1961), Head Mistress 1915–44

Nora Nickalls' own story shows just how different education was for middle-class girls in the last quarter of the nineteenth century. Educated by private governesses until she was ten, Nora then attended a French convent and was 'finished' at an English private school. Her father's idea of a complete education for a girl was that she should be proficient in languages and music, so she was sent to France for six months. She had not expected to work on her return, but found financial problems had overtaken the family and that she had to earn her own living. She began as a student mistress at the private school she had attended and then studied for her Cambridge Teachers' Certificate. She was only able to complete this because she received a loan from the Clothworkers' Company for tuition, and a gift of boarding fees from her uncle, Sir Patteson Nickalls. After seven more years as a teacher, she went to Oxford to read for History Honours. Again, this was possible only because her uncle and his daughter, Ethel Patteson Nickalls, lent her the money for the course at Somerville College, where she matriculated in 1907. Women were not able to receive their degrees at Oxford until 1920, so Miss Nickalls did not finally receive her degree until 1925.

After Oxford, she spent several more years teaching before becoming Head Mistress of Durham County School for Girls, and then, in 1915, Head Mistress of Lady Holles' School.

She made her first visit as Head Mistress elect to the Hackney school on the day after the first Zeppelin raid on London, and retired from the Hampton school after the summer of the flying bombs. This caused a colleague, Miss Hannam, to joke on Miss Nickalls' retirement, 'You came with a bang and you will go with one'.

The financial help which had made such a difference to Nora Nickalls' own life inspired her to start the Nora Nickalls Trust Fund. She recalled that this began in 1920, when the School Captain at Hackney applied to London County Council for a scholarship to the London School of Medicine. However, she was offered only a teacher's training award, because the Council considered a medical training too long and expensive for her to be eligible. Miss Nickalls told her she would pay the fees for a year to see how she got on. Eventually, she won grants, repaid Miss Nickalls and completed her medical training.

Miss Nickalls remembered other cases and set aside £30 a year from her salary for seven years as the basis of the fund. This was added to when she retired, as she asked for subscriptions to be made to the fund instead of having a personal gift. The fund was small, but played an important part in helping some girls to achieve their goals. Barbara Megson, one of the pupils who joined the school in 1936, received a loan from the fund, and, as she said in an interview in 2010, 'it made all the difference'. Without it she would not have been able to go to Cambridge.

Nora Nickalls was remembered for her energy, kindness, understanding and sense of humour. Miss Denney, a member of staff at both Hackney and Hampton, recalled her sense of humour when a Hackney hospital contacted the school. 'The HM had a sense of humour. Requested by a local hospital to find a girl for their office, she was told that the salary was 10s a week and that the girl must be a lady. She replied, "At the salary you offer, you will not get a lady, but I can send you a lady-like girl". The girl she sent got the job!'

Others remembered the strength she gave them to challenge preconceived ideas about which subjects were 'suitable' for women, even in the twentieth century. Isabel Markham remembered the encouragement she received when she chose to study geology. 'Miss Nickalls alone, amongst friends, teachers and family did not dissuade me.'

Nora Nickalls had a wide view of education, believing that it was important for girls to learn from life outside the classroom. She also stressed the importance of an individual's contribution to society and led by example. She was a member of numerous committees, playing an active part in public life at both Hackney and Hampton. She was a member of the Headmistresses' Association (later the GSA) and was Vice-President of the London Branch. In 1922, the Association held its Annual Conference at the school in Hackney. She was a great traveller and continued to travel and teach English throughout her retirement. She died in 1961, aged 84.

The decision to become independent

Once again, as in 1869 and 1902, national legislation was to change the course of LEH's future. The Butler Education Act of 1944 promised a nationwide system of free, compulsory education from the age of 5 to 15 (to be raised to 16 as soon as practicable) and established a system which lasted until almost the end of the twentieth century. At secondary level, three types of school had been envisaged: grammar schools for the academically able, technical schools for those with a practical bent, and new 'modern' secondary schools for the rest. In practice, after the war, most Local Authorities provided only grammar schools for the top 20 per cent of children and secondary modern schools for the rest. Selection for grammar schools was made largely on the basis of the eleven-plus examination, tests of intelligence and attainment in English and arithmetic. In the eyes of the public, children either 'passed' and went to the grammar school, or 'failed' and went to the local secondary modern. Passing or failing was a crucial determinant of life aspirations.[28] Those who passed for the grammar school could take public examinations, the essential qualifications for further education and training for professional careers. Those who did not pass went to schools which, until 1965 and the introduction of the Certificate of Secondary Education, were not allowed to run public examination courses.

The abolition of fees for secondary education promised in the 1944 Act had caused the Governors, along with a number of similar schools, to lobby against its passing. Their views, set out in the minutes were:

Previous page: IIIX in Room 5 with their form mistress Miss Elmslie, 1948.

Opposite page: Main entrance with the charity school girl and boy which came from the Cripplegate schools.

> *There remains a very large section of the community who cannot afford the necessary high fee of the independent school, but who at the same time are in a position to pay something towards the education of their children, and indeed consider it a duty to do so even if it means some privation to themselves. It is for this class that we contend that a school such as ours is of primary importance.*

They argued that their part-grant part-fee schools gave parents choice at an affordable price, representing a middle way between the independent public schools and the free schools of the Local Authorities. Moreover, they argued that schools such as theirs were socially inclusive.

> *In support of what we affirm is our true democratic status, we may say that our pupils are drawn from the professional classes, local tradesmen, and all kinds of residents, and they include the children of many in the humbler walks of life, and we defy anyone to differentiate between one and the other after they have been in our hands for a year or so. They all attain a standard of behaviour and education that befits them to take their place in any walk of life, and we find that their attitude to each other is one of comradeship whether their Parents are drawn from the ranks of peer or peasant.*

However, the Butler Education Act became law, leaving, as the Clerk to the Governors explained to parents in a letter of April 1945, the Governors with two alternatives:

> 1. *To become an Independent Girls Public School under the control of the Governors as to the admission of pupils.*

> 2. *To continue as a Direct Grant Grammar School with the obligation to accept up to half the available vacancies for new pupils from the County Council or other Local Education Authorities, leaving only the other half for free selection.*

The Clerk went on to explain the implications of each alternative. Under the first alternative, the vacancies for upwards of 80 pupils each year would all be available for free selection, subject to the school's test of suitability. Under the second alternative, the Governors would be able to choose only 40, as the remaining 40 would be directed to the school from other bodies.

THIS STONE
WAS LAID BY
SIR WILLIAM BADDELEY, BART.
RMAN OF THE CRIPPLEGATE SCHOOLS FOUNDATION
ON 16TH SEPTEMBER 1936.

TO COMMEMORATE THE REMOVAL OF
THE LADY ELEANOR HOLLES SCHOOL FROM HACKNEY.
FOUNDED IN CRIPPLEGATE 1711 MOVED TO HACKNEY 1878.

Head Mistress,
Miss Mary Richards.

Mr Bruce-Gardyne, the Clerk, made clear the Governors' view that this second alternative would, in time, change the character of the school. He added that under either alternative fees would be payable, but that if the Governors, with the agreement of parents, decided that the school should become independent, the fees would have to be increased by two guineas a term, because the school would no longer receive a government grant. Parents were asked to let the Governors know their views about which alternative to take.

By August 1945, the decision was made. In a second letter to parents, the Clerk reported that a large number of parents had responded and voted that the school should become independent; 'fortified by this', the Governors notified the Ministry of Education 'of their intention to relinquish the grant and to become an Independent Girls' Public School'. He concluded his letter:

> *The Governors would like to repeat that the Lady Eleanor Holles School is not conducted for profit and that the whole of the available income is devoted to its up-keep. Actually the whole cost per pupil is not covered by the fee charged, since this Foundation is in the fortunate position of being able to supplement it from other sources, with the result that the fee is lower than that of other schools of comparable standard. Parents may rest assured that the Governors, whilst maintaining the high standard of the School, will do everything reasonable to keep costs down.*

Now the decision had been made, the Ministry of Education reduced the capitation grant until it was eliminated in three years. So another chapter opened in the history of The Lady Eleanor Holles School. It must now make its way as an independent school.

The Head Mistress, Miss Mary Richards, was optimistic about the future, declaring in her letter in the school magazine of December 1945, 'The School has a great future before it; it hopes to gain its independence so that it may work unhampered to educate the girls who attend it to become thoughtful, useful women, who make all around them happy by their own happy and unselfish attitude to life'. She hoped that all members of the school would 'enhance the reputation of the school, keeping it

free from snobbery and affectation, and making it always a friendly place where each one may develop those special gifts which she possesses'.

At independence in 1946, the school had 531 pupils, with 379 girls in the main school, a VI form of 50 and a Junior Department of 152. Burlington House had 27 boarders. There is much which seems familiar in the school magazine of 1946, which described the events of the school year 1945–6. The end of the war in Europe in May 1945 meant that clubs could take advantage of peacetime conditions to organise expeditions. The Science Club, for

Left: Miss Richards (standing, fifth from the left) with her staff.

Below: School gala at Hampton swimming pool in the 1940s.

example, visited Job's Dairy, Kew Observatory, Hampton Wick Gasworks and the Transformer factory. They went on two all-day expeditions, one to the Pears Soap Factory and the other to Farnham Potteries. The Junior Science Club members made a trip to London Zoo. Meetings at school were also well attended, with Brains Trusts for the juniors and what was described as 'a demonstration of spectacular chemistry to a large crowd of interested and excited Juniors'. VJ (Victory in Japan) Day on 12 November 1945 was added to the regular holiday the girls had been given since Hackney days for the Lord Mayor's Show. Each form collected for its own charity and there were collections for familiar charities, such as the RSPCA, Dr Barnardo's and Great Ormond Street Hospital, as well as more unfamiliar ones, such as the Merchant Navy Comforts Fund. LEH continued to support Hampton Cottage Hospital. There was a full sporting programme of matches for the two lacrosse teams, four netball teams, tennis, rounders and badminton teams. Swimming Sports were held at Hampton Baths. Despite the heaviest rainstorm for ten years, the Open Day on Friday 26 July 1946 was a success, and Miss Richards hoped to see 'a growing desire to make LEH one of the best Schools in the country'.

Colleen Gardener (née MacNamara 1945–56) remembers the Junior Department at the end of the Second World War:

In 1945, thanks to a City Clothworkers' Scholarship, I left my primary school class of 56 boys and girls for the delights of Burlington House, a smart uniform and

Burlington House at the end of the Second World War.

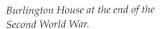
Burlington House at the end of the Second World War.

Boarders c.1937 with several who transferred from Hackney including Dulcie Pyne (fifth from left), Betty Stoodley (second from right), Joan Blythe (third from right) and Peggy Clark (fourth from right).

Right: Cripplegate Secretarial College brooch.

the ineffable wisdom of Miss Hannam. The education there was very Froebel-orientated, with plenty of self-expression – for example making puppets and writing and performing our own playlets, dancing free-style in the 'Iron Room' (which later burned down, to our great sorrow), pond-dipping in Wellies in the Longford River and making 'stables' when the grass was mown in the big field: pairing up as horse and rider, the former neighing volubly and the latter applying adroit control by means of a skipping rope. In the summer of 1947, with Miss Bolwell, we spent weeks constructing a large pit-hut in the garden, digging it out, propping it up and lining and roofing it, then providing ingeniously disguised traps for woolly mammoths and sabre-toothed tigers.

The Second World War had provided many opportunities for women, but when it ended in 1945, women were largely expected to return to their traditional roles as wives, homemakers and mothers. For the most part, jobs were not for life, but until marriage. The majority of girls who left LEH in the 1940s went into some kind of training in traditional areas for women, such as teaching, nursing and secretarial work. A number, among them Jennifer Saunders (née Bush 1947–50), Rosemary Burdett (née Abbott 1943–50), Janet Cody (née Squire 1943–50), Gillian Durham (née Shipley 1940–50), Felicity Farries (née Grant 1942–50) and Ann Reynolds (née Shipley 1940–50), have very fond memories of their time, 1950–1, at the Cripplegate Secretarial and Finishing School in Golden Lane, which was run by the Cripplegate Foundation. The Clerk to the Governors, Mr Hoy, was one of the staff. 'The first thing we noticed, coming straight from a school environment, was how adult we felt and the freedom we were given which helped us to gain confidence.' On the one-year finishing course they learnt Pitman's shorthand and were expected to reach from 100 to more than 160 words a minute. They were also taught typing – 'here we were taught with blank keyboards and gramophone rhythmic-touch method at the beginning' – and, amongst other subjects, bookkeeping, principles and practice of commerce and modern business methods. There were also cultural subjects, which included elocution, deportment and ballroom dancing. 'Miss Malt was in charge of Deportment and we all remember having to walk across the stage one by one while she criticised our deportment. We had to balance books on our heads. Also on the stage we had to learn to sit correctly and to curtsey (not many of us have had the opportunity of using this skill).' They also remember ballroom dancing lessons being made more interesting by a group of young men who came from Upper Canada College in Toronto.

Other leavers went straight into jobs in the Civil Service, banks or at the National Physical Laboratory (NPL) in Teddington. Jean Deacon remembered that, as a result of the war, NPL was

Left: At work in the Biology laboratory, 1948.

Below: Barbara Megson, 2010.

desperate for staff. To begin with, she was the only young person in her section. However, as young men began to return from war, many of the women who worked there, like Jean herself, found husbands at the laboratory.

At this time, only a very few girls from LEH went on to university. In the statistics gathered for the HMI inspection in 1955, it was reckoned that the average number going to university in each of the previous five years was nine. Girls such as Barbara Megson, who, with the support of the Nora Nickalls Trust Fund, went to Girton College, Cambridge in 1948, to read for a History Honours degree, were the exception, not the norm for LEH.

As well as places being more limited for girls, parents were often not convinced university was a worthwhile destination for their daughters. Jeanette Twidle recalls that she was very keen to go to university, but her father said

he would not pay for her, so she went to work at the NPL. The view of Stella Tomlins' (née Buttress 1942–9) mother was also common at this time. Stella is thankful for the role Miss Lacey, Head of Chemistry, 'a really lovely lady', played in helping her to get to university.

She even managed to talk my mother into allowing me to go – my father was keen but mothers in those days just said 'What on earth for, she is only going to get married'! I have been forever grateful to Miss Lacey as after gaining a BSc in Botany, Chemistry and Zoology, I finished with an MSc degree in Biochemistry from UCL in 1952 – yes two years and one year in those days was possible.

Change and continuity 1949–2004

Under the next three Head Mistresses, Ruth Garwood Scott (1949–73), Margaret Smalley (1974–81) and Elizabeth (Liz) Candy (1981–2004), many changes took place at LEH, as the school planned, at the least, to keep abreast of the increased opportunities for women and, at best, to set the pace for the education of girls. Their work in these years saw the steady building up of the school's facilities and reputation, to reach the first division amongst girls' day schools.

Ruth Garwood Scott

The speed of change was particularly apparent during the headship of Ruth Garwood Scott, who took over as Head Mistress when Mary Richards left to marry in 1949. Diana Burns (née Maltby 1954–8) reminds us that it was only later that the Head Mistress became known as Miss Garwood Scott. 'We knew her as Miss G. Scott (one didn't inquire what the G stood for!). Shortly after we left, perhaps in the very early sixties, a new teacher was hired, named Miss Scott. To avoid confusion, the Head Mistress became known officially as Miss Garwood Scott.'

Ruth Scott's first assembly left a lasting impression on those present. Trish White remembers that the girls were harangued from the platform for what Miss Scott described as 'despicable' behaviour, as she had seen three LEH girls outside school leaning up against a wall drinking out of lemonade bottles. Trish, who was 12 at the time, remembers that everyone in her form was terrified. Things were obviously going to be different!

When Miss Scott arrived in 1949, the school numbered just over 500, with about 150 girls in the Junior Department, 47 in the VI form and just over 20 boarders. By her retirement in 1973, the school was 600-strong, with a VI form of 150 pupils. In the almost 20 years between 1954 and the start of a building programme, which provided the Junior Department with a new classroom wing, and Ruth Scott's retirement, there were

Right: Miss Lacey, renowned for producing spectacular lunchtime demonstrations, in the Chemistry Laboratory.

Below: Miss Ruth Garwood Scott.

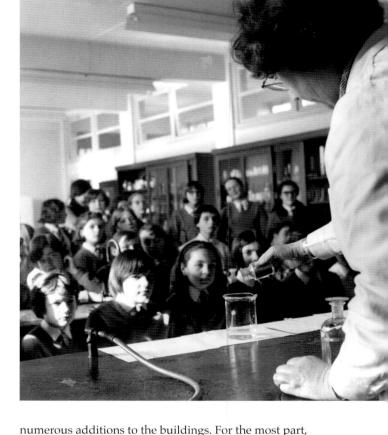

numerous additions to the buildings. For the most part, these were to enable the expansion of the curriculum. The building of laboratories for the study of chemistry and physics at advanced level was a case in point. Much of the money came from a donation from the Industrial Fund for the Advancement of Scientific Education, which was founded to provide independent schools with help towards providing adequate facilities for the study of science. Thanks to Miss Garwood Scott's powers of persuasion, and to the outstandingly high standard of work achieved in the Science Department, under Miss Margaret Lacey, LEH was one of only five girls' schools which gained a grant, and the only one which received the maximum grant the Fund allowed. Thus began an almost continuous programme of construction, which gave the school the west wing, opened by HRH The Duchess of Gloucester on 25 October 1961, housing an art studio, craft, music and additional classrooms; the Great Hall, with a modern kitchen and

Left: HRH The Duchess of Gloucester presenting prizes on her third visit to LEH, 1961.

Below: The Great Hall, 1964.

dining room, and seating for 1,000, and the Chapel of St Anne (the name chosen to remember Anne Watson, Lady Eleanor's executrix), which was dedicated by the Bishop of London when HRH Princess Margaret opened the Great Hall wing in 1964; the Sir Peter Studd Wing, made up of the Pavilion opened in 1968, new changing rooms and enlargement of the Gymnasium in 1969, additional laboratories for biology, geography and geology in 1970, and the library memorial to Miss Lacey and an enlarged Common Room for staff. The entire wing was opened in 1970 by Alderman of Cripplegate Ward, Sir Peter Studd, GBE, then Lord Mayor of London, who made a state visit to the school. In the summer of 1973, Miss Garwood Scott turned the first turfs for what proved to be her final project at the school, the building of an indoor swimming pool.

There were other changes too. The school playing fields and athletics facilities were expanded by buying four and a half acres of former nursery land, named Geard's Acre, to remember the Governor, S Wilfred Geard, who had selected the site at Hampton when the school moved from Hackney in the 1930s. In 1968, the site increased in size again, when the Governors bought some spare ground near the Longford gate where derelict cottages had stood.

One chapter in the school's life ended in 1965. The boarding house, which had provided a home for 35 girls at its busiest, closed and the Junior Department benefited from the extra space.

Previous page: Princess Margaret opened the Great Hall wing and presented prizes, 1964.

Left: Sir Peter Studd (centre holding plaque) with fellow Governors and Miss Garwood Scott opening the Sixth Form Centre in the Pavilion, 1968.

Above: Service of blessing for the swimming pool.

Boarding at Burlington House, 1937–65

When LEH moved from Hackney to Hampton, six pupils came too, including Joan Blythe, who had a Cripplegate Scholarship which could only be used at the school. These girls were weekly boarders, but as time went on girls came as termly boarders, and, during its life as the boarding house, Burlington House housed as many as 35 girls. By the mid-1960s, it was no longer financially viable, and the last boarders left in 1965, leaving the Junior Department in sole occupation.

Boarding during the Second World War

Boarders, of course, needed protection day and night. The windows of Burlington House were sandbagged, and arrangements were made for staff to sleep on the ground floor. There was a bunk system for the boarders in a corridor. The loft in Burlington House was designated 'an emergency hide-out' for the boarders. Ruby Davies, a staff member from 1935 to 1970, recalls, 'if ever the enemy were to arrive at the front porch. The girls were to climb a ladder to the safety of the loft from Miss Nickalls' flat and the resident staff would stand on duty in the hall'.

After the war

Avril Bevins (née Sidney 1946–50) remembers arriving as a 15-year-old boarder in 1946. Food plays an important part in her memories of life at Burlington House. She reflects on the cook's 'wonderful roast dinners' and 'toasting crumpets on the common room fire on a Saturday afternoon'. She also recalls the boarders having a 'Cat's whisker' radio in the wardrobe which the staff never found, and the Sunday evening walks to the Chapel Royal at Hampton Court for evensong.

Lindy Chris (1947–54) became a weekly boarder in the bitter winter of 1947 and a full-time boarder when her parents moved to California. A photograph from 1948 shows boarders on the bridge over the Longford River. Lindy has very clear memories of what life was like in the post-war period.

After WWII conditions generally, and rationing in particular, were worse than during the War; even bread and potatoes were rationed. We each had a little pot for sugar and another one for butter and margarine. I think of them as honey pots as they had a yellow glaze on the inside and were terracotta on the outside. Our names were written on elastoplast and put on each pot. [Scotch tape had not been invented.] The pots were kept on large trays in the big cupboards opposite the windows. I think the pots were replenished on Tuesdays and the measurements were very carefully made (no favouritism at all) and I think the assistant to Mrs Patterson used a balance beam scale.

There were three big tables in the dining room. When we were in the Junior Department we had to go to bed at 6:00pm and the 'Big Girls' ate dinner at 7:00pm.

Outside the dining room was a corridor where we had our gym bags and put our coats and shoes and where we played spelling games and Fizz, Buzz, Bang during the raids. On the other side of the corridor was Miss Cable's room [Head of the Junior Department], which had windows onto the front lawn.

I always liked the main staircase. I liked the wood and the way the staircase turned. At the top of the stairs and to the right were the rooms for Mrs Patterson and then Mrs Burton. Kitty corner across from the top of the stairs was the Common Room where we could gather, read, chat, giggle. I know homework was important and I certainly

Boarders posing on the bridge over the Longford river, 1948.

remember Mrs Patterson checking Joanna Buckland and me prior to a spelling test the next day. She had a strong Scottish accent and when she asked me to spell 'wrath' I got it wrong.

The rest of the rooms upstairs were given over to bedrooms which we shared. Baths were in the evening on a rota basis and minimal hot water. The WCs were separate and were, of course, the old water tank ones, up high near the ceiling, with a pull chain for flushing.

In the mornings we were required to either take Malt or Adexolin (fish oil capsules). The malt came in big brown jars and at first it sounded like a good idea but after a few days it became very dreary very quickly. The adexolin was not fun either and led to serious conversations as to whether to take it first and would the oil rise up through the food and say 'How do you do?' or to take it last and let it sit on top of breakfast as a constant reminder during the morning. After breakfast we had to clean our teeth and make our beds before going to class.

Cheryl Meggitt (née Martin 1956–64) was a boarder in the 1950s and 1960s. She remembers an inspection each morning for 'polished shoes, hair, teeth', and has fond recollections of boarding.

My happy memories of BH were learning to roller-skate and roller-skating on the tarmac junior tennis court and the large car parks at the weekend when the boarders had the run of the place. Boarders were mixed up in teams of all ages in order to play games at the weekend. In the winter, we would come in from the cold to make our own tea and toast, doorsteps of white toast accompanied by large slabs of cake. On Saturday evenings we got dressed up in our best dresses and had a more special dinner. Our favourite was spaghetti bolognaise prepared by a visiting cook. We were only allowed to watch TV on Saturday evenings when we all sat round watching Juke Box Jury. Toasting marshmallows on the open fire of the Junior Common Room at the weekends was fun and, of course, our secret midnight feasts which were often in out of bounds places.

The boarding house.

Prefects in the 1960s.

The 'wind of change' which Harold Macmillan declared was blowing through Africa in 1960 was also blowing for women. In the 1960s, there was a significant expansion of university places, with the building of 23 new universities, including Sussex, Warwick and York. This more than doubled the number of universities, from 20 to 43, and the increase in places resulted in many more women entering university education. At the same time, the development of a reliable form of contraception in the 1960s, the pill, meant that women now had a choice about when, and if, to have children. This helped to erode the argument that further education was wasted on women as they still regularly gave up their jobs and careers when they became pregnant. Miss Garwood Scott's time as Head Mistress coincided with this post-war expansion of education and social developments. She was determined that LEH should be able to equip its pupils to take their places, if they had the talent, at the best universities and to reach the top of their careers. Ruth Garwood Scott was always immensely proud of the achievements of former pupils and regularly referred in the school magazine to the many letters and cards she received each Christmas from former pupils, telling her of their successes at university and in their careers. She always made the point that the worth of the school and

of its pupils would be measured by what they did in their future lives.

This expansion of education resulted in an explosion of the population in sixth forms. When Ruth Garwood Scott was appointed, only 47 girls were following post-O level studies, but by 1973 there were 150 in the VI form. The Sixth Form Centre in the Pavilion, designed to give the VI form a degree of privacy from the rest of the school, was one of the first to be built in the country. Whereas, in 1949, only ten candidates entered for the old Higher Certificate, choosing their courses from ten subjects, in 1973, 53 candidates passed, with a good sprinkling of distinctions, in their chosen subjects, selected from 19 possibilities. As a result, the numbers applying to university increased. In 1950, only 9 girls from LEH went to university; in 1973, 44 girls went to university, 11 with places at Oxbridge, with 2 gaining exhibitions.

In 1951, the School Certificate examinations had been replaced with the General Certificate of Education at ordinary and advanced levels. Another change under Ruth Garwood Scott was the enlarging of the curriculum. Subjects such as Russian, economics, music and pottery were offered at A level, and geology, human biology and anatomy could be O level examination choices.

It was in the early 1960s that Miss Garwood Scott realised that careers advice needed some attention. As Rowena Ellis, a part-time member of the Economics Department, who set up the Careers Department, remembered, 'The existing facilities consisted of a cardboard box on a window ledge which contained leaflets and prospectuses of uncertain age'. As Careers Mistress designate, she listed the facilities she considered essential:

A Careers Room which was used for no other purpose housing appropriate shelving and display areas; tables and chairs so that the material which would be provided could be researched and read comfortably by the girls and, if possible, a separate interview room where girls (and their parents if appropriate) could discuss careers possibilities. The Governors approved of this and the Careers Room was born. The facility was well received by the girls and from this Careers Afternoons developed when former pupils returned to give advice to Sixth Formers.

Ruth Garwood Scott's appointment began 24 years of change and growth, and it was she who, some time in the 1960s, introduced the phrase 'grace and integrity' into the school aims. The phrase first appeared in prospectuses of the 1960s.

The Aims of the School

The School exists not only to provide a good academic education; its chief aim is to help the pupils to become women of grace and integrity, who will make the fullest use of their gifts and will serve the community with a high sense of responsibility.

At the tribute given for her by the Governors on 29 November 1973, it was reported that, from letters received from former pupils from all over the world, 'the aim which Miss Garwood Scott had written for the School prospectus was being achieved. In careers of all kinds and in home-making LEH girls were showing themselves women of grace and integrity'.[29]

As part of this development, Miss Garwood Scott laid strong emphasis on the school helping a girl to develop much more than her academic talents. The VI form curriculum encouraged a breadth of study. In 1973, each girl in the VI form spent one-third of her working week on general studies, choosing those which appealed to her from 15 options, as diverse as philosophy, computer science, a 'hostess' course, women in society, and appreciation of music and art.

Athletics was introduced into the physical education activities in Miss Garwood Scott's time. LEH girls were representing the county and the country in the 1960s and 1970s. School music flourished, and the annual play, produced by Miss Margery Duce for many years, was made part of the official timetable in the last weeks of the summer term for those who had just completed their O and A levels.

Ruth Garwood Scott's fervent emphasis on developing the whole girl included the message that privilege brought responsibility. The Christian ethos was strong in her time and she was keen that girls should serve the community. The Service Volunteers, a joint venture with Hampton Grammar School, was founded in her era as Head Mistress.

Miss Garwood Scott was a flag bearer for the value of independent education, and her contribution to education was recognised in 1973, the year of her retirement, by the award of the OBE. She had presided over some of the greatest changes in the history of the school. In her appreciation of the Head Mistress's work from 1949, Margery Duce wrote, 'Miss Garwood Scott has always tried to preserve the best from the past while looking towards, and planning for, a future, which, however unpredictable, is certain to provide both challenge and opportunity on an ever-increasing scale'.

Ruth Garwood Scott rose majestically to the challenges offered to independent schools, by the 1960s especially, and to the rapidly increasing opportunities for women. She had dedicated herself to the service of the school and had aimed to create 'a good school'. She was always keen to promote the image of the school by encouraging performance at the top level. Marilyn Sparrow (known as Lynne Sparrow 1962–8), a keen member of the Debating Society, remembers her call to the Head Mistress's office:

Miss Garwood Scott told me that Lloyds of London ran an annual public speaking competition and that a few years ago a Head Girl at Holles had been entered for the competition, and won. This year they were going to enter me for the competition. The unspoken, but very clear, implication was that I, too, was to win. I don't remember being asked whether I wanted to enter the competition or not – but those of you who remember Miss Garwood

Miss Garwood Scott in her study.

Miss Garwood Scott admiring farewell gifts with the Head Girl, December 1973.

Scott will recall that that was not her style … Lloyds issued a list of subjects, any one of which the competition entrants could be asked to speak about for five minutes … I can't remember which topic I pulled out of the hat – but I certainly remember winning the competition – the power of Miss Garwood Scott's positive thinking!

The 1950s, in particular, was an era in which parents and staff expected to have a much greater say in 'knowing what was best' for young people. As one pupil from this period remembered, her university course was selected for her. She was told that as she had been educated in Belgium in her early years, 'you are good at French', so this should be her university course. Miss Garwood Scott certainly felt it was her responsibility to point out to pupils the direction in which she believed they should go. This did not always sit easily with a pupil's own aspirations. Two former pupils remembered their disappointment that their interests did not win her encouragement or approval.

Ann Everitt (née Whitfield 1950–6) came to the school when her father, George Whitfield, became Headmaster of Hampton Grammar School. She remembered that, although there was a reasonable choir and a small orchestra, 'one could not take even O level Music, let alone

A level. I remember Miss Scott saying to me, "Keep music in its place, Ann"'.

Celia Brackenridge (1959–68), writing in the *Alumnae News* in the summer of 2010, also remembered the Head Mistress's disapproval. 'My abiding memory of my final year at school was being called in to the office of the then Head Mistress Ruth Garwood Scott to be told in no uncertain terms that I had disappointed her. Why? Because I had chosen to go to PE College instead of applying for university.' Sport, as Celia wrote in 2010, gave her a 'wonderful and fulfilling life'. Retiring from full-time academic life as Professor of Sport Sciences at Brunel University in 2010, she will be organising the 2012 international scientific convention that will precede the 2012 Olympics.

In comparison with the interaction today between a Head Mistress and her pupils and staff, the relationship in the 1950s was much more formal. At the end of each term, there was a ceremonial goodbye to each pupil, with each one going up onto the platform to shake hands with the Head Mistress. Trish White remembers that some even curtsied, which was the standard practice for receiving prizes at Prize Giving. At the end of each school year, formal goodbyes were expected of staff too. Staff waited in the Staff Room until called, one by one, in order of seniority, to the Head Mistress's office.

Ruth Garwood Scott also placed great store by a code of etiquette, which, even in the 1960s, seemed somewhat rarefied to some of the pupils and their parents. Lydia Baker (née Endean 1961–71) recalled this story from her parents, who were 'proud and delighted … that their only child had secured a place at the prestigious Lady Eleanor Holles School', but were so mortified by this incident which took place at an 'At Home',[30] that they did not tell their daughter for many years.

At one of the first 'At Homes', my Father had met my Mother outside school, straight from work. It was customary to line up down the centre of the Assembly Hall in a queue to greet Miss Garwood Scott before going around to the various teachers. As now, there were refreshments, tea and coffee, to one side of the hall. My parents were well down the queue, perhaps 30 or

The Yardley sisters, Gillian (centre) was in the Senior Department. Her sisters Janet and Joan were Juniors.

Miss Garwood Scott was, at the time, much feared as well as respected and it was many years before I recognised how much I owed to her leadership and vision for her 'gels'. She recommended I went to the new Sussex University (in its third year) and visited after a few weeks to find out for herself if it lived up to its reputation as a good place to go – I was amazed when she invited me to dinner at the Old Ship Hotel in Brighton and we drank more than one bottle of wine – she was human after all!

so couples away from the Head Mistress and, having had nothing to drink since lunch time, my Father broke away from the line and picked up a cup of tea, bringing it back to the queue where my Mother waited. Seeing him do this Miss Garwood Scott left her place at the head of the line, walked down to where my parents waited and said, looking at my Father's label, 'Mr Endean, it is customary to greet your hostess before partaking of her refreshments'.

Lydia was later appointed Head Girl by Miss Garwood Scott, so clearly all was forgiven. However, such incidents were a marked contrast to Hampton Grammar next door, attended by many of the brothers of LEH girls, which was seemingly more down to earth in style.

But there could be another side to the Head Mistress. Girls from the 1950s remembered that she had been to New York and brought back a record of *My Fair Lady* as a treat for the prefects, but gave it to them with the warning that it contained some 'inappropriate language'.

At least one former pupil, Elizabeth White (née Sykes 1964–75), remembered her graciousness in an awkward situation. Throughout one Prize Giving, the guest speaker referred to Miss Scott as Miss Smith. 'I have never forgotten the example Miss Garwood Scott set in smiling pleasantly and maintaining complete composure without ever correcting or embarrassing the speaker.'

Not everyone saw other sides to her while they were at school, although some, like Gill Cumberland (née Yardley 1955–63), appreciated later that Miss Garwood Scott had a more human side.

Undoubtedly, by 1973, Ruth Garwood Scott had done a great deal for LEH and many of its pupils. It may well be that she felt her somewhat imperious style was part of the profile necessary for the job. As she said when she was retiring, she was looking forward to casting off the 'unacceptable face of Authority' and enjoying her freedom. We will never know whether similar achievements could have been made with a less authoritarian approach. But her methods got results and the school, from which she retired in 1973, was vastly improved from the one she took over in 1949. This was her legacy and is acknowledged in these two contributions.

First, a former pupil, Diana Burns, who, despite her reservations about Miss Garwood Scott's style, concluded, 'I do think the way she ran the school was appropriate for the times and in keeping with her mandate to prepare us for a career, given that in those days we were just on the cusp of the societal gender role changes that were to come so soon, and that we faced uphill struggles in many areas. She did her best for us'.

Then from Hilda Denney, a well-respected and loved Head of History, who had worked at LEH since Hackney days, and worked for Miss Garwood Scott between 1949 and 1959. Her verdict was that whilst she was not an easy person to work with, 'the school was her whole life and she did great work in it'.

Hilda Denney had a long association with the school. She had first been a pupil at Hackney and then a member of staff, and ended her career in Hampton.

A flavour of school life in the 1950s

Diana Burns (née Maltby 1954–58), see photograph below, remembers some of the day-to-day aspects of school life in the 1950s. As she says, looking back now (2010):

It seems appallingly rigid and my own daughter just rolls her eyes in horror when I tell it as it was. However, we did get a good education, seem mostly to have led happy and productive lives in a wide range of areas, and to be enjoying now our retirement. I loved being at LEH. If we had been in England I would have wanted my daughter to attend.

At the time that I was at LEH, I did not realize quite what superb organizational skills we were absorbing. They were never mentioned as such, but every task or event was very carefully thought through, and then we were either told how to approach it, or encouraged to work out a method ourselves. There was a strong emphasis at all times on method, even if not mentioned as such. The result was that the school ran like clockwork.

There was an LEH-approved style for starting each piece of work, which ensured that 'most girls' work was presentably tidy'. She also recalled a highly organised system for the collection of homework. The movement of pupils around the school was monitored and 'when we walked along the corridors we were required to walk in single file on the right, and a prefect stood at each end of the corridor to ensure that this happened, before and after recess, and between every class'.

Lunch was also well regulated.

When we went in to lunch in the hall, a teacher stood at the door, and we had to show that the palms of our hands were clean. When one reached the Sixth Form one could enter by the centre hall door and not go through this!

For lunch, and we almost all had hot lunch from the school kitchen, the tables were set up for groups of ten, with a Lower Sixth former at each end, and no more than two people from each year level sitting down the sides. Places were assigned at the beginning of term, and

UVA with their form mistress, Miss Ruby Davies (Diana Maltby is circled), 1956.

Miss Maden conducting, with girls standing in what was regarded as the appropriate pose for singing.

one was allowed to choose a friend to sit with. The sixth former served the main part of the meal, although we were allowed to take our own vegetables.

Colleen Gardener recounts the change in atmosphere from Burlington House. 'Senior Department came as rather a shock after the cosiness of BH: going single-file in the long corridors and not talking in the front hall proved particularly trying, as were the awe-inspiring superior beings called Prefects who policed our perambulations.'

'Lessons were very formal on the whole, but enlivened by such marvels as, for example, Miss Denney writing History notes on the left board with her left hand and then continuing seamlessly on the right half with her right.'

Colleen has a particularly vivid memory of the weekly double lesson of singing in the Main Hall, 'with the amazing duo of Miss Maden (deep contralto, small, sturdy but trim, with silver coiffure and always in blue) and, at the piano, Miss Morgan-Brown (tall, thin, grey-haired, taciturn yet benign and usually in grim grey or brown). We always started off with 'vi-o-lets bi-o-lets vi-o-lets bi-o-lets … up and down the scale'.

This was good practice for the carol singing for charity remembered by Pamela Ireland-Brown (née Gummery 1949–57).

In 1955 a group of us from the LEH choir joined with a similar group from Hampton Grammar School to go carol singing. We practised hard for several weeks and were ready to sing every night for the five or six evenings leading up to Christmas Eve. We sang all round Hampton – even when it was foggy! We were good, singing in four-part harmony – sopranos, altos, tenors and bass accompanied by a violin and a recorder. We sang a wide variety of carols and Christmas hymns, singing 'Silent Night' in German as well as English and a German carol 'Es ist ein Ros'. I loved every minute!

They were successful in collecting between £50 and £60 annually for the NSPCC.

Pamela also recalls some more relaxed moments at school. She and friends from LIV, at the end of the summer term in 1952, and friends in UIV, at the end of the

Easter term 1953, held end-of-term 'feasts'. It was agreed between them that only chocolate or homemade toffee was allowed on these occasions, and that Tizer was the official drink. From the photograph above, which Paddy Feddern took of Pamela and her friends, in which several can clearly be seen drinking from bottles of Tizer, it was a good job Miss Garwood Scott did not see them!

Pamela Gummery and friends at their end-of-term 'feast', 1953.

Memories of the 250th anniversary

Painting of the 250th Thanksgiving Service by Joan Alwork, former pupil, then assistant art mistress at LEH.

In 1961, the school celebrated its 250th anniversary.[31] As well as commemorating its foundation as one of the oldest girls' schools in the country, there was much else to celebrate. The work of the 1950s meant that, by 1961, the school was in a strong position. In the school magazine of 1961, Ruth Garwood Scott spelt this out.

That the School is serving well the educational needs of a wide area there can be no doubt.

The demand each year for places in our Junior Department is more than we can meet, and the academic achievements of the Sixth Form, at the other end of the age range, are equally significant. Five State Scholarships, three of which were won by girls who began school in our Preparatory Department, and nineteen entrances to Universities, including six to the Women's Colleges in Oxford, Cambridge and London, make a creditable list.

The 250th anniversary was to be marked by two linked permanent memorials, the founding, in 1960, of The Friends of The Lady Eleanor Holles School (The Friends) which aimed to raise funds for an ambitious building programme. As AR MacKewn, Chairman of the Friends, noted, it was hoped they would build 'something which will outlive us all'. His hope came true. The Friends launched an Anniversary Appeal and is still flourishing more than 50 years later. In 1961, the Friends looked forward to raising money for a spacious new Assembly Hall, partly by offering bricks for sale at half a crown each, a senior library, a swimming pool, a games pavilion, and craft and music rooms. Almost all were built during Miss Garwood Scott's time as Head Mistress.

The celebrations began with a Thanksgiving Service on 22 March 1961 at St Paul's Cathedral, with over 3,000 guests, including 600 girls, and the trumpeters of the Royal Military School of Music. Celebrations continued on 27 April, when the seniors, from the LIV upwards, were taken on a 250th Birthday Party expedition by special train to Stratford-upon-Avon. This event left a lasting impression on all who took part.

Elizabeth Chesman (née Ison), who was in UV, remembers the day.

The most memorable event for me was the visit to Stratford-upon-Avon to see Much Ado About Nothing *with Christopher Plummer and Geraldine McEwan. We were so excited when the steam train with the Lady Eleanor Holles crest steamed into Hampton Station to take about 500 of us to Stratford. How Miss Garwood Scott managed to arrange such an event I have no idea, but it must have been quite an undertaking.*

The train had scarlet letters running along the sides of the coaches, proclaiming 'The Lady Eleanor Holles School'.

Rosemary Price (née Virgo 1950–61) remembers, 'As Deputy Head Girl I got to sit in the Royal Box!' Gill Cumberland also enjoyed the day, but has another memory too. 'My parents, rather strapped for cash, were furious that they had to purchase three pairs of white gloves for this one occasion, as Miss Garwood Scott refused to take any girl not properly attired. However, these did make the long crocodile of girls look rather good, along with the panamas we used to wear in the Summer term'. Three pairs were needed as Gill's two sisters, Janet and Joan, were also at the school. Although we have pictures of the train, what a pity no one seems to have thought to photograph the girls!

The juniors had their own birthday expedition to the Royal Tournament at Olympia.

Finally, as a memento of the year, each girl was presented with a brooch in the design of the school crest.

Above: The special train to Stratford-upon-Avon was decorated with the school badge.

Above left: Refreshments after the service.

Below: Brooch given to each girl as a memento of the anniversary.

Opposite: LEH choir ready to take their places at the 250th Thanksgiving Service.

Left: Miss Margaret Smalley (seated, centre) and staff.

Margaret Smalley, 1974–81

Margaret Smalley had been Head of Music at LEH from 1958 to 1968, and then Senior Mistress from 1968, before she was appointed Head Mistress in January 1974. These were years of consolidation, though she introduced a more relaxed atmosphere to the school as a whole. As the Chairman of Governors (1979–81), Dr Richard Hancock, recalled in his tribute to her, when she retired after ill health in March 1981, this was particularly welcomed on occasions such as Prize Givings.

The Governors, sitting behind her at Prize Giving, were frequently enchanted by her as she always had something appropriate to say about each girl receiving a prize. The remarks were varied, good-humoured and sometimes anecdotal. The trend to less formality on these occasions was one of her aims and this change was widely appreciated, as I can testify through numerous conversations with parents.

Improvements continued during her time, as a result of her successful lobbying of the Governors for additional accommodation for the LVI, the refurbishing of Burlington House, additional rooms for class teaching and administration. Dr Hancock stated that she also 'sowed the seeds in the minds of the Governors for the need to provide improvements in the facilities for either music or science. In the long term she could see that this need not be a matter of choice since if four laboratories were built first, then internal reorganisation might release space for music. Here was the musician putting science first'.

Mary Beardwood, now Assistant Headmistress, initially appointed to the PE Department in advance of the opening of the pool in 1975, to look after swimming, remembered the part Miss Smalley played in getting the finances to install floodlights on the netball courts. These came just after girls had reached their first National Finals in 1979. Girls could now train after the end of school in

A swimming gala in the pool opened in 1975.

the winter months, which played a key part in LEH's future successes.

Miss Smalley was also responsible for making a number of significant appointments during her time, including a Deputy Headmistress; Joanna Braithwaite, the very well-loved Head of the Junior Department in 1976; a number of heads of department; and, beginning with the Art Department, several full-time male members of staff.

Her greatest strength was in interpersonal relationships, as Claire Zisman (1972–9) recalled at the time.

In the lower part of the school, I did not have the opportunity to know her well: all I met was her lively wit, her cheerful smile and the sparkle which she seemed unable to keep out of her eyes, even when telling me off for talking in the front corridor!

As a sixth former I came into closer contact with her and was able to recognise her warmth and care; to experience her kindness. She was, perhaps, at her best when helping individuals, which she found rewarding in a totally unselfish way. Not only did she give sound advice, but she had the rare and wonderful gift of true compassion. She offered me this, and I was able to see

the sympathetic lady behind the rather unorthodox headmistress, who provoked laughter with obedience, and fun with work.

She continued, 'As a Head Mistress, Miss Smalley has never been just a figurehead. She has always shown herself as approachable, not merely on academic matters. By setting an example of care and kindness, she inspires care and kindness'.

Thirty years on (2010), in interviews for this history, everyone from that era who spoke of Miss Smalley, pupils and staff alike, remembered her overwhelmingly for her kindness.

Writing in the school magazine for 1981, Dr Richard Hancock concluded his tribute to her by saying:

Margaret Smalley upheld the fine standards she had inherited, made changes only where she thought the school would become a happier place in which to work, but would not be swayed by a wind which she thought might be of only short duration. The hats for senior pupils could be disposed, but she saw no need to adopt gimmicks to try to prevent girls from leaving after O level for local Sixth Form colleges.

Miss Elizabeth Candy.

Elizabeth Candy, 1981–2004: a 'one-off' for a one-off school

When Elizabeth (Liz) Candy applied for the post of Head Mistress in early September 1980, she had been attracted by a number of factors. Aware of the good reputation LEH already had, she felt that the facilities in 1980 did not quite match up, particularly in her own area of science. She knew there was much that could be done to bring the facilities into the second part of the twentieth century, and relished the potential for development offered by the space of the site. She hoped that at LEH she would have greater scope to achieve improvements, as the Head Mistress there had a greater degree of independence than the Heads of many other day schools in the London area. The one-off nature of LEH's foundation, with its own Board of Governors, really appealed to her.

When Liz Candy took over from acting Head Elizabeth Gill at Easter 1981, there were both opportunities and challenges for independent girls' schools. With the coming to power of a Conservative government in 1979, the hostility to independent education from central government abated, and the Assisted Places Scheme, introduced by Mrs Thatcher's government in 1980, provided money to pay for 30,000 children to go to private schools. In addition, the vast array of legislation affecting the maintained sector introduced by the Conservatives in the 1980s, perhaps most notably the National Curriculum introduced in 1988, attracted a number of parents to the independent sector, seeing it as a bastion of stability. But there were challenges too, from the attractions of

mixed sixth form colleges, and boys' schools which were admitting girls. By 1981, over half of the Headmasters' Conference schools were admitting girls.

To an experienced teacher, Joanna Crooks, newly appointed as Head of English in 1981, the school seemed old-fashioned:

The most old-fashioned aspect was uniform for the Sixth Form, as the Girls' Public Day School Trust high schools I had previously taught in had abandoned that, in some cases over 20 years earlier. The only difference between a Sixth Former and a younger girl at LEH was a plain red tie, and on my first day, while being introduced to the delights of bus duty, I saw the Deputy Head mistake a Sixth Former for a Third Former, proving it was not a very good means of differentiating them. It also seemed old-fashioned that the Sixth Form sat at desks rather than around tables, as my own Sixth Form had done 25 years earlier.

Another member of staff, appointed in 1980, echoed this impression.

I joined the school in 1980, not long before Miss Candy took over. Coming from the state system … it was a bit of a culture shock. It was like stepping back in time. The atmosphere reminded me more of my grammar school in the 1960s than the schools I had taught in … There was, as now, a separate staff dining room, but the rest of the school ate together at set tables. I seem to remember food being collected by designated people for each table – no canteen-style self service, and, this was what most amazed me, no one could start eating until the member of staff on duty had said grace.

School uniform was soon abandoned for the VI form, not without regret on the part of some. 'When Miss Candy arrived, one of the things she insisted upon was that the Sixth Form should no longer have to wear school uniform. Most of the girls accepted the change, some enthusiastically, but not all. At least one defiantly continued to come to school dressed in full school uniform, I believe, right up until she left.'

Top: Miss Candy with the Lord Mayor of London, Sir Peter Gadsden, the Sheriffs of London and the governing body, 1983.

Above: Sir Peter Gadsden at the opening of new science laboratories in 1983.

Right: Adapting the Great Hall to provide additional space for music and drama.

The addition of four new science laboratories, suggested in Miss Smalley's time, was the first of a number of building projects to update the facilities of the school. In Liz Candy's first Prize Giving report, she paid tribute to the attitude of the Governors, who 'realise, much to my joy, that to keep ahead we have to look ahead'. Making sure that the excellence of the facilities matched the excellence of the academic reputation of the school resulted in a number of projects throughout the 1980s, 1990s and into the twenty-first century.

Art, music and drama were chronically short of space. Interviewed in 2010, Miss Candy said that one of the developments which had given her most pleasure during her headship was the expansion of the creative side of the school, especially music and art. The creation of additional space in the Great Hall in 1985, by adding a mezzanine floor, provided much-needed accommodation for music, with individual practice rooms, and for drama. This made much better use of a building which, as Wing Commander Kenneth Newman, MBE DFC, appointed in 1972 as first Bursar at the school, recalled, had considerable shortcomings. The Great Hall had been built originally to be large enough to accommodate all Senior Department pupils and parents for Prize Giving and other school occasions. Unfortunately, as he said, it was built with:

> *a high barrel roof supported by huge curved laminated beams, each of which echoed every sound and made the acoustics completely hopeless. A carol service that was held there on our first Christmas amply demonstrated the problem, as those at the back of the hall were singing at least a line behind those at the front! Consequently this large building was then used only as a dining room and was very costly to heat in the winter.*

The creation of the mezzanine floor meant that for the 'much needed accommodation for Art we must embark only on a relatively small piece of new building, thus saving our much prized open spaces of playing fields'.[32]

The school celebrated its 275th anniversary in 1986, with a service of thanksgiving in St Paul's, and the anniversary appeal raised much-needed money towards building the art block. This was followed by other projects designed to provide state-of-the-art facilities.

Memories of the Junior Department

Jennifer Adams arrived as a newly qualified teacher at Burlington House in 1977 and remained until 1986. She returned in 2002 as Head of the Junior Department. As she recalls, the Junior Department was very different in 1977.

Until this time, there had been a Lower I (LI), one Form I (I) and two each of Upper I, Lower II and Upper II forms. In 1977, however, LI was discontinued and for the first time there were two Form Is, with me teaching Form IY alongside Miss Beckinsale in Form IX. The two forms were always distinguished as X or Y, and you stayed with the same letter throughout your time in the Juniors. There was no academic difference between the forms and the two teachers worked closely together.

The staff consisted of eight form mistresses, one of whom, Miss Beckinsale, was also the Deputy Headmistress; a Music teacher and Mrs Braithwaite. Form teachers all taught almost all subjects, although the top two years had their PE taught by Senior Department PE staff, and all forms' swimming was taught by PE staff. Apart from Miss Willis, the Music teacher, there were no specialist subject teachers in the Junior Department. Nature Study was taught by form mistresses, but Science did not feature on the timetable. Similarly, the girls had Art and Craft lessons with their form mistresses, but DT had yet to be invented.

There was no secretary in the Junior Department, and only two phones – one in the Head of Department's office and one outside the kitchen. During the morning, it would often be answered by Mrs Dudley, a splendid character who had been a lady's maid in the past and fulfilled a variety of roles, including making the staff's break-time pots of coffee and helping to serve lunch to the Form Is. There was no photocopier, but an elderly and rather temperamental Roneo machine, which no one could quite master, in the staff workroom upstairs. There was a small medical room upstairs and a tiny first-aid room downstairs, and teachers had to deal with their own girls' casualties and illnesses. I once sent a girl up to the medical room to rest as she felt unwell, and forgot all about her until she eventually came back down and said she felt better.

Particularly upstairs, Burlington House was a hotch-potch of large and small rooms, several staircases, and corridors that went round corners or up and down a step or two. The previous Head of Department, Miss Cail, had a flat on the first floor and her sitting room has now become a classroom; the top floor was still divided up into staff flats, in one of which lived Miss Dodd, the Bursar's Assistant. The only room on the top floor used by girls was for sixth formers to learn typing.

In the 1970s and 1980s, the girls wore a grey pinafore dress in winter, with a shirt and tie and a red purse belt. They had a scarlet corduroy jockey cap and it was compulsory to wear this, especially on school outings in winter or summer. It certainly made it a lot easier for the staff to keep track of the girls, and anyone who forgot her hat for an outing had to wear it for the whole day in school the next day.

Tiffany Snelling (née Meggitt 1983–90) has fond recollections of the 1980s:

My memories of the Junior Department are as happy as they could be – endless games of rounders in the lunch breaks, playing houses in the 'hedges', lessons outside if sunny and we promised to be good, painting at our easels in the school attic room, xylophone lessons with Miss Willis, the fabulous stamps that Miss Grant used to mark our exercise books if we excelled, reading Tarka the Otter *round the class with Miss Mootham.*

Good fun in the Juniors.

Above: Official opening of the Sports Hall, 2001.

Above right: Junior Department girls leaving St Paul's Cathedral after the 275th Thanksgiving service.

Right: The opening of the Boathouse, 2000.

The Thirties classrooms were rebuilt with the VI form rooms and the Margaret Lacey Library above, and opened in 1992; the tennis and netball courts were re-sited and the staff dining room expanded; the Boat House was officially opened by Steve Redgrave in October 2000; and the Sports Hall was opened in 2001.

This continuing programme of expansion was, as Miss Candy said in 1992, 'a response to increased demand, to perceived need and, dare I say, as earnest of our faith in continuing success and popularity'.

The Junior Department was not forgotten. Burlington House was extensively refurbished in 2003, a project which

Nigel Noble, Bursar from 1998 to 2007, said he would remember to the end of his days, as it was so complex. Liz Candy congratulated him on its successful completion, declaring, 'It is a triumph'.

Not all projects went as well. In 1996, there were heart-felt references from Liz Candy at Prize Giving to the problems of the building and maintenance programme for the summer holiday period.

During the summer holiday period the school suffered a very full programme of building, maintenance and other works. I say 'suffered' because that word is used to describe

Nigel Noble, Bursar 1998–2007.

the process of undergoing and bearing pain. This period provided new practice for me in the art of contractor-speak, the argot of the builder. 'Today' – a misunderstanding, meaning one day. 'We can do that' but we haven't said we will. 'Monday' – well there are fifty-two of those just in this year. 'No sooner said than done' but I hadn't realised you'd said it.

This may well explain why Nigel Noble began to put together a caretaking and facilities team, which could undertake day-to-day maintenance and internal updating and refurbishment.

These projects cost a great deal, and one of the things Liz Candy was most pleased with, looking back on her headship, was putting the finances of the school on a more rational basis, so that a rolling programme of regular updating of facilities and future major developments could be budgeted for. Previously she felt that the Governors were 'trying to run a champagne school on beer money'. Considerable sums were also needed to bring in information technology and set up the networks.

The academic standing of the school developed significantly under her leadership. In 1998, academic results placed LEH within the top ten girls' schools in the country, and the 11th school in the country overall. Miss Candy's hatred of league tables was well known, as she constantly reiterated that what mattered for each individual was that her attainment should be as good as it could be. However, whilst league tables existed, it was always better to be high up than elsewhere. But Miss Candy was always very clear, from the start of her headship, that the school was about much more than academic success. At Prize Giving in 1985, she declared, 'We aim to offer as full an education as possible, and although that must mean good sets of Public Examination results, it should also mean, for everyone, as wide a range of interests and as full a knowledge of the world in which we live as can be had'.

Joanna Braithwaite, Head of the Junior Department from 1976 to 1998, opened the remodelled Burlington House and recalls some memories from her time there.

When I had the honour of opening the newly modernised and refurbished Burlington House I was amazed at the wonderful transformation. How different it all was from when I joined the Junior Department in September 1976. I was, I believe, the first Head of Department who was married with a young family. In those days I was expected to answer and make all the phone calls myself. But by the time I retired in 1998, I had a secretary and computers were a well-established part of the curriculum.

While maintaining the high standards and expectations of my predecessor, I introduced a less formal approach, where my study door was left open, except when I was teaching, so that staff and girls could feel free to come and talk.

I was keen to teach all the classes where possible, and I introduced Drama lessons for each class. These were very popular, and the Drama Competition and end-of-year plays for the UIIs are still a highlight of the Summer Term.

Pupils were encouraged to be independent and resourceful. This was shown when, on a cold January morning before school, a small girl appeared at my door to tell me that one of the girls playing Pooh sticks (leaves actually) on the bridge had overbalanced into the river, but had been rescued by an older girl who had immediately climbed down the bank and pulled her out. On another occasion we found an escaped pony in the garden. A keen horse-riding pupil quickly tethered it to a tree with long skipping ropes and fed it apples until the owner, a neighbour, came to collect it.

Joanna Braithwaite and pupils at her retirement party.

J14 Double Scull Silver medal winners at Junior InterRegional Regatta, 2010.

Right: Gold medals for LEH in Championship Coxless Four at National Schools Regatta, 2011.

By 1998, she was able to say, 'I defy you to show me a day school in which music, sport, the range of extra-curricular activity, the individual and group successes and achievements – and *academic results* – are as good'. She continued:

> There is no doubt that qualifications open doors, doors that lead to the lobby, but what gives access to the penthouse suite is far more than grades on pieces of paper: it is what goes with the grades – the whole person – and, like Heineken,[33] LEH gets to the parts that some other schools don't reach. And it does that by using an age-old recipe in which the best of the past is distilled with new ideas and confidence in the future.

And again in 2001: 'Qualifications may open doors but, ultimately, fulfilment in life relates much more closely to the proper use of interpersonal skills by people who are confident, secure, aware of themselves and sensitive to others'.

In 1982, rowing was added to the sports on offer at VI form level. From the start, LEH girls did well, and enjoyed the opportunity for cooperation with Hampton School (then Hampton Grammar) at a time when links were less developed, as Patsy Taylor (née Moore 1970–83) remembers:

> For most of my time at LEH, although we were next to Hampton Grammar, we were discouraged from having any contact with them. What a surprise we had when we reached the VI form and had a few joint subject options with the boys' school. More surprising was the option in sports to go to the boys' school's boathouse on the Thames and form an LEH rowing club. The first year was an introduction. Then, in the second year, we entered competitions and I was proud to be the first ever rowing captain for LEH, working with the squad to design our T-shirts in the school colours. We did alright through the year as complete novices to the sport and to competing, with the highlight being a win for our coxed four on home ground at the Thames Ditton regatta in the summer of 1983. I have always enjoyed seeing how the current teams at the school have fared over the years, building on the fantastic start we were given by our great coach, Steve Gunn from Hampton Grammar School.

The rowers went from strength to strength, and in 1988 LEH became the top girls' rowing school in the National

Championships, achieving a gold medal, two silvers and a bronze. Girls from LEH represented Great Britain, and the Junior Eight went on to be fifth in the world at the World Championships in Milan. In 1993, Liz Candy remembered, the rowers 'crowned sporting achievements by bringing home the College Cup from Women's Henley: the first school ever to do so and a great tribute to our rowers and their coach'.

Liz Candy relished the independence of the school and both regretted and dismissed the attacks on the independent sector.

Girls here are not chair-bound nor are they slaves to the examination syndrome. They are encouraged to be themselves – though sometimes, perhaps, a little more quietly. We set out to educate them in the true sense of the word and the sad truth is that in trying to do so we, and others like us, have to fight against a system which seeks to narrow, divide, prescribe and set us against our colleagues in other schools with whom we wish to be allied.

She argued fiercely that independent schools should not be seen as elitist and regretted the demise of the Assisted Places Scheme in 1997. In 1995, for example, 39 girls had places under the Assisted Places Scheme, at a cost of £140,322, and the school more than matched this with scholarships, awards and other fee assistance to 225 girls, amounting to £173,099.

As Head Mistress, Liz Candy had a magisterial presence, which could, at first, seem forbidding, but, as Jennifer Hattan (1990–4) pointed out, there was real human sympathy beneath. She describes what happened in 1992, when eight of the UVI asked Miss Candy for permission to use the school's name to raise money to go to Moscow with a charity that was decorating a children's burns unit.

It was always daunting meeting Miss Candy, and, as expected, we sat through a long detailed lecture on how important the A level year was and how the exam results would shape our lives forever. The fundraising was not to distract us at such a vital time. However,

Miss Candy as Captain Hook with Mrs Hazel, Deputy Headmistress, as the parrot in a Sixth Form pantomine.

when we thought she had finished, her body language changed in the way only Miss Candy could carry off and she softened as she said, 'Well that's the Head Mistress talk over' and proceeded to tell us how she believed that our project was going to give us the kind of learning school never could. She still stood by the warning of how important the exams were, but she could not have been more supportive and enthusiastic about the project.

Liz Candy was always prepared for fun in the right context. Who will ever forget her pantomime appearance as Dr Evil, with her sidekick Mini Me, aka Mrs Hazel, her Deputy? Or the two of them as Edina and Patsy from *Absolutely Fabulous*? Former pupils from the time certainly have not, and at least one pupil, newly arrived at the school, took this performance as a sure sign that things were going to be a great deal better than at her old school. 'My main memory is of you [Miss Candy and Mrs Hazel] dressed up as Eddie and Patsy from *Ab Fab*. When you started falling up the stairs, I can actually recall thinking, "This school is not going to be like my old one". And it wasn't! But in the best possible sense.'

The Lady Eleanor Holles School provides an excellent education. Its pupils are highly successful in public examinations and they have outstandingly good achievements in a wide range of activities, including sport and music. Throughout the school the standards of pupils' work are well above average and their attainment is high in relation to their capabilities.

Pupils' attitudes and progress in learning are very good and represent a major strength of the school. The quality of teaching is also very good.

The school has strong and effective leadership.

Ofsted Report, 1995

The Lady Eleanor Holles School is a very successful school, with many significant strengths, particularly examination success and few areas for improvement. The head mistress, with humour and charismatic leadership, has ensured the school's very effective evolution over several years. The school has responded to new initiatives with drive and enthusiasm, for example in the use of information and communication technology by the pupils, and has in hand a number of curriculum improvements. Traditional values, however, of excellent discipline, pride in one's own endeavour and success, and the need to strive to maintain the highest possible standards, have been retained and promoted.

Independent Schools Inspectorate, 2001

Miss Candy's legacy

Inspection reports from Ofsted (Office for Standards in Education) in 1995 and the Independent Schools Inspectorate in 2001 spoke of the school in glowing terms.

In the view of the Head of English, who had been Miss Candy's first appointment, 'If league tables had existed in 1981, LEH would not have shone, but by the time I left it had, in the *Daily Telegraph*'s phrase, premier league status, besides having made enormous progress, especially in art and music and the introduction of rowing'.

There were many tributes paid to Liz Candy at the end of 23 years as Head Mistress. The Senior Department assembly, 'ABC of being Head', arranged in honour of Miss Candy's time as Head Mistress (1981–2004), by the Deputy Headmistress, Mrs Lesley Hazel, on 30 June 2004, gives a real flavour of the respect and affection in which she was held.

Miss Candy with Mrs Lesley Hazel, Deputy Headmistress.

A is for assemblies

'I know that we'll all remember her for her "Good morning to you", "Will you stand in silence", and "I don't want to end this assembly on a bad note BUT ..."' (UVI)

D is for Dr Evil

An old girl says that teaching Mrs Hazel and Miss Candy the Doctor Evil dance from *Austin Powers* was just hysterical, and a very bizarre experience for her! They both performed so fantastically in the panto, the producers could not have wished for a more accurate impersonation!

F is for finance

The bursar, Nigel Noble, writes:

'F' is for Finance – or Fees, to our parents!
LEH is a brilliant school but it is also a business, and a multimillion pound business at that. The Bursar does the day-to-day work, but the Head Mistress must know the business and ensure that all the numbers add up. Miss Candy, therefore, checks the Bursar's sums and ensures he makes every pound do the work of two! She enquires, demands, pleads, cajoles and encourages in equal measure.
She discourages waste but encourages thrift.
She accepts advice with grace and ensures that her own is accepted – without fail!
She knows the bottom line and keeps to it!
Miss Candy does all this in her own unique way. With style, with good humour – and with the odd stern look.
Yes, 'F' is for Finance, but in her case you can also add Fun, Finesse and Fiscal Common Sense!
She is quite simply a Great Lady with the numbers!

H is for humour

An old girls recalls, 'One of the nice things we discovered later about Miss Candy was that under the stern exterior lay a fantastic and sometimes quite irreverent sense of humour'.

S is for scary

In the Assembly Hall, on the first day of IIIs being sorted into forms, one old girl remembers the following exchange:

Miss Candy: Stephanie Walton III.
Stephanie (under her breath): Yesss!
Miss Candy: If you say 'Yes' like that one more time, Stephanie, it will be NO!
Very scary.

V is for visionary

Without Miss Candy's support and vision, LEH Boat Club would not enjoy the victorious reputation it has. Her role in the building of the Millennium Boat House has led to the creation not only of a state-of-the-art facility, but also to the development of a community in which girls are encouraged to succeed. The Boat House stands forever as a testament to Miss Candy's dedication to the pursuit of perfection. (Rebecca Bligh, Boat Club Captain 2003–4)

W is for work

'It would be stating the obvious to say that **working** with Miss Candy was never dull!' (Anna Stribley, PA to the Head Mistress 1993–2003)

W is for Wisdom

'Whether dealing with parents, staff or pupils, Liz was able to sum up any situation, get to the heart of the matter with incredible speed and deal with anything that landed on her desk with insight and decisiveness'. (Anna Stribley)

W is for Wit

'Hers was razor sharp, and went together with a **whacky** sense of humour! (Anna Stribley)

Z is for zizzing into retirement (As if ...!)

An old girl concludes, 'She was an exceptional headmistress who contributed enormously to my schooldays being some of my happiest. And I have realised since leaving school what an apparently rare thing that is to be able to say, so I feel very lucky indeed!'

City links, 1710–1998

In the 1990s, it was decided to move the governance of the school entirely to Hampton, rather than having two centres, at Hampton and in the City. In 1998, Nigel Noble became Bursar and Clerk to the Governors of the school, who now met at the school instead of in the City. This loosened the links with the City of London, though the Corporation, Cripplegate Foundation and City University continued to nominate Governors. The move caused some regret, even amongst those who could appreciate that it was more practical for Governors' meetings to be held at the school, and for Governors to have a more hands-on feel for the school.

The links reached back to the school's foundation in the parish of St Giles', Cripplegate, in the Cripplegate Ward of the City of London. Some of the school's early Trustees became Aldermen of the Ward, and from 1875 the Alderman of Cripplegate was named as one of the Governors of the school. The Mare Street school had been opened in 1878 by the Lord Mayor and the Sheriffs of London, and, from then on, girls at the Mare Street school received regular invitations to the Lord Mayor's Show. When the Alderman of Cripplegate became Lord Mayor, as Henry Knight did in 1882, invitations to tea at the Mansion House also followed. In 1904, after the closure of the Cripplegate boys' school, the administration of the school was run by the Cripplegate Schools' Foundation from the Cripplegate Institute in Golden Lane. This worked well when the school was in Hackney. The Alderman of Cripplegate and the Vicar and churchwardens of St Giles' were on the Board of Governors, to keep the connection between the school and the parish and ward of the original foundation. However, once the school had moved to Hampton, it made less practical sense. Initially, in the 1960s, an administrative assistant, Miss Dodd, was appointed, and then, in 1972, Wing Commander Newman, MBE DFC became the school's first Bursar. Close connections with the City were maintained until the 1990s, with regular visits from Aldermen of Cripplegate and Lord Mayors of London, especially in Miss Garwood Scott's time. In 1967, and again in 1970, the Lord Mayor made a ceremonial state visit to LEH, bringing with him the two Sheriffs, the City Marshal, the Common Cryer and the Sword Bearer.

Right: A treasured photograph sent in by Mrs Christine Brown (née Kidd, 1944–53) shows what she describes as 'Four good pals' – left to right, Barbara Davies, Ann Lewis, Norma Jones and herself – about to cycle home. Many pupils in the 1950s regularly cycled for half an hour or more to and from school.

Across the years, the LEH experience

The LEH experience is wide. Girls from every decade in the twentieth and twenty-first centuries have valued the friendships formed at school and appreciated a set of values and aspirations which encouraged them to believe in themselves and in what women could do.

Lasting friendships

Ann Everitt started in the LIV when her father moved to Hampton to become Headmaster of Hampton Grammar School.

It might have been difficult to settle in, as I had had a good year at Manchester High School, but in fact I was happy from the start, mainly I think because on my first day a girl came up to me and asked, 'Would you like me to be your friend?' Gillian Higlett (now Wilder) and I became firm friends from that day onwards and see each other at least once every year, although she has lived in Vancouver since 1962.

Sarah Sheppard (2000–8) states, 'Friends for life were made there'.

For others, friendships have been renewed after retirement. Dinah Alsford (née Henley 1951–6) recalls how

she and another friend, Yvonne Vintiner (née Wooton-Whitling 1947–58) began, in 1997, to trace school friends from their year group. By 1999, they had found 65 of the 76 girls they remembered. Since then, a group has met annually for a short break together, with 'girls' travelling from South Africa, Canada and Australia. The photo above was taken at the 2010 reunion in Shaftesbury.

Lessons for life

Now I am retired and a pensioner, the seven years I spent at LEH seem such a small episode in my life, but they gave me what I now know was a solid foundation for the rest of my life. Some of the guiding principles of the school at that time may seem a little old-fashioned now, but the self-discipline (which I found hard!), sense of duty, and pride in achievement in whatever area that might be, have enabled me to survive life's problems on many occasions. (Sheila Woodhouse, née Britton 1955–62)

Madeline Macdonald (née Appleby 1946–55) agrees about the importance of self-discipline: 'We senior alumnae in our great wisdom and maturity now are agreed on one thing; we were imbued at LEH with the strength of *self*-discipline.'

Anything's possible

LEH was very much a feminist school and the teachers were good role models. (Cheryl Meggitt)

There were no boundaries to learning or aspirations, and it was quite a shock on leaving school to find that others in the world felt that women were somehow different to men in this respect – the school, however, had given me sufficient confidence to disregard this. (Elizabeth White)

Above all, I think that I was encouraged to do whatever I wanted with my life, irrespective of whether girls were supposed to do it or not! I have always been determined to work hard to achieve what I want, and to say what I think if I think something is wrong; this confidence stems from my time at LEH, where I always felt valued and safe. (Sian Hendrie, née Evans 1976–83)

Most importantly, LEH made me feel like it wasn't 'a man's world'. We were taught that we could achieve anything we set our minds to. Aside from the education,

Left: Reunion in Shaftesbury, 2010.

Below: UVY with their form mistress, Miss McKittrick, outside the Geography room, Summer 1960.

Vara Fitzhugh's enthusiasm for school drama developed into a lifelong interest. She is seen here in 1956 (inset) playing one of the knights in Murder in the Cathedral.

it was the confidence as women they instilled within us, that stays within me through all these years. … It was quite a shock really when I entered the workplace after graduating and realised women are viewed differently. (Ania [Anne at LEH] Markham 1983–90)

My time at LEH has taught me to deal with my peers and superiors with confidence, a skill which has been invaluable in my working life, and pretty effective in my social life as well! (Tiffany Snelling 1983–94)

Truly memorable and inspiring teachers … my overwhelming impression was of strong women who wished to inspire us to aim high. (Sarah Sheppard 2001–8)

Lifelong interests
Music

Christine Ewing (née Osborne 1946–54) describes how her musical experiences at LEH provided her with a lifelong interest. Her happiest memories were music lessons with Miss Morgan Brown and the choir under Miss Maden. Organising trips to Sadler's Wells and the Royal Opera House as President of the Music Club, and going to her first opera, *Die Fledermaus*, with the Music Society established her love of music and choral singing.

Chemistry

I remember the 'magical' chemistry display culminating in the fountain experiment Miss Lacey put on for third formers to encourage us to take an interest in science. It certainly worked for me. I went on to read Chemistry at Oxford followed by a career in the water industry. (Mary Sykes, née Saunders 1946–56)

Drama

Vara Williams (née Fitzhugh 1952–9) recalls: 'My most favourite memories of Lady Eleanor Holles are being in the school plays.' She was in every school production from 1956 to 1959, and particularly remembers being chosen as one of the knights in *Murder in the Cathedral* in 1956 (see photo on left), when she was still in UV – 'usually only Sixth Formers performed'. She remembers that 'apart from the joy of being in a play, something I have continued to do all my life ... actors for the last three weeks of the summer term were allowed to miss nearly all classes to learn parts and rehearse'. When Vara left LEH she went on to a teacher's drama course at the Royal Academy of Music and has been acting in or directing amateur productions ever since.

Russia

Jennifer Hattan (1990–4) recounts a memorable incident:

I think it was summer 1992 when the History Department bravely took a group from our year to Russia. It was a fabulous trip that led to a long love of the country. During one eventful outing two of our group were lost on the Moscow underground. I can recall the sheer horror of the teachers who had to deal with the reality of this and the absolute delight when the girls returned having offered a taxi driver a handful of US dollars to drive up and down until they recognised the hotel. A statue of Yuri Gagarin was the only landmark that helped them find their way home! [34]

Responsibility to society

Cheryl Meggitt (1956–64):

Miss Garwood Scott, who had a reputation for being very strict, also said we were very fortunate to receive such a good education which was denied many other girls and we should give back to society what we had been given.

Sarah Sheppard (2001–8) remembers:

Other initiatives such as the Charity Week, the Charity Committee, Amnesty International Group, Sixth Form Cafe, Make Poverty History Group, which rapidly expanded into a general social action committee, all meant I left the school with a keen interest in the world around me and a desire to make changes.

Margaret Warmington (3rd from left), Stella Tomlins (4th from left) and Jane Ross (3rd from right) enjoying catching up at a Holly Club lunch.

All-round education

Tessa Sauven:

When I was given a place at the Junior Department I remember being told how very lucky I was and at the time had no conception what that would mean to me. I look back on that comment now and realise just what a great gift those 11 years at LEH were. Not that I was one of the most talented or gifted pupils, but alongside all the academic work there was so much more to that education that has helped me ... I now realise, having children of my own, what a great influence a happy time at school can be and just how 'lucky' I was.

Jennifer Hattan (1990–4) says:

LEH provided me with an exceptional education. Not only were exceptional talents supported, encouraged and developed, but the importance of all-round education was valued on a par with excellent exam grades.

Dining Room, 1980s.

Food

After the rigours of wartime rationing, which continued until 1951, girls in the 1950s relished food which today might be approached with more caution. In 1947, the newly established School Council successfully petitioned Miss Richardson for ice cream, a treat after wartime austerity.

Madeline Macdonald remembers 'the scrum that used to break out in the 1950s dining hall when there were sausages and chips for lunch', and 'the race to fill up with a second portion of chips before they had run out'.

Most LEH girls from this period fondly remember the sticky buns available at break time, and judging by their youthful appearances and, for the most part, slim physiques, such 'treats' did not do them lasting damage. As so many cycled or walked to school, they clearly used up the calories. Dinah Alsford asks, 'Has anybody mentioned the buns we used to buy at recess? They were gorgeous when they were fresh, not so good if they were

yesterday's. I think they were bath buns; they had a lot of sugar on top and the prefects sold them from a door into the hall by the gym'.

And Colleen Gardener (1945–56) recalls:

One of the favourite societies was the German Club, not so much because of the language content… but because the Head of German was married to the Chief Patissier at the Lyons' Corner House group; consequently the highlight of each meeting was being able to sample the most delicious Torten of cartwheel dimensions such as had never been seen, let alone tasted, in the drab post-war years.

But perhaps things have not changed that much in 50 years or so. Here is Sarah Sheppard, at school in the first decade of the twenty-first century: 'My VI form tutor's weekly supply of cookies on Wednesday mornings added to my parents' conviction that LEH ran on food bribery!'

Three generations at LEH. Patricia Longmore (née Spindler 1942–9) on the right, pictured with, on the left, one of her daughters, Juliet Harris (née Longmore 1974–6), and, centre, her granddaughter Charlotte Harris (2007–).

After 75 years in Hampton, the LEH experience has now often reached two, if not three, generations in some families. Patricia Longmore (née Spindler 1942–9) was followed by her three daughters in the 1970s, and a granddaughter started in 2007.

Another former pupil, Margaret Warmington (née Osborne 1943–52), not only sent her daughter, Victoria, to the school, but also returned to work as School Secretary and Admissions Registrar between 1978 and 1999. Is anyone else still using one of the many shoebags she embroidered and sold in aid of school funds?

Others, too, have returned to teach. The LEH experience could also lead to partnerships for life, as a number of girls across the years have met their husbands 'over the fence'. Colin Jones, an Old Hamptonian who met his

future wife Janet (née Hollands, 1944–53) when she was a pupil at LEH, recalled at least eight other couples who met in this way in their era, the 1940s. Janet Ridgeway (née Lawrence 1942–9) remembered her friendship with Peter, who became her husband, developed at the Friday evening ballroom dancing classes, recalled here by Trish White:

Who can forget those Friday evening dancing classes with the Hampton Grammar boys under the stern but excellent guidance of Mr James? Those Friday evenings were anticipated with a mixture of excitement and dread. Would I be able to avoid 'the Clutcher' and 'Baby Hippo' this week? Would Mr James's eagle eye fall upon my partner and me? The cry of 'I could drive a bus between you two, stand closer together' was mortifying.

Setting the pace for the twenty-first century

When Mrs Gillian Low became Head Mistress in 2004, she was keenly aware that the school must continue to earn its place in the premier rank of independent schools by providing the highest quality in every respect. Since then, there have been a significant number of developments across the whole range of school life, from the introduction of an enhanced curriculum and the creation of opportunities for the development of educational, leadership and extra-curricular skills to enhancing the school's role, profile and influence both locally and nationally.

LEH was one of the first schools to embrace the AQA Baccalaureate in the Sixth Form. A particular attraction for introducing this new qualification was the emphasis, through the Extended Project Qualification, on individual research and scholarship. Also in the Sixth Form, an enrichment programme is now offered to ensure that all girls have the opportunity to develop their subject understanding and skills beyond the confines of their examination specifications. These developments, along with a programme of support in preparation for university entrance, have helped to nurture the school's ethos of intellectual curiosity and ensure that girls are academically robust for the rigors of university life.

Keeping pace with the twenty-first-century curriculum and the importance of computer literacy brought about

Previous page: Senior Department girls.

Right: Mrs Low chatting with Sixth Formers.

Opposite page: Junior girls in one of the 'hedge homes'.

Above: The Learning Resources Centre is a popular place for a quiet read.

Above right: Newsletters celebrate the many activities girls and staff participate in each term.

the Learning Resources Centre (LRC). This created a much larger space for the number of girls in the school than the previous library had been able to accommodate. By incorporating a much-needed area for sufficient additional computers to allow for class use, the space became a true resources centre. It is a really attractive place for girls to use. Staff competence in the use of smartboards and computers has grown hugely in the last few years. In line with identifying future needs are the plans for the new Arts Centre. This is designed to provide larger and enhanced facilities for art, music and drama, including a large theatre for performances, lectures and meetings, and improved teaching and rehearsal space. In addition, the scheme will provide refurbished dining facilities, new classrooms, the replacement of the LVI Common Room and landscaping.

Developing communications internally and externally was always high on Mrs Low's agenda. Individual interviews with staff, an 'open door' for girls, and meetings for parents quickly helped her to identify

areas to develop. Keen to utilise the latest technology to make information about the school, its expectations and opportunities readily available, the school website was launched. This now offers a more reliable way of providing extensive information about the school. A range of booklets, from the parents' handbook to extra-curricular activities, also provides a quick and easy reference for parents. Each term, newsletters, *Senior Focus* and *Junior Focus*, celebrate the huge array of activities and achievements of students, and keep parents and pupils in touch.

Plans were initiated to improve the environment too. The lines of the not particularly attractive 1930s building were softened with additional planting, and a reception area created off the entrance hall to provide a welcoming space, with a receptionist and seating for parents and other visitors. The internal environment is continually being modernised and made more attractive, with projects such as carpeting and soft furnishings bought by The Friends for the Sixth Form Common Rooms and the refurbishment of the

Senior pupils at
Annual Gymnastics
Display.

" The school radiates with positivity, drive and enthusiasm: the girls are a positive delight to teach and their genuine curiosity and love of learning is infectious. LEH buzzes with energy and creativity, with the sheer variety of activities happening throughout the building and beyond. "

Anna-Marie Wright, Teacher of English

Richard Nicholson took particular responsibility for developing the extra-curricular programme and forging links with the wider community.

The twenty-first-century school is a wonderful place to work:

> LEH is without doubt the most enjoyable and rewarding position I have held in my 20-year teaching career. Within weeks of joining the school I felt part of a unique community: one which is supportive, caring and incredibly dynamic. Working with colleagues who are not only highly professional and incredibly dedicated, and girls who strive to give of their best in everything that they do, is a real privilege. At LEH the expectations are high but the rewards are immense: it is indeed a very special place to work. (Stephen Bicknell, Teacher of Resistant Materials and Assistant Head of Holles House)

Staff Room. Working conditions have been vastly improved for the pastoral team, with the creation of separate offices for the Heads of Year, providing much-needed private space for conversations with students and parents.

LEH has always placed great emphasis on providing the best conditions not only for teaching and learning, but also for girls to develop interests, character and personality. Mrs Low wanted to build on this with the creation of a new senior management post, in which

Those who knew of the quality of education that LEH was providing were frustrated for many years that the name of the school was not more widely known outside London. Now The Lady Eleanor Holles School is much more widely recognised nationally, not least as a result of Mrs Low's year as President of the Girls' Schools Association in 2010. That the school is a very special place has been recognised in successive inspection reports over many

Above: Junior School drama.

Right: De Vere house at Sports day.

"

Academic success and a rich extra-curricular experience of aesthetic, creative and physical activities combine with an effective pastoral structure to provide an excellent educational experience.

The staff have created a happy school in which the quality of pastoral care is outstanding and in line with the school's aim. It ensures that pupils feel confident, valued and encouraged to take advantage of the opportunities offered.

Pupils are happy in their school and speak of it with affection and pride. "

Independent Schools Inspectorate report 2007

years. The most recent Independent Schools Inspectorate report, of 2007, praised the school for providing 'outstandingly well for its pupils'. Further, it noted that 'in a community in which pupils and staff are individually valued and in which expectations are high, pupils achieve excellent standards, not only in public examinations, but also in sporting, cultural, social and charitable activities'. The report also commented that 'pupils grow up to be confident, thoughtful and courteous young women'. The school was delighted to feel that the inspection team had captured the values at the heart of the school so well, and indeed that 'grace and integrity' remained a notable characteristic of the girls.

For the future

In 1710, the Lady Holles' School for 50 poor girls, with one mistress, began in a schoolroom in Redcross Street, in the parish of St Giles', Cripplegate, City of London. In 2010, The Lady Eleanor Holles School has almost 900 pupils, with over 110 teaching staff across the senior and junior departments, with a similar number of visiting and non-teaching staff, on a 24-acre site in Hampton. As the school gives thanks for the past 300 years, what of the future?

Mrs Low's hope is that girls at LEH will be 'happy, engaged and have achieved their dreams and aspirations'. She wants the school to be a vibrant place, with a purposeful, supportive and outward-looking community; a place in which there is lots of fun; a place to which girls really 'aspire', and which helps girls to be 'resilient and flexible' to face the challenges of their lives.

In 1936, when the school moved from Hackney to Hampton, then Head Mistress Nora Nickalls wrote, 'A school blessed with a tradition cannot live on its past, and can only justify its existence if it plays its part with a will in an ever-changing world'. The past 300 years have shown how well the school has played its part in responding to an ever-changing world. In the twenty-first century, the pace of change is increasingly fast. Experience gives us confidence that those responsible for the direction of the school will live up to this tradition, and that the school will continue to be the living legacy of Lady Eleanor Holles.

Pupils in the Senior Department.

In their own words

Junior Department
What was the highlight of 2010 for you?

"

... when our netball team won the Bute House netball tournament ... it felt like a wonderful honour when we were presented with our medals and our school name engraved on the winners' cup, which had never been won by the school before.

Ellie Williams (UII)

... going to Richmond Theatre and having a behind-the-scenes tour. We got to look at the orchestra pit, go in the wings and see the dressing rooms. But the best bit was definitely going on stage and pretending that you were an actress, performing a play!

Phoebe Spence (UII)

... when we went to Junior Citizenship in Bushy Park. We did all sorts of things, like how you would save somebody if they were stuck in the Thames or any other rivers.

Sophie Dunley (UII)

... being elected as a member of Pupil Parliament. I was thrilled when I heard my name being called out in assembly. I'm proud of myself for being chosen, and will stand up for the rights of all LEH girls in the year to come.

Elena Salvoni (UII)

... jumping off a 40ft pole onto a trapeze. I conquered my fear of heights and got a really good view of PGL.

Gabriella Nunes (LII)

... our end-of-year party. We all got to dress up as celebrities and famous people. We ate party food and had a great time. It was a fabulous end to the year.

Phoebe Cummings (UII)

... when we started handbells in music. The bells have their own sleeping bags and numbers. The music reading is very different from piano or violin, but just as fun.

Helena Atkin (LII)

... when we were in UI and Mrs Bass would make fractions fun by dividing cakes. That was an enjoyable maths lesson.

Rahima Aziz (LII)

... definitely the African Children's Choir. The songs were really energetic and I was standing on my seat clapping my hands above my head practically before they even started!

Emma Pollock (UI)

"

It is an honour to be an ambassador for such an amazing school; I am proud to represent LEH. The support and teaching from staff have been phenomenal, and I have always been able to rely on the special friendships I have made here. LEH provides endless opportunities for everyone to fulfil their dreams, whatever they may be.

Polly Teuten, Head Girl 2010–11

I appreciate how the teachers know everyone individually and how you feel that they really take pride in making lessons fun.

Victoria Sayer (LIV)

The sense of community and friendship in the school.

Lisa Asher (UV)

I really like the fact that there's always an activity or club for you, whether it's science, sport, drama or something else.

Olivia Edward (III)

Great opportunities for sport.

Ellie van Klaveren (LVI)

... that LEH is more than examination results. It's the things outside of the classroom, like friendships and the encouragement to be independent and to think for ourselves.

Karen Ang (UV)

The great effort teachers put in to help you achieve.

Sarah Choi (LVI)

... the way we are encouraged to stand up and speak for ourselves.

Beth Molloy (UV)

The combination of exceptional academic excellence with bustling extra-curricular programme.

Paige Reynolds (LVI)

Each student can become her own person, developing confidence.

Tahira Mohamed (LVI)

... the extra-curricular activities because they are fun and challenging.

Hannah Bartholomew (III)

Next page: Artist's impression of the new front elevation of LEH showing the proposed Arts Centre in the foreground.

Endnotes

1. Soprano, Alto, Tenor, Bass.

2. The Hampton Independent and State Schools' Partnership, along with similar groups nationally, was set up initially through direct government funding, to develop academic links and build community cohesion between local schools. The Partnership currently comprises seven schools: Hampton School, The Lady Eleanor Holles School, Hampton Academy, The Hollyfield School, Teddington School, Orleans Park School and Tolworth Girls' School.

3. SHINE: Support and Help in Education was founded in March 1999 to support additional educational initiatives, which encourage children and young people to raise their achievement levels.

4. The Holly Club celebrated what it believed was its centenary in 1986. However, the first reference in the minutes to an Old Pupils' Association was in December 1889, when Miss Ruddle reported its formation in her termly report to the Governors. She would not have been able to agree to its formation without the approval of the Governors.

5. John Holles, 4th Earl of Clare, married Margaret, heiress of Henry Cavendish, 2nd Duke of Newcastle, and thus acquired Welbeck Abbey. He left Haughton for Welbeck and Haughton Hall fell into decay. All that remains of Haughton today are the ruins of the chapel of St James and the burying place which is almost certainly where Eleanor was buried.

6. In compiling the database of Court Officers, Professor Robert Bucholz examined every extant admissions register of the royal household for the period, both official and unofficial. In an email he told me, 'I can state categorically that Lady Eleanor Holles was never a sworn servant in ordinary to Queen Anne'.

7. Account written by the Trustees of the boys' school.

8. Although the Decree of the High Court of Chancery, 1710, refers to 'Lady Eleanor Holles's Charity School', the school was known as Lady Holles' School throughout its time in Redcross Street.

9. In 1710, the parish Trustees were William Gardiner, Citizen and Distiller of London; Edward Buckley of the same parish of St Giles', Cripplegate, Brewer; Charles Feltham of the same parish, Brewer; Felix Feast of the same parish, Brewer; Isaac Tillard of the same parish, Merchant; Henry Lowth of the same parish, Upholder (sic); and William Edwards of the same parish, Weaver.

10. Quarter days were the four dates in each year on which servants were hired, rents were due and bills were paid. They fell on four religious festivals, roughly three months apart. In England, the quarter days were Lady Day (25 March), Midsummer Day (24 June), Michaelmas (29 September) and Christmas (25 December).

11. During the time of the school at Redcross Street, at least two were referred to as widows. Several left 'to improve my situation', which, it is clear from the context, means they were leaving to marry.

12. Between 1704 and 1877, an annual service was held, usually in Whitsun week, to celebrate the founding of charity schools under the auspices of the SPCK in the London and Westminster area.

13. In 1811, the National Society for Promoting the Education of the Poor in the Principles of the Established Church was set up, and, for obvious reasons, became generally known as the National Society.

14. Tippets were very large collars, covering the shoulders and coming down some distance in front. See the engraving from *The Graphic* on page 63.

15. A guinea was a pre-decimal amount of £1 and 1 shilling. It was considered a more genteel amount than £1. You paid tradespeople in pounds, but asked the middle classes to settle their school bills in guineas.

16. Walthamstow County High School for Girls, Church Hill, was opened as a private school in 1890 by a committee of subscribers.

17. The Skinners' Company bought a site in Stamford Hill in 1883 and opened a girls' school in 1890, The Skinners' Company's School for Girls.

18. The Taunton Report had recommended the setting up of three grades of school to serve the middle classes. A first-grade school for the upper-middle class, a second-grade school for the middle of the middle class, and a third-grade school for the lower-middle class. Lady Holles' School in Mare Street was a second-grade school, serving the middle of the middle class.

19. Until the end of its time in Hackney, girls were required to wear white dresses at all school functions.

20. Many thanks to Ceridwen Roberts and Rosemary Cole for their work in compiling details of admissions from the first of the Hackney registers.

21. The entire school, in their white dresses and straw hats, attended Miss Clarke's wedding on 7 July 1915 in St Giles', Cripplegate. The reception was held at the school. As well as giving 100 guineas and a pair of silver candelabra as wedding presents, the Governors presented an illuminated testimonial to Miss Clarke's work which is now in the school archives.

22. Reference to a German Zeppelin which had been bombing north London and was attacked and destroyed by aircraft fire in the early hours of 3 September 1916. The blazing wreckage fell to ground in a field in Cuffley, hence the name Cuffley Zepp. Thousands of Londoners had watched as the Zeppelin was attacked and there was huge rejoicing at its destruction.

23. She recalled later that gas masks were non-existent, 'but we kept handkerchiefs in an appropriate solution in every classroom cupboard'.

24. Some time between 1910 and the 1920s, the school changed its name from Lady Holles' School to The Lady Eleanor Holles School.

25. There seem to have been some changes in the 1920s, to white blouses, navy and silver ties and hat badges. In winter girls wore black velour hats, and in summer white panama hats edged with navy binding. Summer dresses were striped with white colours and cuffs. In 1931, gym slips changed to navy pinafore dresses.

26. An example of the loyalty the Trustees, and then the Governors, if they felt they were well served. Another example is the firm of solicitors, Baylis and Pearce, whose service to the Foundation dated back to the eighteenth century.

27. Lady Eleanor's great-great-grandfather.

28. It is one of the author's most vivid childhood memories, being told, on the eve of the eleven-plus examination, that performance in the tests would 'make or mar' her life. She passed.

29. This phrase does not appear in any documents relating to the school before its appearance in the school prospectus in the 1960s.

30. Name given to parents' evenings at the time.

31. Some time between 1928 and 1936 it came to be believed that the school had been founded in 1711 rather than in 1710. For more details, see 'Myths about the school' on page 188.

32. Liz Candy, Prize Giving report, 1985.

33. Classic marketing slogan for Heineken beer in the 1980s and 1990s: 'Heineken refreshes the parts other beers cannot reach.'

34. Author: As one of the staff on this trip, this memory brought back the horror of the moment when we realised that our Russian guide, having taken us on a tour of some of the unique murals and decorations in Moscow's metro stations, during rush hour and at breakneck speed, was not giving us time to head-count at each stop.

Myths about the school

The school began in 1711

The eighteenth-century Trustees always referred to 1710 as the start of the school. On several occasions, they took legal advice about aspects of the trust and each time went over and recorded details of the foundation, which was always referred to as 1710. All the early records, including the settlement made by Anne Watson, were kept in the Treasurer's home, first in a 'tin box' and then in an iron chest, and were handed on from Treasurer to Treasurer. The Trustees who built the Hackney school in 1878 also referred to the foundation as dating back to 1710, and this is the date they put on the stone plaque on the front of the Mare Street school.

The view of when the school started seems to have changed between 1928 and 1936. The Order of Service for the Jubilee Service of Thanksgiving for the Mare Street school in 1928 referred to the foundation of Lady Holles' School in 1710, whereas the foundation stone laid in 1936 by Sir William Baddeley for the new building in Hampton referred to 1711. How did this happen? My guess is that the Governors in the 1930s came to believe that a lease, signed on 19 November 1711 between the Trustees of the boys' and girls' schools, which is referred to in the 1905 book by Robert Pearce on the Charities of St Giles' without Cripplegate, marked the start of the school. In this document, the Trustees of the boys' school leased the schoolroom and two ground-floor rooms used by the girls for 900 years, from Christmas 1710, to the Trustees of the girls' school, at a yearly rent of 1 shilling. The girls' school Trustees also agreed to bear half the cost of repairs to the entire building. It is evident, however, from the *Account of the Rise of the Society* which set up the boys' school that there had been an earlier lease signed in 1709, as soon as the Redcross Street school was built. The question of when the school began is settled by the Treasurer's account book, from which it is clear that the girls' school under the name of the Lady Holles' School was operating from 25 March 1710.

Lady Eleanor Holles was a lady-in-waiting to Queen Anne

Although this seemed to be a common idea when I taught at LEH between 1992 and 2008, no one knew where the idea came from. The only written reference I have found was in a Prize Giving speech by Sir William Baddeley in the 1930s. As Professor Bucholz, Loyola University Chicago has indicated, as Lady Eleanor does not appear in any of the court records in this role, it is safe to conclude she was not a lady-in-waiting to Queen Anne.

Lady Eleanor left money in her will for a school to be built

What she actually did was to direct that any money left, 'the overplus', after her executrix, the Honourable Anne Watson, had distributed all the bequests made in Eleanor's will, should be used for charitable purposes. She did not specify a school.

Julia Maria Ruddle opposed the building of a gymnasium

In 1889, the Governors were considering building a gymnasium and swimming bath at Mare Street. In a letter dated 21 June, which was copied into the Governors' Minutes, Miss Ruddle gives her view that 'there is no doubt that so excellent a plan should be looked upon as a great boon by the parents of the pupils', and she submitted the prospectus and photographs of the Swedish gymnasiums at Hampstead and Regent Street.

The Governors eventually gave up their plans, but this appears to have been on the grounds of cost, as the school started to run at a loss, and not because the plan was opposed by Miss Ruddle.

This portrait was bought in Miss Garwood Scott's time as Head Mistress in the mistaken belief that the Eleanor Holles in the picture was the Eleanor whose legacy had started the school. It is however, a portrait of Eleanor's Aunt (d.1681) who married Oliver Fitzwilliam, 1st Earl of Tyrconnell (d.1667).

Still a puzzle …

When did the name of the school change from Lady Holles' School to The Lady Eleanor Holles School?

This seems to have taken place between 1910 and 1926. In the 1910 Board of Education scheme, the school is called 'The Lady Eleanor Holles School' for the first time, but this does not seem to have been used by the school itself for some time. The 1913 prospectus still called the school 'Lady Holles' School for Girls'. Even the title page of the University of London report in 1917 uses this title, though, at the end of the report, it writes of the fine work being done at 'Lady Eleanor Holles' School'. Prospectuses have not survived for every year, but the next we have for 1926 calls the school 'The Lady Eleanor Holles School for Girls'.

Even more puzzling!

There is a late nineteenth-century photograph of the Redcross Street school, built in the 1860s, in which 'Lady Holles' School for Girls Instituted 1702' can clearly be read in the stonework.

It may well be that girls were being educated in the Cripplegate boys' school before 1710. The boys' school occupied several sites before moving into the new building in Redcross Street at Christmas 1709. When the Trustees of the boys' school raised sufficient money to build the Redcross Street school, they were planning to include a schoolroom and accommodation for girls and a schoolmistress, so it may be that girls were already being taught. However, the accounts for a separate girls' school with the name of Lady Holles' School start in 1710, so it seems safe to conclude that this is when Lady Holles' School first began.

The phrase 'grace and integrity' appeared in one of the earliest documents relating to the school
The earliest document relating to the school is the Orders and Rules. The phrase does not occur there, and it does not ring true for an eighteenth-century charity school, which was founded to educate and clothe poor girls destined to become domestic servants. Qualities of grace and integrity are genteel characteristics that would be expected from polite society, not from domestic servants. Qualities of honesty and respectability were the traits to be encouraged in the hard-working poor. So where did the phrase come from? It begins to appear in prospectuses from the mid-1950s, and by Miss Garwood Scott's own admission it was she who invented the phrase to reflect her aspirations for her pupils.

Head Mistresses

Redcross Street school

1710	Mistress Martindale
1712	Mistress Garland
1713	Mistress Tuliday
1722	Mistress Peak
1723	Mistress Bargrave*
1735	Mistress Mary Bargrave**
1764	Mistress Ann Bland
1772	Mistress Dorothy Cotton+
1779	Mistress Allen
1795	Mistress Susanna Simmons
1799	Mistress Dorothy Clayton
1823	Mistress Charlotte Clayton++
1848	Miss Sarah Chaff✦
1858	Miss Caroline Hoare‡
1876	Miss Mary Frampton•
1878	Miss Maria Kavanagh✗
1883	Miss Mary Price
1884	Miss Jane Ewens▲

1899 Redcross Street school closed

1878 Mare Street school started

	Miss Julia Maria Ruddle
1895	Miss Ada Beatrice Clarke
1915	Miss Nora Nickalls

1936 Mare Street school closed and LEH moved to Hampton

1944	Miss Mary Richards
1949	Miss Ruth Scott, later known as Ruth Garwood Scott
1974	Miss Margaret Smalley
1981	Miss Elizabeth Candy
2004	Mrs Gillian Low

Right: Mrs Low congratulates Charlotte Lawson, Head Girl 2009–10 at Sixth Form Graduation. Mark Tompsett, Head of Sixth Form, in the background.

*Widow. **Daughter of previous mistress. +Resigned, 'declined that office on account of her marriage'. ++Retired with a pension, probably as a result of changes the Trustees were proposing of adding the duties of matron to those of teacher. Served 32 years in total at school, 25 as mistress. ✦Resigned in 1857, probably because of the introduction of the infants' school. ‡Mistress and Superintendent of both infants' and girls' schools. Resigned in 1876 because of ill health and given a pension by Governors. •Left to marry ✗Left because of illness, lung disease. ▲Last Head Mistress of the Redcross Street school until it closed in 1899.

Timeline

1707	Lady Eleanor Holles wrote her will, stating that any 'overplus' from her estate should be used for charity.
1708	In June, Lady Eleanor died in the parish of St Giles-in-the-Fields, London.
1708/9	The Honourable Anne Watson decided to use the 'overplus' to support a school for girls.
1710	A decree of the High Court of Chancery set out the details of how Lady Holles' School was to be funded and organised.
	Lady Holles' School for 50 poor girls was opened in three rooms of the boys' school in Redcross Street in the parish of St Giles', Cripplegate.
1711	On 19 November, the Trustees of the boys' school leased the rooms used by the girls' school to the Trustees of the girls' school for 900 years.
1832	The girls moved into their own purpose-built premises on another site in Redcross Street.
1858	The infants' school was added to the existing girls' school.
1860s	Further additions were made to the buildings.
1869	Endowed Schools Act.
1870	Elementary Education Act.
1875	The Redcross Street school became a public elementary school.
1878	Lady Holles' Middle School was opened in Mare Street, Hackney, with Julia Maria Ruddle as first Head Mistress.
1895	Ada Beatrice Clarke became Head Mistress at Mare Street.
1899	The girls' and infants' schools in Redcross Street were closed and the site sold to the London County Council.
1902	Under the 1902 Education Act, Mare Street became a secondary school for girls.
	First issue of school magazine, *Our Magazine*.
1903	Kindergarten was set up.
1914–8	First World War.
1915	Nora Nickalls appointed Head Mistress at Mare Street. Beginnings of VI form work.
1928	Jubilee celebrations were held to mark 50 years in Hackney.
	Votes were given to women over 21, on the same terms as men.
1936	The Mare Street school was closed and LEH moved to temporary premises, Summerleigh, in Teddington.
1937	The new, purpose-built school in Hampton was opened by the Duchess of Gloucester. LEH was now a direct grant-aided, grammar school for day girls, with some boarding facilities.
1939–45	Second World War.
1944	The Butler Education Act made secondary education free and available to all.
	Nora Nickalls retired and Mary Richards became Head Mistress.
1946	The Lady Eleanor Holles School became independent.
1949	Ruth Garwood Scott was appointed Head Mistress.
1965	The boarding house at Burlington House was closed.
1974	Margaret Smalley was appointed Head Mistress.
1981	Elizabeth Candy was appointed Head Mistress.
2004	Gillian Low was appointed Head Mistress.

Education Acts and LEH

1869 The Endowed Schools Act, a direct result of the Taunton Commission Report, created the Endowed Schools Commission and gave its members considerable powers. Their brief was to discuss with trusts, such as the one running Lady Holles' School, ways in which their endowments could be most usefully applied for the future. The Commission was charged with drawing up new schemes of government for endowed schools such as the Lady Holles' School, and, in particular, to extend the benefits of endowments to girls.
The Endowed Schools Commission was merged into the Charity Commission in 1874.

1870 The Elementary Education Act was designed to provide a national, universal system of elementary education for 5- to 13-year-olds. The Act set up School Boards to provide schools in areas where there was not adequate provision for all resident children. Existing schools, such as Lady Holles' School, were to be integrated into the provision for the area.
All schools would be subject to government inspection.
Parents were given the right to withdraw their children from religious instruction.
Education was not free and school fees, 'school pence', were charged. Nor was attendance compulsory.

1880 School attendance was made compulsory.

1891 Elementary education was to be provided free.

1899 The Board of Education Act set up a government department to oversee education.

1902 The 1902 Education Act abolished the School Boards and created Local Education Authorities. The Act laid the basis for a national system of secondary education. Under this Act, Lady Holles' School became a state-aided secondary school.

1944 The Butler Education Act set up a nationwide system of education in three stages: primary, secondary and further, for students up to the age of 18.
The principle behind the Act was that a child's education should be based on capacity and promise, and not on the circumstances of the parent. So fees were not to be charged for admission to schools.
Schooling was made compulsory between the ages of 5 and 15, and the Act said the leaving age should be raised to 16 as soon as possible. In the event, the school leaving age was not raised to 16 until 1972.

Next page: Pupils cheering the arrival of the Duchess of Gloucester on her second visit to LEH in 1947.

List of Subscribers

This book has been made possible through the generosity of the following subscribers:

Jennifer Adams	Staff 1977–86 and 2002–11
Maria-Teresa Addison (née Moon)	1983–94
Sophie Emma Agambar	2010–
Janet Airey (née Bazley)	1965–75
Ferrie Al-Chalabi	
Ann Allen (née Barling)	1947–55
Robyndra Jessica Kaur Allen	2010–
Susan Allen (née Wells)	1940–50
Joanna Allsop (née Pollock)	1964–74
Dinah C Alsford (née Henley)	1951–6
Jasmine J Amaria	1987–94
Elizabeth and Ameet Ambekar	
Amy Amissah	2010–
Emily Anderson	1986–95
Julia Anderson (née Hatherall)	1969–76
Victoria Anderson	1990–2001
Anne Marie Angliss	Staff 1988–
Yasmin Persia Anwer	2010–
Sheila Anzarut (née Howitt)	1946–56
Rosemary Arthur (née Warren)	1944–53
Martina Clara Asmar	1974–81
Emily Atkin	2010–
Helena Atkin	2008–
Melanie Atkins	1979–90
Helen Atkinson	1993–2000
Antonia Austyn	2007–
Jennifer Baird (née Cabeldu)	1953–62
Pamela Baker	Staff 1959–64
Anjuli Bali	2008–
Amanda Ball Eccleston	1984–6
Hannah Ball	2004–11
Helen Ballard (née Govett)	1988–95
Sarah Balsom (née Henley)	1954–61
Charlotte Hannah Banks	2007–
Florence Leah Banks (née Mason)	1922–7
Anne Y Barker	1962–5
Ella Barker	2010–
Judith M Barker	1946–52
Lucy Barnes	2008–
Joanna Barzycki	2006–
Mary Beardwood	Staff 1974–
Frances Beaton	1998–2009
Lydia Beaton	1994–2004
Jean Beckinsale	Staff 1957–84
Brenda Beckman (née Marshall)	1946–51
Helen Beedham	Staff 1993–
Emma Bennett	1981–91

Jemima Benstead	2003–10
Claire Ellen Bernard	1994–2001
Luisa Betts	1982–93
Catherine Bevington (née Edwards)	1974–86
Avril Bevins (née Sidney)	1946–1950
Steven G Bicknell	Staff 2007–
Pamela Bingham	1942–9
Margaret Bingham (née Westmoreland)	
	1960–8
Eva Black	2008–
Moira Black	1958–67
Simone Blaskey (née Engelsman)	1970–80
Henrietta Blundell	2007–
Jane Blunden (née Hunter)	1955–1966
Joan Blythe	1932–8
Diana Boesch (née Marshall)	1946–56
Eileen Jane Bolitho	1949–56
Judith Boot	
Emily and Florence Booth	1995–2009
Joyce Boucher	Staff 1979–90
Janet Boullin (née Bill)	1954–64
Margaret Boulton Smith	1944–51
Eve Bowden	2011–
Louisa Bowman	1985–94
Gill Brackenbury (née Huddart)	1972–82
Celia Brackenridge	1959–68
Catherine Bradley (née Rennie)	1963–73
Lucy Bradley	2009–
Kirstin Brady	2009–
Joanna Braithwaite	1976–98
Elizabeth Bramley	2009–
Christine Branagan (née Obank)	1951–8
M Breckon	Governor 2003–11
Catherine Briggs	1978–89
Emily Brighton	2003–10
Sheila Britton	1955–62
Victoria Broadway (née Warmington)	1976–83
Amber Broekhuizen	2009–
Christine Brown (née Kidd)	1944–53
Tabitha Brown	2001–
Eleanor Brzeskwinski	2010–
Lydia Brzeskwinski	2008–
Sophia Brzeskwinski	2010–
Flora Buckley	2009–
Anna Budd (née Woodman)	1990–7
Claire Burchett	2007–
J Hazel Burkett (née Gill)	1944–9

Brooke Burkhart	2011–
Fiona Mary Butler (née Morrison)	1956–66
Stephanie Butler	1956–62
Stella Buttress (Wright / Tomlins)	
	Pupil 1942–9, Staff 1965–78
Olivia Cahill	2011–
Helena Caldon (née Beynon)	1984–91
Her Honour Ann Campbell DL	1960–8
Dawn Cameron	1978–85
Lauren Campbell	2007–
Niamh Campbell	2009–
Claudia Caravello	2007–
Alexandra Carden	2004
Nicola Carden	2010–
Mimi Carlton	2005–
Sally-Anne Carpenter-Smith (née Judge)	
	1956–62
Alison Carr	1954–62
Mary Carr	1954–64
Talia Carter	2008–
Emma Louise Cates	2007–
Celia Chalmers (née Davies)	1950–8
Dr Rosemary Evans (Mrs R Chapman)	
	1956–63
E J Chesman	1953–63
Chloe Cheung	2006–
Daisy May Childs	2000–7
Harriet Alice Childs	1996–2005
Lauren Childs	2006–
Lindsey Childs	2009–11
Carolyn (Lindy) Chris	1941–54
Erica Clark	1938–43
Peggy Clark	1927–39
Caroline Clarke	2007–
Valerie Clarke	1955–61
Sarah Clohessy (née Welch)	1983–94
India Clutterbuck	2009–
Georgina Coates	2009 –
Janet Cody	1943–50
Gabriela Cohen	2009–
Ingrid Colclough	Staff 1996–
Fiona Colhoun	1967–78
Julia Comber (née Farrow)	1957–63
Sadie Connolly	2008–
Myra Beauchamp Conway	1958–63
Imogen Cook	2009–
Joanna Cook	1991–2002

Martha Cook	2008–	Sarah Felger (née Webster)	1982–91	Vivienne Laura Hay	2003–10
Phillippa Cook	1991–2002	Katharine Fenn	1969–81	Andrew Hayter	Staff 2008–
Sophie Cook	2009–	Anna Fernandez	2011–	Lesley Hazel	Staff 1979–
Annabel Cooper	2007–	Agnes Fife	1947–50	Philippa Healy (née Warrington)	1969–81
Judy Cooper (née Raven)	1945–50	Hannah Foley	2008–	D D Heaney	
Lucy Cooper	2006–	Francesca Foster	2007–	Alice Heath	2001–8
Mary Corbould (née Gordon)	1947–53	Margaret Fotheringham (née Rogers)	1971–8	Murray Hedgcock	
Mary Cordle (née Ryan)	1956–67	Rosemary Fox	1947–8	Sian Hendrie (née Evans)	1976–83
Alison Corley (née Downes)	1957–64	Peggy Franklin	1945–52	Elizabeth Henshaw	2008–
Lucy Emma Cornwell	2008–	Jade Fricot	2010–	Alys Herbert	2008–
Mary Court	School Nurse 1996–2010	June Fuller	1943–9	Lisa Aileen Herde	2009–
Alison Cox	1970–8	Melanie Furnell-Jones (née Knight)	1962–9	Sarah Hewlett (neé Calvert)	1984–95
G A Cox	Governor 2004 –	Judy Gale	1962–70	Christina Hill	2008–
Simon Croft	1978–85	Sue Gamblin	Staff 2000–10	Deborah Hilton	1968–79
Gill Cumberland (née Yardley)	1955–63	Colleen Gardener	1945–56	Kate Holder	1990–2001
Phoebe Cummings	2007–11	Betty D Garrard Evans (née Bird)	1938–44	P Holland	
Vanessa Cutts	1979–84	Marilyn Garrod (née Virgo)	1951–63	Isabel Holme	2008–
Rosalind Pyne D'Albert	1959–68	Freya Gascoigne	2009–	Sheelagh Hope	1963–71
Emily Louise Daglish	1998–2009	Fiona Geiger (née Roddan)	1967–77	Sacha Hopkins Powell	2005–
Joanne Dancey	2005–	Bethan George	2002–	Leigh Stock	1962–9
Rebecca Dancey	1999–2006	Elinor George	2010–	Alix Hopper	1992–9
Dr Shilpa Dave	1981–91	Ella George	2006–	Lauren Hopper	1991–8
J M Davies	Staff 2005–	Grace George	2003–	Elizabeth Anne Horne	1993–2004
Louise Davies (née Kingsley)	1972–84	Lisa and Nigel George		Amy Horrell	2005–
Zara Davies	2010–	Paulina Sophia Gerchuk	2011–	Elizabeth M Hossain	Staff 1992–2008
Hatty Day	1996–2003	Tushna Ghadially	1982–94	Sophia Hossain	1986–97
Dr Samantha de Silva	1986–97	Ann Gibbons		Annette Hovsepian	2008–
Juliet Dehnel (née Cox)	Staff 1971–86	Gill Gibbs	1964–73	Alison Howard (née Shattock)	1964–71
Rosemary A Dellar (née Soutter)	1947–55	Pam Gidney (née Hornsby)	1939–44	Anne Howell (née Macfarlane)	1960–62
Frances Dent (née Wyllie)	1962–69	Assisi Gifford	2011–	Philip M G Hubbard	
Ankita Deo	2010–	Poppy Gilbert	2008–	Bernard Hughes	Staff 1998–
Ramandeep Deol	2009–	Janet Gill-Hooton	1945–54	Elizabeth Hughes	1959–70
Jessica Deverson		Joan Gillingham (née Tapley)	1938–43	Mrs A Meyrick Hughes	Governor 2002–
Emily Devine	2008 –	Anna Gilroy	2006–	Phoebe Hughes	1998–2005
Emily Dexter	1995–2006	Caroline Gilroy-Scott	Staff 1995–	Dayle Hume	Staff 1995–
Catherine Dibble	1996–2007	Alison Goodyear (née Rae)	1953–62	Dawn Reynolds	1983–9
Norma Jesty Dinnage	1950–53	Sara Gordon	1997–2004	Anne Louise Hunter	1957–67
Maureen P Dodd	1937–43	Amelia Gosztony	2009–	Margaret Hurll	1952–61
M R Donaghy		Jill Grant	Staff 1975–2004	Nicole Hussein	2006–
Lauren Donaldson	2009–	Lady Sonia Grant (née Landen)	1938–45	Zara Hussein	2009–
Lucy Douglas	1999–2006	Alderman David Graves		Becky Hutton	2007–
Rosamund Downer	2003–	P M Gray	Governor 2010–	Pam Ireland (née Gummery)	1949–57
Rachel Dresner (née Lutz)	1988–95	Imogen Green	2006–	Nicola Irens (née Charlton)	1980–92
Damneek K Dua	2008–	Cecily Green	2011–	Jessica Irvine	1995–9
Cara Duckworth	2004–11	Carolyn Greensmith		Georgia Isaac	2006–
Rosie Duckworth	2001–8	Judy Greenwood (née Strang)	1957–67	Erika Izawa	1996–2006
Esther Victoria Duffy	2006–	Judith M Greig	1958–64	Suzannah Jackson (née Fox)	1972–84
Ellen-Kristina Dunkley	1976-88	Caroline Grieveson	Staff 1998–	Becksy James	2002–
Alexia Dunley	2007–	Laura N Griffin	2009–	Katherine Jeffery	Staff 1991–
Sophie Dunley	2007–	In memory of Pamela M Griffin	1944–50	Katherine Jenkins	2002–9
Sonia Dunn (née Baldwin)	1946–57	Amy V L Griffiths	2007–	Jasmine Jewell	2011–
Beth Dunnett (née Carter)	1996–2002	Olivia Grumitt	2009–	Kate Jillings	1987–98
Melissa Dunnett (née Barltrop)	1989–96	Jane Haigh	1966–76	Christine Johnson (née West)	1953–65
Judy Dunt (née Corderoy)	1949–54	Fiona Hall (née Stark)	1977–87	Julia Jolliffe	2001–9
Elizabeth Ede (née Harding)	1959–64	Judith Halls (née Pett)	1957–67	Brenda Jones	Staff 1980–2003
Caroline Edwardes Jones	1943–55	Harriet I Haly	2008–	Shirley A Jones	1942–54
Margaret Ellwood	1951–8	Lydia R Hamill	2004–	Oriana Emily Grace Jopling	2011–
Claire Emerson	1982–93	Susan Harman (née Gilbert)	1956–64	Hanna Joseph (née Gingell)	1993–2000
Hannah F Evans	2010–	Dr Jane Harpur (née Mathie)	1958–64	Tanya Joshi	2008–
Heidi J S Evans	1995–2002	Yolanda Harris	1972–84	Ann Joyce	
Sue and Martin Evans		June Hart	2004–11	Warsha Kale (née Prabhu)	1978–89
Ann Everitt (née Whitfield)	1950–56	Hazel Harvey (née van Rest)	1946–53	Anisha Kamat	2004–11
Paradis Farahati	2011–	Alice Harwood	2009–	Raina Kamat	2006–
Shirley Farnsworth (née Grattan)	1940–50	Laetitia Hawkins	2007–	Ria Kamboj	2008–
Venice Amelia Farr	2009–	Nadia Haworth	2008–	Sohmika Kandhari	2011–
Felicity Farries (née Grant)	1942–50	Jasmine Nancy Hay	2001–8	Lucy Kean	2007–

Veronica Kean	Staff 2006–	Georgina Macrae	2009–	Linda Morte (née Piggott)	1960–70
Christine Keeble	1968–79	Caroline Mactaggart (née Williams)	1971–81	Alice Isabella Mosely	2004–
Fizzy Keeble	2003–10	Madeline Macdonald (née Appleby)	1946–55	Elizabeth Kailin Moules	2008–
Lucy Astrid Keeler	2005–6	S B Moeko Maiguma-Wilson	2003–10	Dr Joanne E Moxey	1977–84
Fiona Keeling (née Fletcher)	1981–8	Margaret Main (née Hamlin)	1939–45	Judy Mulholland (née Flight)	1965–74
Diana Keiller (née Swain)	1964–70	S P Maloney	Staff 2009–	Giles Murphy	
Gillian Keller (née Pulford)	1963–70	Diana Maltby	1954–8	Caroline Murray (née Seeman)	1948–58
Frances Kelly	2006–	Prina Mandavia	1995–2003	Mrs M I Nagli	Governor 1997–
Judith Kendall (née Erlebach)	1953–63	Harry and Clare Mann		Ilisha Nangla	2008–
Moira Kendall (née Mackenzie)	1956–63	Isabelle Mann	2010–	Rosemary Netscher (née Briars)	1952–61
Claire Kendrick	1980–7	Mr and Mrs G Marks		Charles and Susannah Nettleton	
Fiona Kent	1981–9	Joanna Markbreiter	1999–2010	WG CDR & Mrs K J Newman	Bursar 1972–87
Pamela Kent (née Brown)	1960–7	Anne M Markham	1983–90	Dr Valerie Newman (née Turnbull)	1957–67,
K J S Kerr	Governor 2011–	Isabel Markham (née Davis)	1938–46		Governor 2001–
Emily Khatib	2005–	Val Martin-Long (née Moore)	1967–72	Doreen Newton (née Ritchie)	1947–52
Ying Ying Khong	2002–9	Ann Martin Criss	1961–6	Richard J J Nicholson	Staff 2006–
Catherine King	2007–	Catherine T Martin	1964–6	Helen Ann Nicks	1986–95
Gemma King	2007–	Jessica Charlotte Eden Martin	2005–	S A Nightingale	1997–2008
D Kingston		Lesley Massingham (née Baldwin)	1956–62	R Niven	Governor 2002–11
Zoë Kirby (née Tebbutt)	1989–94	Pat M Matthes (née Sheath)	1945–50	Nigel Noble	Bursar 1998–2007
Freya Krol	2010–	D R Mayes		Joy Norgate	1970–82
Rebecca Krol	2006–	Faye Maynard (née Palmer)	1948–54	Hester Norman	2005–
Aria Kumar	2009–	Charlotte Mayne	1997–2008	Gabriella Nunes	2008–
Irene Kwok	2009–11	Midge Mazzier	2008–	Lena Nwana	2007–
Alexandra Laidlaw	2007–	Phoebe Mazzier	2010–	Margaret Obank	1951–61
Jessica Laidlaw	2003–10	Jane McAusland	1953–9	Patricia Oliver	Staff 1979, 1982–95
Louise Lambert (née Nagli)	1990–7	Julia Dowden	2010–	Christine Osborne	1946–54
Elly Lambourn	2008–	Susan McCartney		Susan J Owen	1964–72
Olivia Lambourn	2005–	Madeleine McClean	2011–	Margaret Oxley (née Arnold)	1949–61
Alison Lane	1981–8	Dr S McCormick	Governor 2009–	Margaret A Packer	1949–58
Emily Langton	2009–	Emma McDonald	1980–91	Lesley Helen Page-Wilson	1948
Wendy Lansdown (née Forrest)	1947–52	Fiona McDougall	1990–9	Esther Park	2009–
Alicia Lau	2010–	Sarah McEwen	1978–90	Alison and Peter Parkin	
Jenny Laverack	1985–92	Dr Patricia McFadden	1947–56	Sylvia Parkin	1980–96
Maddie Lawless	2008–	Carole McGraw (née Alexander)	1945–55	Caline Parsons	1957–68
Charlotte Lawson	2003–10	Cheryl Meggitt (née Martin)	1957–64	Amber Rajvir Patara	2009–
Sheila Leach	1943–9	Barbara E Megson	1937–48	A Patel	2000–11
Gina Lee	2009–	Alice Melotte	1995–2006	Rhianna Patel	2011–
Janine Lees	1959–66	Katherine Melotte	2000–11	Harriet Patton	2006–
Christine Leigh	1998–2005	Sarah Melotte	1997–2008	Emily Paul	1998–2005
Gabriella Lewis	2010–	Rosemary E Coleridge Middleton	1953–7	Clarisa and Roberto Paultroni	
N D Lewis	Governor 2011–	Isobel Miles	2009–	Hilary Pearce	1973–83
Jane Lines (née Shutes)	1945–54	Mr and Mrs K Miles		Jenny Pearcey	1964–68
Kelly Little (née Dawson)	1978–87	Ellen Miller	2006–	Desirée Pedersen	2007–
Abigail Lloyd	1997–2008	Judith Mills	1983–90	Josephine Pedersen	2005–10
Georgina Lloyd	2002–	Fiona Miln	1988–99	Louise Pedersen	2003–10
Isobel Lloyd	2002–	Imogen Grace Misso	2007–	Soren H Pedersen	
Rosamund Lloyd	2003–10	Enid G D Mitchell FRBS	1937–47	Rosemary Pegram (née Reed)	1951–60
Shirley M Lloyd	1939–49	Glendon Mitchell (née Stock)	1953–64	Olivia Triantafillou Perosa	2011–
Morag Lomax	Governor 2000–	Tahira Mohamed	2005–	Jennifer Perrier	1989–99
Catherine Long	1998–2005	Rosemary Irene Money (née Norton)	1937–43	Marjorie G Perry (née Reynolds)	1951–61
Cecilia Long	2004–11	Janet Monteil	Staff 1990–	Charlotte Pexton	2009–
Dorothy and David Long		Lauren Monteil	1995–2006	Kate Phillips (née Colman)	1986–93
Felicity Long	2000–7	Pascale Monteil	1994–2005	Alice Picton	2005–
Jenny Long	2008–	Pamela Moore (née Mobbs)	1944–52	Elise Piercy	2008–
Matilda Long	2002–9	Katharine Morgan	2005–	Dilly Pirgon	2002–6
Patricia Longmore	1942–50	Isabella Morgante	2008–	Melek Pirgon	2001–5
Marie Lovatt (née Screech)	1955–65	Charlotte Morley	1978–85	Mr & Mrs T Pitcher	
Gillian Low	Head Mistress 2004–	Hannah Morrill	2002–9	A J Pitchers	Bursar 2007–
Sarah Luddington	1965–76	Laura Morrill	2000–7	Clementine Pizzey-Gray	2006–
Róisín Alice Lynch	2011–	Ros and Nick Morrill		Stephen Pizzey and Jenny Gray	
Thea Lysons	Staff 1961–90	Sophie Morrill	2005–	Lirios Pla-Miró	Staff 2006–11
Eileen Macchi (née Stamp)	1941–6	Jennifer Morrison	1984–2000	Catherine Pochkhanavala-Cleeve	
Eileen M Mackay (née Cameron)	1950–5	Judy Morrison (née Marshall)	1959–66	(née Cleeve)	1989–96
Hazel Mackervoy (née Parkyn)	1949–54	Lucy Morrison	1991–2002	Amy Polglase	2008–

Katherine Pollitt	1970–81
Sarah Pollitt	1975–85
Amy Porton	2006–
Marian Louise Postgate (née Thorne)	1951–8
Amy Powell	2009–
Stephanie Powell	2006–
Jean Preston	1957–64
Emelia Price	2009–
Lucy Prior	2003–
B C R Pugh	
Marion Putland	1960–7
Katherine Pyne	2006–
Loveday Quarry	2010–
Pippa Quincey	2006–
Lizzi Radford	2007–
Lamya Rais	2008–10
Grace Ramsay	2008–
Laura Ramsay	2004–
Rachel Ramsay	1998–2005
Eloise Rose Rattle	2005
Susan M Rees (née Brinton)	1947–56
Anna E Reeve	1979–87
Dr Catriona Reid (Mrs Rowe)	1951–62
Julia Rennie	1992–2003
Sara Reynolds (née Davies)	1978–89
Georgia Richard	2005–
Joanna Richards (née Govett)	1992–9
Ceridwen Roberts	1957–66
Ellie Roberts	2003–
Emma Roberts	2005–
Margaret Roberts	1964–75
Sian C L Roberts	1962–7
Florence Robertson	2000–11
Isobel Robertson (née Grant)	1970–82
Rose Robertson	1995–2006
Rosie Robson	2000–11
Cara Rodger (née Willmott)	1963–73
Barbara Rodgers (née Woods)	1959–66
Hannah Rogers	2000–11
Lucy Rogers	2003–
Amanda Rolfe (née Lisle)	1971–82
Elizabeth Rose (née Harvey)	1949–56
Mrs J Ross (née Lester)	1957–64,
Governor 1997– , Chair of Governors 2002–	
Joanna Russ	1977–87
Victoria Russ	1975–85
Joy Russell	1956–69
Kate Russell	2009–
Lucy Emma Victoria Russell	2001–8
Patricia Russell	1956–69
Jean Sadgrove	1949–55
Natalie Sadovska	
Lily Sanderson	2007–
Aditi Satija	2007–
Alison Saunders	1959–67
Tessa Sauven (née Sherriff)	1961–72
Beatrice Shah Scott	2010–
Madeleine Shah Scott	2010–
Homa Sebi	
Wendy Seigel (née Grumbar)	1959–68
Sonal Shah	1991–2002
Hanna Sharif	2000–11
Samirah Sharif	2011–
Zaina Sharif	2000–11
Maureen Sharman (née Denham)	1944–9

Pamela Sharp	Staff 2001–
Claudia Shek	2011–
Rosemary Shepherd (née Coxon)	1951–8
Susan Shepherd (née Harding)	1955–64
Linda Shepley	1959–61
Sarah Sheppard	2001–8
Dr L Sherski	Governor 2000–11
Sarah and Nicholas Sherwin	
Juliet Short (née Waters)	1950–60
Isabelle Silver	2010–
Susannah Simon	1973–82
Ileesha Singh	2010–
Sue Sleight (née Reynolds)	1954–60
Hannah Jayne Smith	2002–9
Jessica Smith	2009–
Lucinda Annetta Kelly Smith	2005–
Raquel Snajdar	1987–98
Dr Christine Averil Snodgrass	
(née Poole)	1945–52
Anna Sparrow	2004–11
Benedicte Sparrow	1989–2000
Catriona Sparrow	2006–
Marilyn (Lynne) Sparrow	1962–8
Sarah Spencer-Brown (née Govett)	1989–96
Tessa Stanworth (née Westcott)	1940–53
Nadia Starr	2006–
Sasha Stewart	2009–
Marilyn Stock	1952–62
Una Stock	1950–61
Celia Stockton	1957–66
C S Stokes	Governor 2010 –
Joanna Stokes	1997–2004
Cynthia Stone	
Annabelle Stoney	2007–
Louisa Stoney	2009–
Anne-Louise Stoupe (née Wallis)	1957–68
Lucinda Stuart	2011–
Isobel Stuart-Webb (née Kay)	1938–45
Aamiya Sanna Suri	2011–
Mary J Surrey (née Bruce)	1942–52
Louise Swanwick	2006–
O and R Swarbrick	
Mary Sykes (née Saunders)	1946–56
Hilary J Symm	
Pamela Symonds (née Fish)	1946–54
Chayna Tae	2010–
Hannah Tankaria	2008–
Elizabeth Taylor (née Lewis)	
Daphne Taylor	1941–6
P E Taylor	
Abigail Thellusson	2009–
Catherine Thomas	1990–7
Jacqueline Thomas	Staff 1978–89
Michelle Thomas (née Knight)	1958–66
Valerie Thomson (née Taylor)	1949–61
Melissa Thorne	2005–
Hannah Thurston	2011–
M P Tibbs	
Nicky Timperley	1969–80
Olivia Kay Tolson	2009–
Charlotte Tolson (née Weaving)	1983–7
Matilda (Tilly) Toseland	2005–
Kristin Townsend	2011–
Alexandra H S Travers	2008–
Ann M Travers	Staff 1988–

Victoria C S Travers	2010–
Georgina Treen	2000–10
Alison Troake	1978–85
Sarah Tunnicliff-Ford	1961–72
Gillian Turnbull	1959–70
Mary Turner	1963–9
Amelia Turner	2010–
Georgina Turner	2006–
Roseanna Turner	2010–
Mary Tyler (née Hall)	1971–9
Zoë G van den Bosch	1981–90
Eleanor van Klaveren	2005–
Edna May van Leeuwen	1934–9
Rosemary Virgo	1950–61
Hilary Vit	1972–9
Amy Vogel	Staff 2009–
Thea Vukasinovic	2000–11
Helen Walker (née Austin-Sparks)	1970–7
Ann Walter	Staff 1968–2005
Charlotte Walton	2007–
Barbara Want (née Crane)	1939–42
Jonet Ward (née Glennie)	1949–59
Kelly J Warren	
Margaret Waters	Staff 1992–
Stephen Waters	Staff 2001–
Enid Wayman (née Copp)	1948–56
Revd Barbara Webb	Staff 1979–89
Kathryn Webb	2009–
Victoria Webb	1989–95
Helen S Webber	2009–
Jemima Webster	2008–
R T Welch	Governor 2010–
Jennifer Wells (née Cumming)	1956-63
Elizabeth White (née Sykes)	1964–75
Patricia White (née Bush)	Pupil 1947–55,
Staff 1958–60 and 1967–96	
Bryony Ellie Whitemoor	1986
Adelaide Wieland (née Snelling)	1971–6
Kate Wieland	2005–
Megan Wieland	2011–
Elizabeth Williams (née Giles)	1960–7
Vara Williams (née Fitzhugh)	1952–9
Holly Wilson	2006–
Diana Winterforde-Young (née Cook)	1941–9
Amalie Woergaard Smidth	2005–10
Lauren Jung-Hyun Woo	2011–
Olivia Wooldridge	2008–
Camille Wouters	2009–11
Anna-Marie Wright	Staff 2010–
Frederica Wright	2011
Katie Wright	2008–
Maureen Wright (née Knight)	1953–62
Victoria Wyatt	2007–
Jean Wynd	1946–57
Caroline Yalden (née Rowland)	1970–80
Yasmin M Y Yau	2008–
Jessica C Yim	2006–
Katherine M Yong	1981–92
Karolyn Yoon	2010–
Anne D Yorke	1946–51
Sally Young (née Beard)	1966–77
R A P Young	Governor 2002–
Jennifer Zarek	1958–69
Allia Zubaidi	2006–

Index

This index is compiled on a word-by-word basis rather than letter-by-letter so that, for example, Spital Square precedes Spitalfields. Principal sections for an entry are denoted in **bold**. Page numbers in *italics* denote illustrations.